Theory & Practice of THERAPEUTIC MASSAGE
Fifth Edition Workbook

Mark F. Beck

to be used with

Theory & Practice of Therapeutic Massage

Fifth Edition

CENGAGE Learning™

Australia Canada Mexico Singapore Spain United Kingdom United States

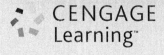

CENGAGE Learning™

Theory & Practice of Therapeutic Massage Workbook 5th Edition by Mark F. Beck

President, Milady: **Dawn Gerrain**

Publisher: **Erin O'Connor**

Acquisitions Editor: **Martine Edwards**

Senior Product Manager: **Philip Mandl**

Editorial Assistant: **Maria Hebert**

Director of Beauty Industry Relations: **Sandra Bruce**

Executive Marketing Manager: **Gerard McAvey**

Production Director: **Wendy Troeger**

Senior Content Project Manager: **Angela Sheehan**

Senior Art Director: **Joy Kocsis**

For product information and technology assistance, contact us at
Professional & Career Group Customer Support, 1-800-648-7450

For permission to use material from this text or product, submit all requests online at **www.cengage.com/permissions**
Further permissions questions can be emailed to
permissionrequest@cengage.com

Library of Congress Control Number: 2009938144

ISBN-13: 978-14354-8525-9

ISBN-10: 1-4354-8525-4

Milady
5 Maxwell Drive
Clifton Park, NY 12065-2919
USA

Cengage Learning products are represented in Canada by Nelson Education, Ltd.

For your lifelong learning solutions, visit **milady.cengage.com**

Visit our corporate website at **www.cengage.com**

Notice to the Reader
Publisher does not warrant or guarantee any of the products described herein or perform any independent analysis in connection with any of the product information contained herein. Publisher does not assume, and expressly disclaims, any obligation to obtain and include information other than that provided to it by the manufacturer. The reader is expressly warned to consider and adopt all safety precautions that might be indicated by the activities described herein and to avoid all potential hazards. By following the instructions contained herein, the reader willingly assumes all risks in connection with such instructions. The publisher makes no representations or warranties of any kind, including but not limited to, the warranties of fitness for particular purpose or merchantability, nor are any such representations implied with respect to the material set forth herein, and the publisher takes no responsibility with respect to such material. The publisher shall not be liable for any special, consequential, or exemplary damages resulting, in whole or part, from the readers' use of, or reliance upon, this material.

Printed in the United States of America
5 6 7 8 9 18 17 16 15

Contents

How to Use This Workbook

This *Theory & Practice of Therapeutic Massage Fifth Edition Workbook* has been written to meet the needs, interests, and abilities of students receiving training in therapeutic massage.

This workbook should be used together with *Theory & Practice of Therapeutic Massage,* Fifth Edition. This workbook directly follows the information found in the student textbook.

Students are to answer each item in this workbook with a pencil after consulting their textbook for the correct information. Items can be corrected and/or rated during class or individual discussions, or on an independent study basis.

A variety of question formats are included to emphasize essential facts found in the textbook and to measure the student's progress.

Part 1

The History and Advancement of Therapeutic Massage

Historical Overview of Massage

CHAPTER 1

COMPLETION: In the space(s) provided, write the word(s) that correctly complete(s) each statement.

1. The term *massage* was first used in American or European literature to denote using the hands to apply manipulations to the soft tissues during the ______________ century.

2. Two terms the Chinese use for systems of massage are ______________ and ______________ .

3. There is documentation that the Chinese have practiced massage since ______________ .

4. The Japanese style of massage that uses finger pressure is ______________ .

5. A sacred book of the Hindus written around 1800 B.C. is the ______________ .

6. The Hindu practice of bathing and massage that included kneading the extremities, tapotement, frictioning, anointing with perfumes, and cracking the joints of the fingers, toes, and the neck was known as ______________ .

7. The ________________ is a code of ethics for physicians and those about to receive medical degrees that binds them to honor their teachers, do their best to maintain the health of their patients, honor their patients' secrets, and prescribe no harmful treatment or drug.

8. The word that Hippocrates used to denote the art of rubbing upward, not downward, is ______________ .

MATCHING: Match the name with the best description. Write the letter of that name in the space provided.

A. Asclepius	G. Dr. Douglas O. Graham	M. Mathias Roth
B. Avicenna	H. Hippocrates	N. Charles Fayette Taylor
C. Celsus	I. Albert J. Hoffa	O. George Henry Taylor
D. Dr. James H. Cyriax	J. Per Henrik Ling	P. Dr. Emil Vodder
E. Elizabeth Dicke	K. Dr. Johann G. Mezger	Q. John Harvey Kellogg
F. Maria Ebner	L. Ambroise Paré	

_____ 1. Popularized use of the word *massage* in America

_____ 2. Credited with popularizing the terms *effleurage*, *petrissage*, *tapotement*, and *friction*

_____ 3. The Greek physician later worshipped as the "god of medicine" who founded the first gymnasium

_____ 4. The Greek physician who became known as the father of medicine

_____ 5. The name of the Roman physician who wrote *De Medicina*

_____ 6. The Persian philosopher/physician who wrote the *Canon of Medicine*

_____ 7. The French barber/surgeon who was one of the founders of modern surgery and who described in his publications the positive effects of massage in the healing process

_____ 8. Known as "the father of physical therapy"; developed a system of movements he called "medical gymnastics"

_____ 9. The English physician who published the first book in English on the Swedish movements

_____ 10. Established the first institute in England to teach Swedish movement gymnastics

_____ 11. The New York physician who introduced the Swedish movements to the United States in 1858

_____ 12. Physician's brother who published the first American textbook on the Swedish movements

_____ 13. Acknowledged by many of the authors of his day as "the founder of scientific massage"

_____ 14. Considered by some to be "the father of Swedish massage in the United States"

_____ 15. The distinguished German physician who published *Technik Der Massage*

_____ 16. The Austrian who developed a method of lymph massage

_____ 17. Developed *Bindegewebsmassage*

_____ 18. An author, magazine editor, and the director of the Battle Creek Sanitarium.

_____ 19. Popularized *Bindegewebsmassage* in England

_____ 20. The English orthopedic physician credited with popularizing deep transverse friction massage

MATCHING: Match the term with the best description. Write the letter of the appropriate term in the space provided.

A. acupressure	C. Rolfing	E. sports massage
B. reflexology	D. shiatsu	F. Swedish massage

_____ 1. Based on the Western concepts of anatomy and physiology, and uses effleurage, petrissage, vibration, friction, and tapotement

_____ 2. A method based on the traditional Oriental medical principles for assessing and treating the physical and energetic body order to regulate *chi* (the life force energy)

_____ 3. A finger pressure method based on the Oriental concept that the body has a series of energy (*tsubo*) points

_____ 4. A method of massage especially designed to prepare an athlete for an upcoming event and to aid in the body's regenerative and restorative capacities following a rigorous workout or competition

_____ 5. Developed out of the technique of structural integration, it aligns the major body segments through manipulation of the fascia or the connective tissue

_____ 6. A method based on the idea that stimulation of particular points on the surface of the body has an effect on other areas or organs of the body

COMPLETION: In the space(s) provided, write the word(s) that correctly complete(s) each statement.

1. The oldest professional massage organization in the United States is ______________ ______________________________.

2. The first time that massage was offered at the Summer Olympics was ________ .

3. Chair massage or seated massage was developed by ______________ and introduced to the profession in the year ________ .

4. The agency in the United States recognized for certifying massage therapists is

____.

5. The agency named in No. 4 began testing and certifying massage therapists in the year

________.

6. Another phenomenon that was initiated in the 1990s that validates the effects and benefits of massage is ________________.

7. In the year ________, the Federation of State Massage Boards formed to create a licensing examination called the ___________.

8. Numerous research projects that study the effects of touch on human well-being have been conducted at the ________________________ under the direction of Dr. Tiffany M. Fields.

9. The National Center for Complementary and Alternative Medicine was established in the year ________ by the __________________________.

MULTIPLE CHOICE: Carefully read each statement. Choose the word or phrase that correctly completes the meaning and write the corresponding letter in the blank provided.

1. The systematic manual or mechanical manipulation of the body's soft tissues is called ________
   a) shiatsu
   b) massage
   c) physical therapy
   d) chiropractic

2. Increased circulation, muscle relaxation, and pain relief are ________
   a) problems of massage
   b) benefits of massage
   c) medical conditions
   d) massage movements

3. Massage has been part of Western medical traditions for at least ________
   a) 10 years
   b) 200 years
   c) 3000 years
   d) 10,000 years

4. Modern Chinese massage is called ________
   a) *anmo*
   b) shiatsu
   c) *chi gong*
   d) *tui-na*

5. The use of the term *massage* to denote the practice of manipulating the soft tissues first appeared in American or European literature around ______
   a) 1875 c) 1774
   b) 1925 d) 1850

6. A finger pressure technique used by the Japanese is called ______
   a) shiatsu c) *tsubo*
   b) *tui-na* d) acupuncture

7. The popularity of bathing and massage lessened with the ______
   a) decline of the Roman Empire c) invention of electricity
   b) invention of hot tubs d) Inquisition

8. Much of Greco-Roman culture was preserved by the ______
   a) Spanish c) Turks
   b) Romans d) Persians

9. The father of physical therapy is ______
   a) Charles Fayette Taylor c) Asclepius
   b) Hippocrates d) Per Henrik Ling

10. The Swedish Movement Cure was brought to the United States by ______
    a) Douglas Graham c) the Taylor brothers
    b) Ambroise Paré d) Dr. Johann Mezger

11. The Greek physician/priest credited with founding the first gymnasiums in the seventh century B.C. was ______
    a) Homer c) Herodicus
    b) Hippocrates d) Asclepius

12. Much of modern massage terminology is based on terms from this language: ______
    a) Italian c) Greek
    b) Chinese d) French

13. Public interest in massage began to reemerge in the United States around ______
    a) 1950 c) 1960
    b) 1970 d) 1980

14. National certification in massage and bodywork has been available in the United States since ______
    a) 1961 c) 1985
    b) 1972 d) 1992

15. The idea that stimulation of particular body points affects other areas is called ______
    a) chiropractic
    b) reflexology
    c) Rolfing
    d) Trager

16. Neuromuscular techniques were developed in the 1940s by ______
    a) Dr. Leon Chaitow
    b) Paul St. John
    c) Boris Chaitow and Stanley Lief
    d) Janet Travell

17. A national organization that certifies massage therapists is the ______
    a) AMTA
    b) NCBTMB
    c) ABMP
    d) FSMTB

WORD REVIEW: The student is encouraged to write down the meaning of each of the following words and titles. This list can be used as a study guide for this unit.

American Massage Therapy Association (AMTA)

____

____

The American Organization for Bodywork Therapies of Asia (AOBTA)

____

____

anatripsis

____

____

ascete

____

____

Association of Bodywork Professionals (ABMP)

____

____

Bindegewebsmassage

chirurgy

craniosacral therapy

deep transverse friction massage

Esalen massage

Federation of State Massage Therapy Boards (FSMTB)

Federation of Therapeutic Massage, Bodywork and Somatic Practice Organizations

gymnasium

Hippocratic Oath

MBLEx

manual lymph drainage

massage

medical gymnastics

National Center for Complementary and Alternative Medicine (NCCAM)

National Certification Board for Therapeutic Massage and Bodywork (NCBTMB)

neuromuscular therapy

Polarity therapy

Rolfing

shiatsu

Swedish Movement Cure

Touch Research Institute

Trager method

tsubo

tui-na

CHAPTER 2

Requirements for the Practice of Therapeutic Massage

SHORT ANSWER: In the spaces provided, write short answers to the following questions.

1. What is meant by "the scope of practice"?

2. In states that have massage licensing, how is the scope of practice defined?

3. In the United States, which jurisdiction might oversee regulations for massage?

4. What is the major reason for licensing massage therapists?

5. What is the role of national or state regulatory boards?

6. Besides massage licensing laws and ordinances, what other laws must be followed when operating a massage business?

____

____

TRUE OR FALSE: If the following statements are true, write *true* in the space provided. If they are false, write *false.*

__________ 1. If a massage therapist is nationally certified, she can practice anywhere in the United States.

__________ 2. Reciprocity means that if a massage therapist has a license in one place, she can practice anywhere.

__________ 3. In a state that has massage licensing, if a licensed nurse or chiropractor wants to practice massage, she must obtain a massage license.

__________ 4. The scope of practice for massage is clearly defined by national standards.

SHORT ANSWER: Of the following statements, put a check mark in front of the ones that may be grounds for revoking, canceling, or suspending a massage license.

_____ 1. Having been convicted of a felony

_____ 2. Being guilty of fraudulent or deceptive advertising

_____ 3. Being engaged currently or previously in any act of prostitution

_____ 4. Practicing under a false or assumed name

_____ 5. Being accused of making sexual advances or attempting sexual acts during the course of a massage

_____ 6. Prescribing drugs or medicines (unless you are a licensed physician)

_____ 7. Charging extremely high fees for the services provided

_____ 8. Being addicted to narcotics, alcohol, or like substances that interfere with the performance of duties

_____ 9. Being guilty of fraud or deceit in obtaining a license

_____ 10. Selling nutritional products or other non – massage-related items

_____ 11. Being willfully negligent in the practice of massage so as to endanger the health of a client

COMPLETION: In the space(s) provided, write the word(s) that correctly complete(s) each statement.

1. A _____________ is issued by a state or municipal regulating agency as a requirement for conducting a business or practicing a trade or profession.

2. A document that is awarded in recognition of an accomplishment or for achieving or maintaining some kind of standard is a _____________.

3. Ongoing training that is required to renew a license or certification is termed _____________.

MULTIPLE CHOICE: Carefully read each statement. Choose the word or phrase that correctly completes the meaning and write the corresponding letter in the blank provided.

1. *Scope of practice* defines _______
   a) legally acceptable professional activities
   b) medical ethics
   c) specific techniques
   d) geographical boundaries

2. If a client's condition is outside the massage technician's scope of practice, the technician should _______
   a) schedule extra sessions
   b) refer the client to the proper professional
   c) take more training
   d) refer to textbooks

3. The main reason for massage licensing is _______
   a) to make sure that only people who graduate from special schools practice
   b) to ensure that only certain kinds of massage are practiced
   c) to protect the health, safety, and welfare of the public
   d) to close down massage parlors

4. Testing and licensing of massage professionals is generally overseen by _______
   a) a regulatory board
   b) the legislature
   c) a professional massage association
   d) a local law enforcement agency

5. Being licensed in one city or state _______ validation in another location. _______
   a) does not guarantee
   b) requires
   c) guarantees
   d) assumes

6. The education standard recommended by the National Certification for Therapeutic Massage and Bodywork is ______
   a) 300 hours
   b) 150 hours
   c) 1000 hours
   d) 500 hours

7. A document awarded in recognition of achieving or maintaining a set standard is a/an ______
   a) recommendation
   b) license
   c) certificate
   d) diploma

8. Completing a course of study or passing an examination results in ______
   a) certification
   b) licensing
   c) a diploma
   d) job security

9. Certificates can be awarded by ______
   a) schools
   b) professional organizations
   c) institutions
   d) all of the above

10. A document issued by a regulatory agency that is required to practice a trade or profession is a ______
    a) certification
    b) permit
    c) ordinance
    d) license

11. A document awarded for achieving or maintaining some standard or accomplishment is a ______
    a) commendation
    b) certificate
    c) license
    d) promotion

12. *Scope of practice* is defined in ______
    a) textbooks
    b) licensing regulations
    c) professional organizations
    d) medical dictionary

WORD REVIEW: The student is encouraged to write down the meaning of each of the following words and titles. This list can be used as a study guide for this unit.

certification

____

____

continuing education

license

National Certification Board for Therapeutic Massage and Bodywork (NCBTMB)

National Certification Examination for Therapeutic Massage and Bodywork (NCETMB)

scope of practice

Professional Ethics for Massage Practitioners

CHAPTER 3

COMPLETION: In the space(s) provided, write the word(s) from the list below that correctly complete(s) each statement.

confidential	fairness	a satisfied customer
courtesy	honest	sexual
ethics	professional	tactful

1. The standards and philosophy of human conduct or code of morals of an individual, group, or profession is known as ____________.
2. One of the best forms of advertising in a personal service business is ____________.
3. A person engaged in a vocation or occupation requiring advanced training to gain knowledge and skills is considered a ____________.
4. All clients should be treated with ____________ and ____________.
5. All communications with clients should be ____________ and ____________.
6. Be respectful of the therapeutic relationship and maintain appropriate ____________ boundaries.
7. To handle a client who is overly critical, finds fault, and is hard to please, the therapist must be ____________.

MATCHING: Match the term with the best description. Write the letter of the appropriate term in the space provided.

A. personal boundary	D. dual relationship	G. countertransference
B. professional boundary	E. power differential	H. supervision
C. therapeutic relationship	F. transference	

_____ 1. A client-centered relationship in which all activities benefit and enhance the client's well-being

_____ 2. A relationship in which one person is more vulnerable

_____ 3. Defined by our experiences, beliefs, and upbringing

_____ 4. Practitioner personalizes the relationship with the client

_____ 5. Practice that protects the client and therapist

_____ 6. A shame-free environment in which to sort out emotional or boundary issues

_____ 7. Client projects attributes of someone from a former relationship onto the practitioner

_____ 8. A social or romantic relationship outside or beyond the therapeutic relationship

_____ 9. Practitioner/client relationship free of physical, emotional, or sexual impropriety

_____ 10. Parent/child, therapist/client, teacher/student relationships exhibit this characteristic

_____ 11. Provide a framework to function safely in the world

_____ 12. Client seeks more out of the relationship than is therapeutically appropriate

_____ 13. Creates a safe environment and stable framework from which to practice

_____ 14. Unconscious phenomena that occur in therapeutic relationships in which there is a power differential

_____ 15. A secondary relationship that extends beyond the massage practitioner/client relationship

_____ 16. Conferring with a mentor, a colleague, or a peer group regarding ethical issues

SHORT ANSWER: In the spaces provided, write short answers to the following questions.

1. List nine attributes that are helpful for developing good communication between therapist and client.

   a. ____________________

   b. ____________________

   c. ____________________

   d. ____________________

   e. ____________________

   f. ____________________

   g. ____________________

   h. ____________________

   i. ____________________

2. The most effective tool to prevent or clarify boundary issues is

   ____________________.

3. List eight major areas to consider when establishing professional boundaries.

   a. ____________________

   b. ____________________

   c. ____________________

   d. ____________________

   e. ____________________

   f. ____________________

   g. ____________________

   h. ____________________

4. Name three ways to stay current in the massage profession.

a. ______________________________

b. ______________________________

i. ______________________________

MULTIPLE CHOICE: Carefully read each statement. Choose the word or phrase that correctly completes the meaning and write the corresponding letter in the blank provided.

1. The code of morals of a profession, group, or individual person is called ______
   a) values
   b) attitudes
   c) morals
   d) ethics

2. A person in an occupation that requires advanced training to gain skills and knowledge is considered a ______
   a) journeyman
   b) professional
   c) skilled laborer
   d) veteran

3. A massage therapist's best method of advertising is ______
   a) satisfied clients
   b) newspaper
   c) radio
   d) Internet

4. Intimate or sexual relationships between client and practitioner are ______
   a) avoided
   b) done only with full consent
   c) not done in the massage facility
   d) done only for therapeutic reasons

5. Keep your knowledge current by ______
   a) attending seminars
   b) reading trade journals
   c) joining professional associations
   d) doing all the above

6. Professional standards are determined by educational requirements, codes of ethics, and ______
   a) standards of practice
   b) scope of practice
   c) state and local regulations
   d) all of the above

7. Guidelines that help to define us emotionally and spiritually, are determined by our experiences and beliefs, and act as a safety net and personal protection are ______
   a) personal boundaries
   b) codes of ethics
   c) morals
   d) professional boundaries

8. ________ are preliminarily outlined in policy and procedure statements and protect the safety of the client and the therapist. ________

a) Codes of ethics
b) Professional boundaries
c) Standards of practice
d) Personal boundaries

9. A(n) ________ relationship is a practitioner/client relationship that is client centered, in which all activities are to benefit and enhance the client's well-being and maintain or promote their welfare. ________

a) intimate
b) unhealthy
c) therapeutic
d) medical

10. In a practitioner/client relationship, the foundation that provides an environment of safety, trust, and respect for the client to relax, open, release, and heal is ________

a) confidentiality
b) a thorough assessment
c) clear policies and procedures
d) being well educated

11. A relationship in which more authority is held by the person on one side of the relationship, whereas the other person is in a more vulnerable or submissive role is ________

a) an abusive relationship
b) a therapeutic relationship
c) a power differential
d) countertransference

12. When a client unconsciously projects attributes of someone from a former relationship onto a therapist or seeks more out of the relationship than is therapeutically appropriate, it is called ________

a) countertransference
b) projecting
c) fantasizing
d) transference

13. When a practitioner begins to personalize or take a therapeutic relationship with the client personally it is called ________

a) transference
b) a power differential
c) countertransference
d) unethical

14. Any situation that combines the therapeutic relationship with a secondary relationship that extends beyond the massage practitioner/client relationship is ________

a) unethical
b) therapeutic
c) a dual relationship
d) illegal

15. In a therapeutic relationship, whose responsibility is it to maintain appropriate boundaries? ________

a) the therapist or practitioner
b) the client
c) both the client and therapist
d) all of the above

16. When a therapist becomes involved in instances of transference, countertransference, or dual relationships, she should ______
    a) discontinue the relationship
    b) quit her practice
    c) feel ashamed
    d) seek supervision

WORD REVIEW: The student is encouraged to write down the meaning of each of the following words and titles. This list can be used as a study guide for this unit.

boundaries

Code of Ethics

confidentiality

countertransference

dual relationship

duty to warn and protect

ethics

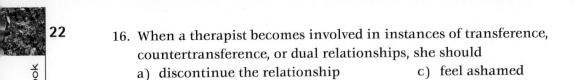

personal boundaries

power differential

professional

professionalism

professional boundaries

supervision

therapeutic relationship

transference

Part 2

Human Anatomy and Physiology

CHAPTER 4

Overview

COMPLETION: In the space(s) provided, write the word(s) that correctly complete(s) each statement.

1. The study of the gross structure of the body or the study of an organism and the interrelations of its parts is ____________.
2. The science and study of the vital processes, mechanisms, and functions of an organ or system of organs is ____________.
3. The study of the structural and functional changes caused by disease is ____________.
4. The scientific study of muscular activity and the mechanics of body movement is ____________.
5. The delicate physiologic balance that the body strives to maintain in its internal environment is ____________.
6. The abnormal and unhealthy state of all or part of the body where it is incapable of carrying on its normal function is ____________.
7. A ____________ of a disease is perceived by the victim whereas a ____________ of a disease is observable by another person.

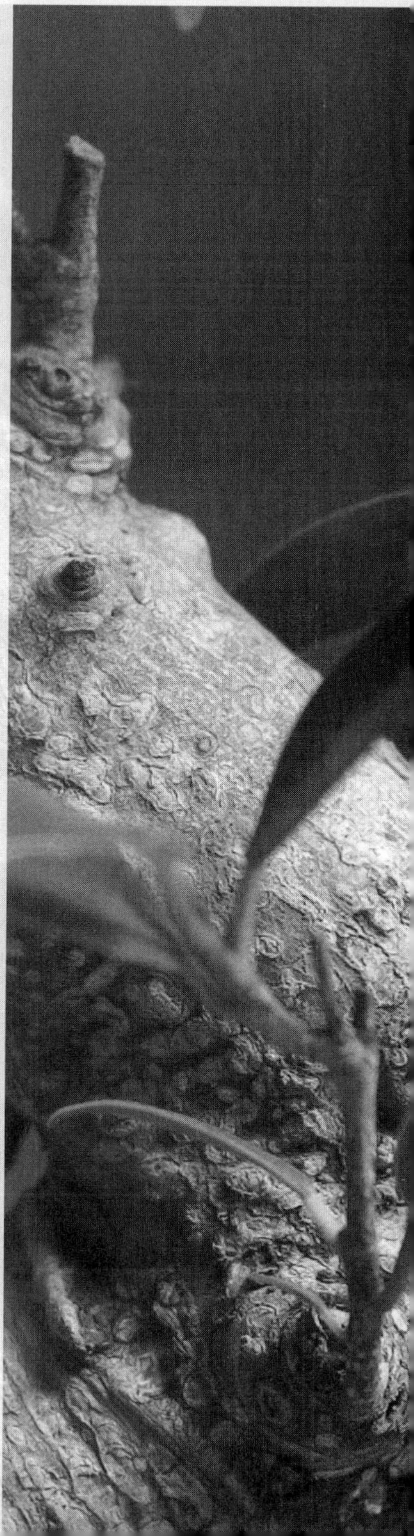

KEY CHOICES: Massage can have a direct, an indirect, or a reflex effect on various functions of the body. Put the appropriate key letter for each of the following phrases in the spaces provided.

D = Direct effect

I = Indirect effect

R = Reflex effect

_____ 1. Increased circulation to the muscle and internal organs

_____ 2. Stretching of muscle tissue

_____ 3. Slower, deeper breathing

_____ 4. Loosening of adhesions and scar tissue

_____ 5. Reduced heart rate

_____ 6. Reduced blood pressure

_____ 7. Increased local circulation of venous blood

_____ 8. General relaxation of tense muscles

KEY CHOICES: Most diseases have signs and/or symptoms. Put the appropriate key letter for each of the following phrases in the spaces provided.

X = Symptom

O = Sign

_____ 1. nausea

_____ 2. abnormal skin color

_____ 3. pain

_____ 4. chills

_____ 5. elevated pulse

_____ 6. severe itching

_____ 7. abdominal cramps

_____ 8. fever

_____ 9. dizziness

_____ 10 skin ulcers

COMPLETION: In the space(s) provided, write the word(s) that correctly complete(s) each statement.

1. Two hormones that are secreted by the adrenal glands are ____________ and ____________.

2. The protective body sensation that warns of tissue damage or destruction is ____________.

3. The two reactions to pain are ______________ and ______________.

4. Inhibited blood flow to an area of the body is known as ____________.

5. A syndrome that often starts as a simple muscle spasm that is complicated by muscle splinting and constricted circulation is the ____________________.

6. Much of the discomfort in the condition of the previous question is from ________________.

7. Psychologically, skillfully applied therapeutic massage helps to reduce pain by relieving ____________ and ____________.

8. In a pain-spasm-pain cycle, pain is intensified because of ____________.

9. Therapeutic massage on contracted ischemic tissue relieves ______________ and restores ____________.

10. Pain is an indication of ______________ or ________________.

11. Generally, the more severe the pain, the more severe the ______________.

12. Bacteria, viruses, fungi, and parasites are ________________.

13. If pathogenic organisms enter the body in large enough numbers to multiply and become capable of destroying healthy tissue, they cause ____________.

14. If these organisms are confined to a small area, the condition is considered a ________________, but if they spread throughout the body, the condition is termed a ________________.

15. When tissue is damaged from invading organisms or physical injury, substances are released that cause ________________.

16. The four signs and symptoms of inflammation are ______________, ______________, ______________, and ______________.

17. An elevated body temperature that accompanies infectious diseases is a ______________.

18. The fibrous connective tissue formed as a wound heals is ______________.

19. Connective tissue fibers are produced in healing tissue by ______________.

SHORT ANSWER: In the spaces provided, write short answers to the following questions.

1. List six possible direct causes of disease.

   a. ________________________________

   b. ________________________________

   c. ________________________________

   d. ________________________________

   e. ________________________________

   f. ________________________________

2. Stress is most notably associated with the adrenal glands and their secretion of the "fight or flight" hormones. Briefly describe what happens to the following body functions during the "fight or flight" reaction.

   1. Muscle tone ________________________________

   2. Blood pressure ________________________________

   3. Digestion ________________________________

   4. Circulation to skeletal muscles ________________________________

   5. Circulation to digestive organs ________________________________

   6. Red blood cells ________________________________

3. Different types of tissue heal at different rates. Number the following from 1 to 5 according to how fast they mend: 1 is the fastest, 5 is the slowest.

_____ nerve tissue

_____ bone

_____ skin

_____ muscle

_____ ligament

COMPLETION: In the space(s) provided, write the word(s) that correctly complete(s) each statement.

1. Physiologically, skillfully applied therapeutic massage helps to reduce pain by providing ____ ____.

2. If massage increases the overall intensity of the pain, the therapist should ______________ ____.

3. A wellness-oriented person attempts to maintain a balance between ______________, ______________, and ______________.

4. In medical terminology, compound words are constructed of ______________, ______________, and ______________.

MATCHING: In the following six exercises match the term in the first column with the meaning in the second column. Write the letter of the appropriate term in the space provided.

WORD ROOTS I

_____	1. arth(ro)	A. lung
_____	2. chondr/o	B. tissue
_____	3. cyt	C. joint
_____	4. hem	D. nerve
_____	5. hist	E. cell
_____	6. my(o)	F. heat
_____	7. neur(o)	G. blood
_____	8. oss, ost(e)	H. vessel
_____	9. phleb	I. bone
_____	10. pulmo	J. cartilage
_____	11. therm	K. vein
_____	12. vas	L. muscle

WORD ROOTS II

_____	1. brachi	A. head
_____	2. cardi	B. kidney
_____	3. cephal	C. foot
_____	4. derm	D. stomach
_____	5. gastr(o)	E. arm
_____	6. gyn	F. woman
_____	7. hepat	G. skin
_____	8. labi	H. lung
_____	9. nephr(o)	I. liver
_____	10. ocul	J. heart
_____	11. pneum	K. eye
_____	12. pod	L. lip

PREFIXES I

_____	1. ab-	A. beyond, outside of, in addition
_____	2. ad-	B. against
_____	3. anti-	C. against, counter to
_____	4. ante-	D. away from
_____	5. bio-	E. inside
_____	6. contra-	F. above, in addition
_____	7. ex-	G. before
_____	8. infra-	H. out of
_____	9. extra-	I. to, toward
_____	10. intra-	J. beneath
_____	11. sub-	K. under, below
_____	12. super-	L. life

PREFIXES II

_____	1. ect-	A. under, below
_____	2. end-(o)	B. one, single
_____	3. epi-	C. inside, within
_____	4. hyper-	D. around
_____	5. hypo-	E. stupor, numbness
_____	6. mega-	F. upon, over, in addition
_____	7. micr-(o)	G. large, extreme
_____	8. mon-(o)	H. outside, without
_____	9. narc-	I. pertaining to disease
_____	10. path-	J. small
_____	11. peri-	K. false
_____	12. pseud-(o)	L. above, extreme

PREFIXES III

_____	1. hemi-	A. many, much
_____	2. hetero-	B. middle, midline
_____	3. hom-	C. the other
_____	4. medi-	D. together, along with
_____	5. multi-	E. four
_____	6. para-	F. single, one
_____	7. poly-	G. common, same
_____	8. quad-	H. many, multiple
_____	9. retro-	I. half
_____	10. syn-	J. three
_____	11. tri-	K. next to, resembling, beside
_____	12. uni-	L. backward

SUFFIXES

_____	1. -ase	A. diseased
_____	2. -algia	B. study of, science of
_____	3. -ectomy	C. forming an opening
_____	4. -graph	D. surgical removal of body part
_____	5. -ia	E. denoting an enzyme
_____	6. -itis	F. tumor
_____	7. -ology	G. write, draw, record
_____	8. -oma	H. morbid fear of
_____	9. -ostomy	I. excision, cutting into
_____	10. -otomy	J. painful condition
_____	11. -pathic	K. inflammation
_____	12. -phobia	L. a noun ending of a condition

MULTIPLE CHOICE: Carefully read each statement. Choose the word or phrase that correctly completes the meaning and write the corresponding letter in the blank provided.

1. The scientific study of body movement is ________
   a) anatomy
   b) kinesiology
   c) pathology
   d) physiology

2. Normal functions of body systems are studied in ________
   a) physiology
   b) histology
   c) anatomy
   d) pathology

3. The study of the gross structure of the body or an organism and its parts is known as ________
   a) physiology
   b) histology
   c) anatomy
   d) pathology

4. Describing how the organs or body parts function and relate to one another is ________
   a) physiology
   b) histology
   c) anatomy
   d) pathology

5. The study of structural and functional changes caused by disease is ________
   a) physiology
   b) histology
   c) anatomy
   d) pathology

6. Lower blood pressure and general relaxation are ________ effects of massage. ________
   a) recurring
   b) indirect
   c) direct
   d) reflex

7. The body's internal balance is called ________
   a) blood chemistry
   b) breathing
   c) homeostasis
   d) physiology

8. Perceived conditions such as dizziness, nausea, or pain are called ________
   a) symptoms
   b) diseases
   c) homeostasis
   d) signs

9. Observable indications such as fever, abnormal pulse rate, or abnormal skin color are ________
   a) symptoms of disease
   b) illnesses
   c) signs of disease
   d) psychosomatic

10. The adrenal hormone that acts as an anti-inflammatory and antiallergenic in stressful situations is ________
a) DMSO
b) cortisol
c) estrogen
d) adrenaline

11. Prolonged adrenal excretions make the body ________
a) exhausted
b) energetic
c) strong
d) ecstatic

12. The pain-spasm-pain cycle is associated with ________
a) headaches
b) heart attacks
c) muscle spasms
d) mental health

13. The condition in which contracted muscles inhibit blood flow to an area is called ________
a) constriction
b) ischemia
c) hypertension
d) bruising

14. The existence of disease-producing organisms throughout the body is termed a/an ________
a) microorganism
b) inflammation
c) systemic infection
d) local infection

15. A protective tissue response characterized by swelling, redness, heat, and pain is ________
a) ischemia
b) spasm
c) sunburn
d) inflammation

16. In medical terminology, the root word usually indicates the ________
a) number
b) body part
c) condition
d) treatment

17. The medical term prefix "a" means ________
a) one
b) many
c) without
d) after

18. The medical term prefix "ambi" means ________
a) in twos
b) both
c) walking
d) movement

19. The medical-term prefix "infra" means ________
a) beneath
b) above
c) inside
d) outside

20. The medical-term suffix "algia" means
    a) three
    b) binding
    c) inflammation
    d) painful condition
    ____

21. The medical-term suffix "itis" means
    a) inflammation
    b) old
    c) resembling
    d) tumor
    ____

22. The medical-term suffix "pathic" means
    a) germs
    b) tumor
    c) toxic
    d) diseased
    ____

23. The medical term root "arth(ro)" means
    a) joint
    b) bone
    c) blood
    d) lung
    ____

24. The medical term root "derm" means
    a) teeth
    b) bone
    c) skin
    d) lung
    ____

WORD REVIEW: The student is encouraged to write down the meaning of each of the following words. The list can be used as a study guide for this unit.

adrenaline

---

anatomy

---

cortisol

---

disease

---

fever

homeostasis

infection

inflammation

ischemia

ischemic pain

kinesiology

medical terminology

microorganisms

pain

pain-spasm-pain cycle

pathology

physiology

scar tissue

sign of disease

stress

symptom

____

____

wellness

____

____

Human Anatomy and Physiology

CHAPTER 5

INTRODUCTION

COMPLETION: In the space(s) provided, write the word(s) that correctly complete(s) each statement.

1. The submicroscopic particles that make up all substances are called

   _____________.

2. These are arranged in specific patterns and structures called

   _____________.

3. In the human organism, the basic unit of structure and function is the

   _____________.

4. These are organized into layers or groups called _____________.

5. Groups of these form complex structures that perform certain functions.

   These structures are called _____________ and are arranged in

   _______________.

6. All living matter is composed of a colorless, jellylike substance called

   _____________.

7. The cytoplasm contains a network of various membranes called

   _______________________, which perform specific functions necessary for cell survival.

8. Cell reproduction is controlled by the _____________ and the _________.

9. During the early developmental stages of an organism, the repeated division of the ovum results in many specialized cells that differ from one another in composition and function. This process is called ________________.

10. In the human organism, as a cell matures and is nourished, it grows in size and eventually divides into two smaller cells. This form of cell division is called __________.

SHORT ANSWER: In the spaces provided, write short answers to the following questions.

1. Name four ways in which cells differ from one another.

   a. ______________________ c. ______________________

   b. ______________________ d. ______________________

2. Name the four principal parts of a cell.

   a. ______________________ c. ______________________

   b. ______________________ d. ______________________

MATCHING: Match each term with its associated function. Write the letter of the appropriate term in the space provided.

A. cell membrane	F. Golgi apparatus	K. nucleolus
B. centrosome	G. lysosome	L. nucleus
C. chromatin	H. microtubules	M. ribosome
D. endoplasmic reticulum	I. mitochondria	N. vacuole
E. fibrils	J. nuclear membrane	

_____ 1. converts and releases energy for cell operation

_____ 2. contains cellular material and transports materials between the inside and outside of the cell

_____ 3. produce lipids or proteins for cell utilization and transport

_____ 4. supervises all cell activity

_____ 5. synthesizes carbohydrates and holds protein for secretion

_____ 6. involved in the rapid introduction or ejection of substances

_____ 7. divides and moves to opposite poles of the cell during mitosis

_____ 8. controls passage of substances between the nucleus and cytoplasm

_____ 9. composed of RNA and protein molecules that synthesize proteins

_____ 10. fibers of protein and DNA that contain the genes

IDENTIFICATION: Identify the structures indicated in Figure 5.1 by writing the letter of the structure next to the appropriate name in the space provided.

_____ 1. cell membrane

_____ 2. chromatin

_____ 3. smooth endoplasmic reticulum

_____ 4. Golgi apparatus

_____ 5. lysosome

_____ 6. pinocytic vesicle

_____ 7. mitochondria

_____ 8. nucleolus

_____ 9. nucleus

_____ 10. ribosomes

_____ 11. vacuole

_____ 12. rough endoplasmic reticulum

_____ 13. cytoplasm

_____ 14. centrioles

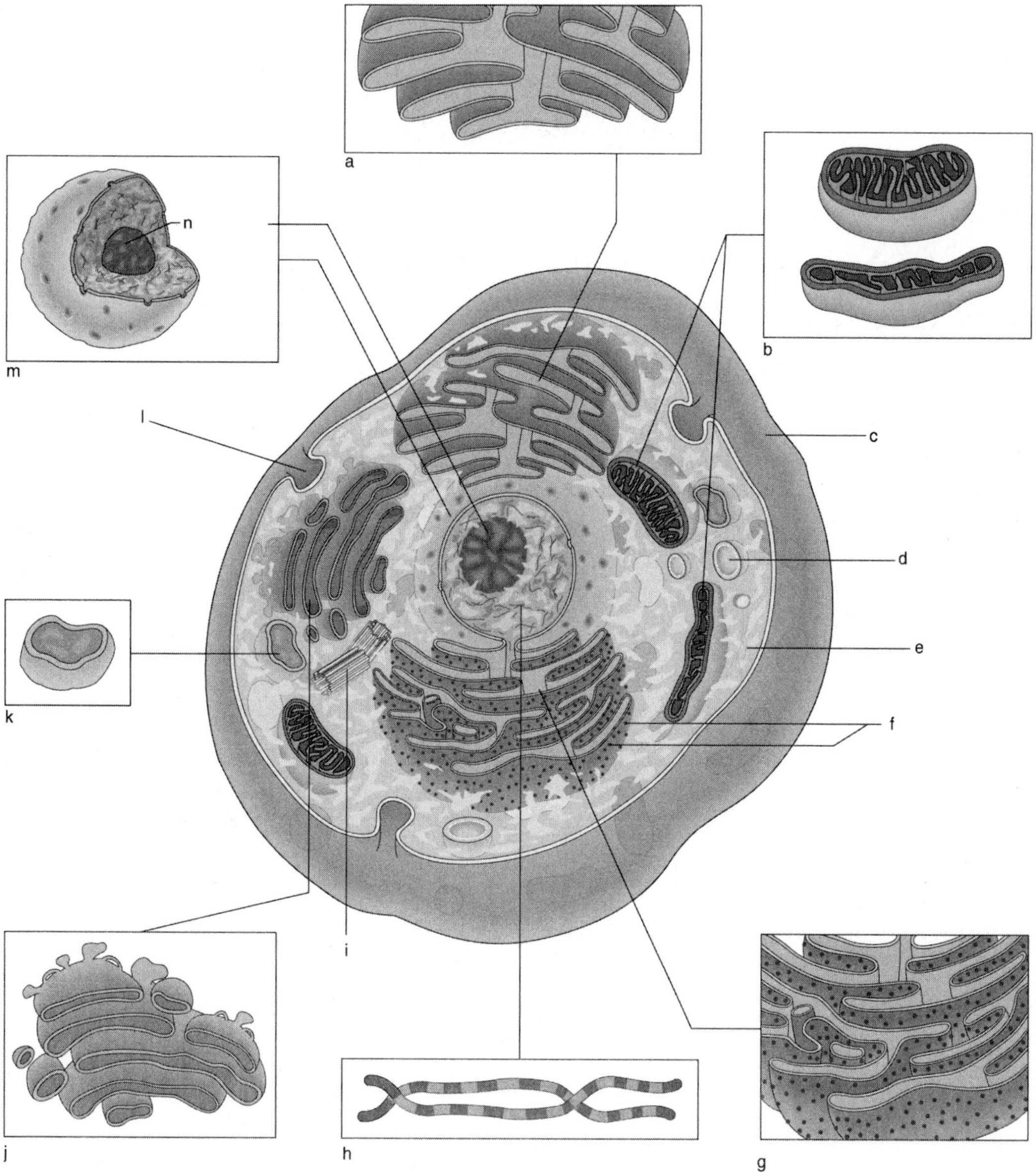

Fig. 5.1 Structure of a typical animal cell.

SHORT ANSWER: The five phases of cell division are listed below. Number the phases from 1 to 5 to indicate the correct order in which they occur.

_____ metaphase _____ interphase _____ anaphase

_____ telophase _____ prophase

MATCHING: Match the term with the best description. Write the letter of the best description in the space provided.

_____ 1. metaphase

_____ 2. telophase

_____ 3. interphase

_____ 4. prophase

_____ 5. anaphase

A. Chromosomes become larger and can be seen as two coiled strands called *chromatids*.

B. This is the normal state of the cell during growth.

C. Cytoplasm divides into two cells.

D. Chromosomes arrange along the equatorial plane.

E. The chromatids are separated and are again called chromosomes.

COMPLETION: In the space(s) provided, write the word(s) that correctly complete(s) each statement.

1. The chemical reactions within a cell that transform food into nutrients used for cell growth and operation are broadly termed _____________________.
2. Two phases of metabolism are ____________ and ____________.
3. The process of building up larger molecules from smaller ones is ____________.
4. The process of breaking down larger substances or molecules into smaller ones is ____________.
5. Protein substances that act as organic catalysts to initiate, accelerate, or control specific chemical reactions in the metabolic process are called ____________.
6. Collections of similar cells that carry out specific functions of the body are called ____________.

SHORT ANSWER: In the spaces provided, list the four main categories of tissues.

1. ______________________________

2. ______________________________

3. ______________________________

4. ______________________________

IDENTIFICATION: In the space provided, write the name of the tissue type that best fits the description.

_____________ 1. represented by blood and lymph

_____________ 2. functions in the process of absorption, excretion, secretion, and protection

_____________ 3. binds structures together and serves as a framework

_____________ 4. acts as a channel for the transmission of messages

_____________ 5. forms the skin, the covering of the organs, and the inner lining of all the hollow organs

_____________ 6. carries nutrients to the cells and carries away waste products

_____________ 7. deep fascia, superficial fascia

_____________ 8. initiates, controls, and coordinates the body's adaptation to its surroundings

_____________ 9. contracts and causes movement

_____________ 10. always has a free surface that is exposed to outside influences

_____________ 11. responsible for the movement of food through the digestive tract, the constriction of blood vessels, and the emptying of the bladder

_____________ 12. bones, cartilage, and ligaments

_____________ 13. cells classified by shape as squamous, cuboidal, and columnar

_____________ 15. provides support and protection

_____________ 16. covers all the surfaces of the body

_____________ 17. responsible for pumping blood through the heart into the blood vessels

_____________ 18. composed of neurons

_____________ 20. makes up the major tissue of the glands

_____________ 21. responsible for facial expression, speaking, and other voluntary movements

COMPLETION: In the space(s) provided, write the word(s) that correctly complete(s) each statement.

1. Two categories of membranes are _____________ membranes and _________________________ membranes.

2. ____________________ produce a thick, sticky substance that acts as a protectant and lubricant.

3. ____________________ produce a more watery, lubricating substance that lines the body cavities and sometimes forms the outermost surface of the organs contained in those cavities.

4. Three major serous membranes are the _____________ that encases the lungs, the _____________ around the heart, and the _____________ that lines the abdominal cavity.

SHORT ANSWER: In the spaces provided, write short answers to the following questions.

1. List three fascial membranes associated with the muscles.

   a. ____

   b. ____

   c. ____

2. Name three types of skeletal membrane and state where each is found.

   a. ____

   b. ____

   c. ____

MATCHING: Match the term with the best description. Write the letter of the best description in the space provided.

_____ 1. elastic cartilage

_____ 2. areolar tissue

_____ 3. osseous tissue

_____ 4. adipose tissue

_____ 5. ligaments

_____ 6. fibrocartilage

_____ 7. fibrous connective tissue

_____ 8. tendons

_____ 9. hyaline cartilage

A. impregnated with mineral salts, chiefly calcium phosphate and calcium carbonate

B. found between the vertebrae and in the pubic symphysis

C. found in the external ear and the larynx

D. found on the ends of bones and in movable joints

E. fibrous bands that connect bones to bones

F. composed of collagen and elastic fibers that are closely arranged

G. cords or bands that serve to attach muscle to bone

H. binds the skin to the underlying tissues and fills the spaces between the muscles

I. has an abundance of fat-containing cells

COMPLETION: In the space(s) provided, write the word(s) that correctly complete(s) each statement.

1. The three types of muscle tissue are ____________, ____________, and ____________.

2. ______________________________ are usually attached to bone or other muscle by way of tendons, and they can be controlled by conscious effort.

3. Because these muscles have alternating light and dark cross markings, they are called ________________.

4. Muscle tissue found in the hollow organs of the stomach, small intestine, colon, bladder, and the blood vessels does not have the cross markings and is called ____________ or ____________ muscle.

5. ______________________ is found only in the heart.

MULTIPLE CHOICE: Carefully read each statement. Choose the word or phrase that correctly completes the meaning and write the corresponding letter in the blank provided.

1. All substances are made from subatomic particles that form ________. ________
   a) molecules
   b) tissues
   c) atoms
   d) cells

2. The basic structure in human organisms is the ________. ________
   a) organ
   b) tissue
   c) cell
   d) molecule

3. Cell division, which produces new identical daughter cells, is called ________. ________
   a) mutation
   b) mitosis
   c) amitosis
   d) gestation

4. The complex chemical and physical process that nourishes organisms is called ________. ________
   a) mitosis
   b) metabolism
   c) homeostasis
   d) nutrition

5. Microscopic structures in the cytoplasm of the cell that produce energy needed for cellular work are called ________. ________
   a) lysosomes
   b) mitochondria
   c) Golgi bodies
   d) endoplasmic reticulum

6. Anabolism and catabolism are closely regulated to maintain ________. ________
   a) prophase
   b) enzymes
   c) amitosis
   d) homeostasis

7. Which of the following is not one of the five main human tissue types? ________
   a) epithelial
   b) connective
   c) nervous
   d) skeletal

8. A special molecule that stores energy for use in muscular activity is ________. ________
   a) adenosine triphosphate
   b) fatty acids
   c) glucose
   d) protein

9. Bone, adipose tissue, epimysium, and hyaline cartilage are ________. ________
   a) areas of fat storage
   b) kinds of connective tissue
   c) skeletal structures
   d) common sites of inflammation

10. The thin tissue layer that forms the skin, organ coverings, and inner lining of all the hollow organs is the ________. ________
    a) epithelial tissue
    b) connective tissue
    c) muscular tissue
    d) skin

11. Fibrous tissue between muscle bundles is called ________. ________
    a) cartilage
    b) fascia
    c) muscular tissue
    d) perichondrium

12. The ________ membrane lines the inner joint cavities. ________
    a) synovial
    b) adipose
    c) mucous
    d) serous

13. The bands that attach muscles to bone are ________. ________
    a) tendons
    b) ligaments
    c) cartilage
    d) aponeurosa

14. The tough, fibrous bands that connect bones to bones are ________. ________
    a) tendons
    b) ligaments
    c) cartilage
    d) fascia

15. Skeletal muscles are also known as ________. ________
    a) voluntary muscles
    b) nonstriated muscles
    c) tendonous muscles
    d) smooth muscle

16. Cardiac muscle tissue occurs only in the ________. ________
    a) liver
    b) blood vessels
    c) heart
    d) skeletal muscles

WORD REVIEW: The student is encouraged to write down the meaning of each of the following words. The list can be used as a study guide for this unit.

adipose tissue

____

____

amitosis

____

____

anabolism

anaphase

anatomy

areolar tissue

atoms

cardiac muscle tissue

catabolism

cell

cell membrane

cellular metabolism

centrosome

columnar

connective tissue membranes

cuboidal

cytoplasm

cytoplasmic organelles

differentiation

fibrocartilage

fibrous connective tissue

enzymes

epithelial membranes

epithelial tissue

fascia

histology

hyaline cartilage

interphase

ligaments

metaphase

mitosis

molecules

mucous membranes

nerve tissue

neurons

____

____

nucleus

____

____

organ system

____

____

organs

____

____

perichondrium

____

____

periosteum

____

____

physiology

____

____

prophase

____

____

protoplasm

reticular tissue

serous membranes

skeletal muscle

smooth muscle

squamous

striated muscles

superficial fascia

synovial membrane

telophase

tendons

tissues

voluntary muscles

THE ANATOMIC POSITION OF THE BODY

COMPLETION: In the space(s) provided, write the word(s) that correctly complete(s) each statement.

1. In the anatomic position, the body ________________ with the palms of the hands facing ____________.

2. Anatomists divide the body with three imaginary planes called the ________________, the ________________, and the ________________ planes.

3. The ______________ divides the body into left and right parts by an imaginary line running vertically down the body.

4. The ______________ is an imaginary line that divides the body into the anterior (front) or ventral half of the body and the posterior (back) or dorsal half of the body.

5. The ________________ is an imaginary line that divides the body horizontally into an upper and lower portion.

6. ____________ refers to the plane that divides the body or an organ into right and left halves.

MATCHING: Match the term with the best description. Write the letter of the best description in the space provided.

_____ 1. cranial or superior aspect

_____ 2. caudal or inferior aspect

_____ 3. anterior or ventral aspect

_____ 4. posterior or dorsal aspect

_____ 5. transverse plane

_____ 6. sagittal plane

_____ 7. coronal plane

_____ 8. medial aspect

_____ 9. lateral aspect

_____ 10. distal aspect

_____ 11. proximal

A. situated in front of

B. situated farther from the crown of the head

C. farthest point from the origin of a structure or point of attachment

D. situated in back of

E. on the side, farther from the midline

F. nearest the origin of a structure or point of attachment

G. situated toward the crown of the head

H. dividing the body into right and left sides

I. the frontal plane dividing it into front and back halves

J. pertaining to the middle or nearer to the midline

K. a plane through a body part perpendicular to the axis

IDENTIFICATION: Identify the indicated cavities in Figure 5.2 (a diagram of the various body cavities) by writing the correct names in the numbered space that corresponds to the number on the figure.

1. ______________________________

2. ______________________________

3. ______________________________

4. ______________________________

5. ______________________________

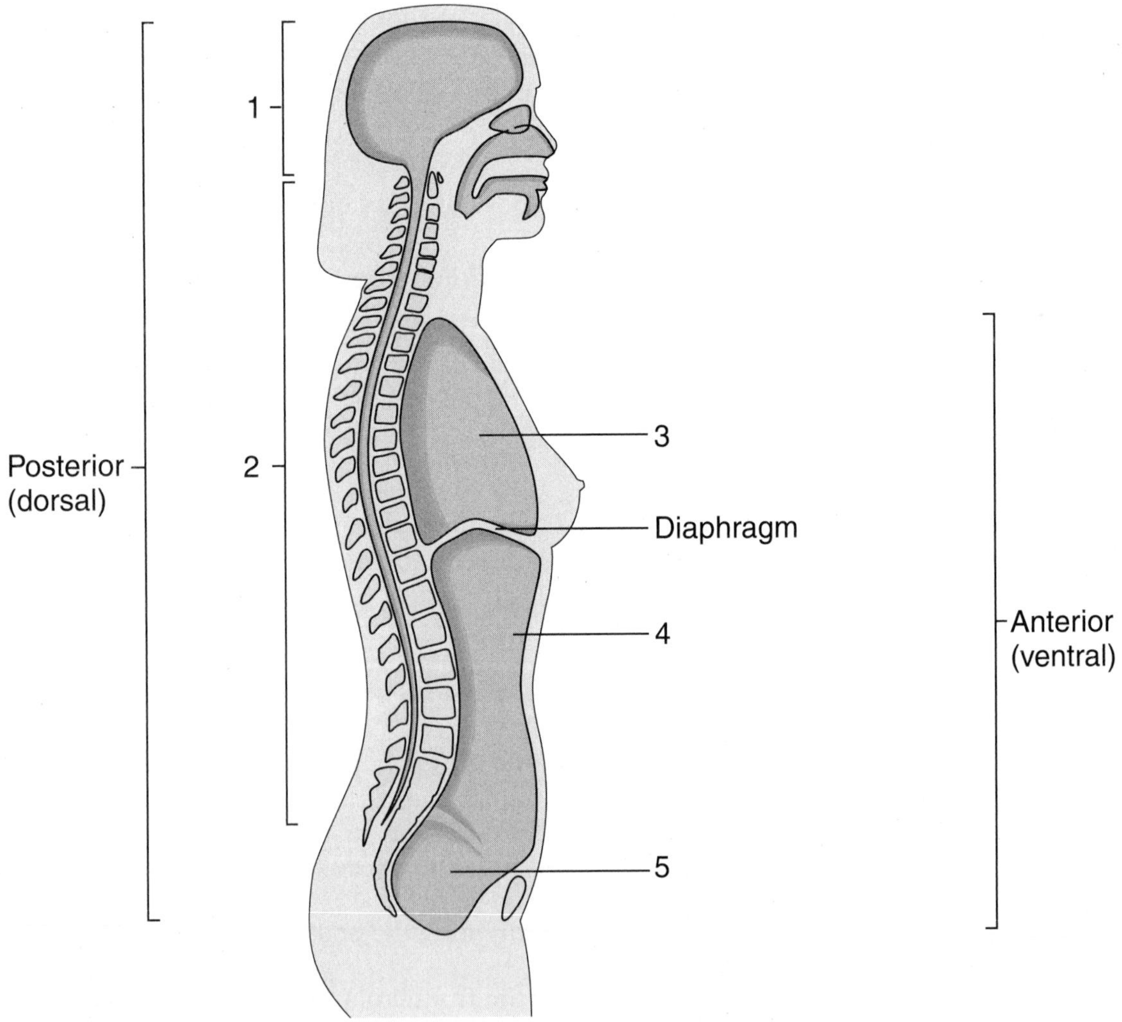

Fig. 5.2 Body cavities.

MATCHING: Match the term with the best description. Write the letter of the best description in the space provided.

_____ 1. hypogastric	A. region of the temples
_____ 2. inguinal	B. region of the neck
_____ 3. temporal	C. region of the shoulder joint and deltoid muscle
_____ 4. scapular	D. region of the armpit
_____ 5. frontal	E. region between the elbow and shoulder
_____ 6. brachial	F. region of the abdomen lateral to the epigastric region
_____ 7. cervical	G. region of the navel
_____ 8. deltoid	H. region inferior to the umbilical region
_____ 9. umbilical	I. region of the kneecap
_____ 10. epigastric	J. region of the thigh
_____ 11. lumbar	K. region of the groin
_____ 12. gluteal	L. region of the lower back
_____ 13. patellar	M. region of the abdomen
_____ 14. popliteal	N. region of the breast and chest
_____ 15. pectoral	O. region of the head, posterior to the frontal region and anterior to the occipital region
_____ 16. parietal	P. region of the temporal bone behind the ear
_____ 17. axillary	Q. region of the muscles of the buttocks
_____ 18. femoral	R. region of the back of the shoulder or shoulder blade
_____ 19. mastoid	S. an area behind the knee joint
_____ 20. hypochondrium	T. region of the forehead

IDENTIFICATION: Identify the anatomic areas indicated in Figures 5.3 and 5.4 by writing the letter of the anatomic area next to the appropriate term in the space provided.

_____ 1. axillary

_____ 2. brachial

_____ 3. cervical

_____ 4. epigastric

_____ 5. femoral

_____ 6. frontal

_____ 7. gluteal

_____ 8. hypochondrium

_____ 9. hypogastric

_____ 10. inguinal

_____ 11. lumbar

_____ 12. occipital

_____ 13. parietal

_____ 14. patellar

_____ 15. pectoral

_____ 16. popliteal

_____ 17. sacral

_____ 18. scapular

_____ 19. temporal

_____ 20. umbilical

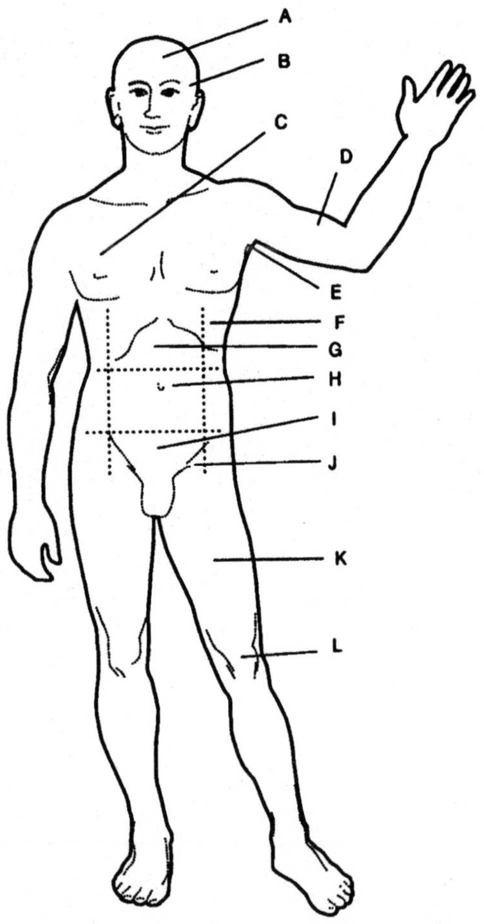

Fig. 5.3 Regions of the body, anterior view.

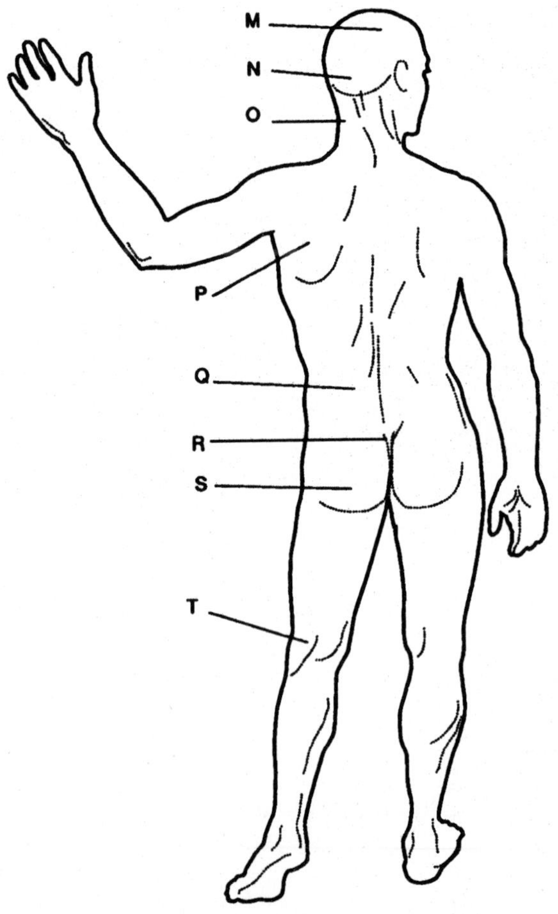

Fig. 5.4 Regions of the body, posterior view.

COMPLETION: In the space(s) provided, write the word(s) that correctly complete(s) each statement.

1. The dorsal cavities include the ____________ cavity and the __________________ cavity.
2. The ventral cavities are the ____________ cavity and ____________ cavity.
3. The liver, stomach, spleen, pancreas, and small and large intestines are located in the ____________ cavity.
4. The ____________ contains the bladder, rectum, and some of the reproductive organs.
5. The four main anatomic parts of the body are ____________, ____________, ____________, and ____________.
6. Body structures containing two or more different tissues that combine to perform a definite function are called ____________.
7. When several organs work together to perform a body function, they constitute an ____________.

SHORT ANSWER: In the spaces provided, list ten organ systems.

1. ____
2. ____
3. ____
4. ____
5. ____
6. ____
7. ____
8. ____
9. ____
10. ____

IDENTIFICATION: In the spaces provided, write the name of the related major body system.

_______________ 1. carries oxygen and nutrients to all parts of the body

_______________ 2. is damaged with a scratch or burn

_______________ 3. provides a rigid structure and attachment for muscles

_______________ 4. breaks down food into absorbable particles

_______________ 5. includes the pituitary, thyroid, and ovaries

_______________ 6. produces heat and movement

_______________ 7. removes uric acid from the system

_______________ 8. provides for continuation of the species

_______________ 9. allows for the absorption of oxygen into the body

_______________ 10. includes the liver, lungs, kidneys, and colon

_______________ 11. provides information about where the body is in the environment

_______________ 12. produces hormones

MULTIPLE CHOICE: Carefully read each statement. Choose the word or phrase that correctly completes the meaning and write the corresponding letter in the blank provided.

1. The imaginary line that divides the body into front and back halves is the ________. ________
   - a) coronal plane
   - b) sagittal plane
   - c) midsagittal plane
   - d) transverse plane

2. The liver and stomach are contained in the ________. ________
   - a) dorsal cavity
   - b) pelvic cavity
   - c) abdominal cavity
   - d) cranial cavity

3. The elbow is ________ to the wrist. ________
   - a) proximal
   - b) medial
   - c) lateral
   - d) distal

4. The ribs are lateral to the ________. ________
   - a) arms
   - b) scapula
   - c) pelvis
   - d) sternum

5. Lumbar refers to the region of the ________. ________
   a) temple
   b) skull
   c) lower back
   d) pelvis

6. The epigastric area is ________. ________
   a) the location of the bladder
   b) inferior to the diaphragm
   c) the region of the tongue
   d) anterior to the scapula

7. The human body has ________ important organ systems. ________
   a) two
   b) five
   c) ten
   d) twenty

8. The axillary region of the body is ________. ________
   a) at the bend of the elbow
   b) the armpit
   c) near the groin
   d) on the head

9. The ________ region of the body is behind the knee. ________
   a) patellar
   b) parietal
   c) popliteal
   d) femoral

10. A sagittal cut through an organ or body divides it into ________. ________
    a) right and left portions
    b) superior and inferior portions
    c) dorsal and ventral portions
    d) three or four lateral portions

11. The bladder is located in the ________. ________
    a) dorsal cavity
    b) crainial cavity
    c) abdominal cavity
    d) pelvic cavity

12. A transverse section in the parietal area would show ________. ________
    a) the inside of the knee
    b) one side of the brain
    c) both sides of the brain
    d) both lungs

WORD REVIEW: The student is encouraged to write down the meaning of each of the following words. This list can be used as a study guide for this unit.

abdominal cavity

anatomic position

anterior

circulatory system

coronal plane

cranial cavity

digestive system

distal

dorsal cavities

endocrine system

excretory system

inferior

integumentary system

lateral

medial

muscular system

nervous system

organ system

pelvic cavity

posterior

proximal

respiratory system

sagittal plane

skeletal system

superior

thoracic cavity

transverse plane

ventral cavities

vertebral cavity

SHORT ANSWER: In the spaces provided, list six functions of the skin.

1. ______________________________
2. ______________________________
3. ______________________________
4. ______________________________
5. ______________________________
6. ______________________________

MATCHING: Match the term with the best description. Write the letter of the appropriate term in the space provided.

A. papillary layer
B. reticular layer
C. subcutaneous tissue
D. stratum corneum
E. stratum spinosum
F. stratum germinativum
G. dermis as a whole
H. epidermis as a whole

_____ 1. the deepest layer of the epidermis

_____ 2. contains fat cells, sweat and oil glands, and hair follicles

_____ 3. contains conelike projections made of fine strands of elastic tissue extending upward into the epidermis

_____ 4. site of keratin formation

_____ 5. contains blood and lymph vessels and nerve endings

_____ 6. serves as a protective cushion for the upper skin layers

_____ 7. contains melanocytes that produce the pigment melanin

_____ 8. contains collagen, reticulum, and elastin fibers

_____ 9. consists of cells containing melanin

IDENTIFICATION: Identify the structures indicated in Figure 5.5 (a cross-section of skin) by writing the letter of the structure next to the appropriate name in the space provided.

_____ 1. arrector pili muscle

_____ 2. dermis

_____ 3. epidermis

_____ 13. sebaceous gland

_____ 14. stratum corneum

_____ 15. stratum germinativum

_____ 4. hair root

_____ 5. adipose

_____ 6. papilla of hair

_____ 7. capillaries

_____ 8. pacinian corpuscle

_____ 9. vein

_____ 10. hair shaft

_____ 11. Meissner corpuscle

_____ 12. reticular fibers

_____ 16. stratum granulosum

_____ 17. subcutaneous tissue

_____ 18. dermal papilla

_____ 19. sudoriferous gland

_____ 20. stratum lucidum

_____ 21. stratum spinosum

_____ 22. artery

_____ 23. nerve

_____ 24. sweat pore

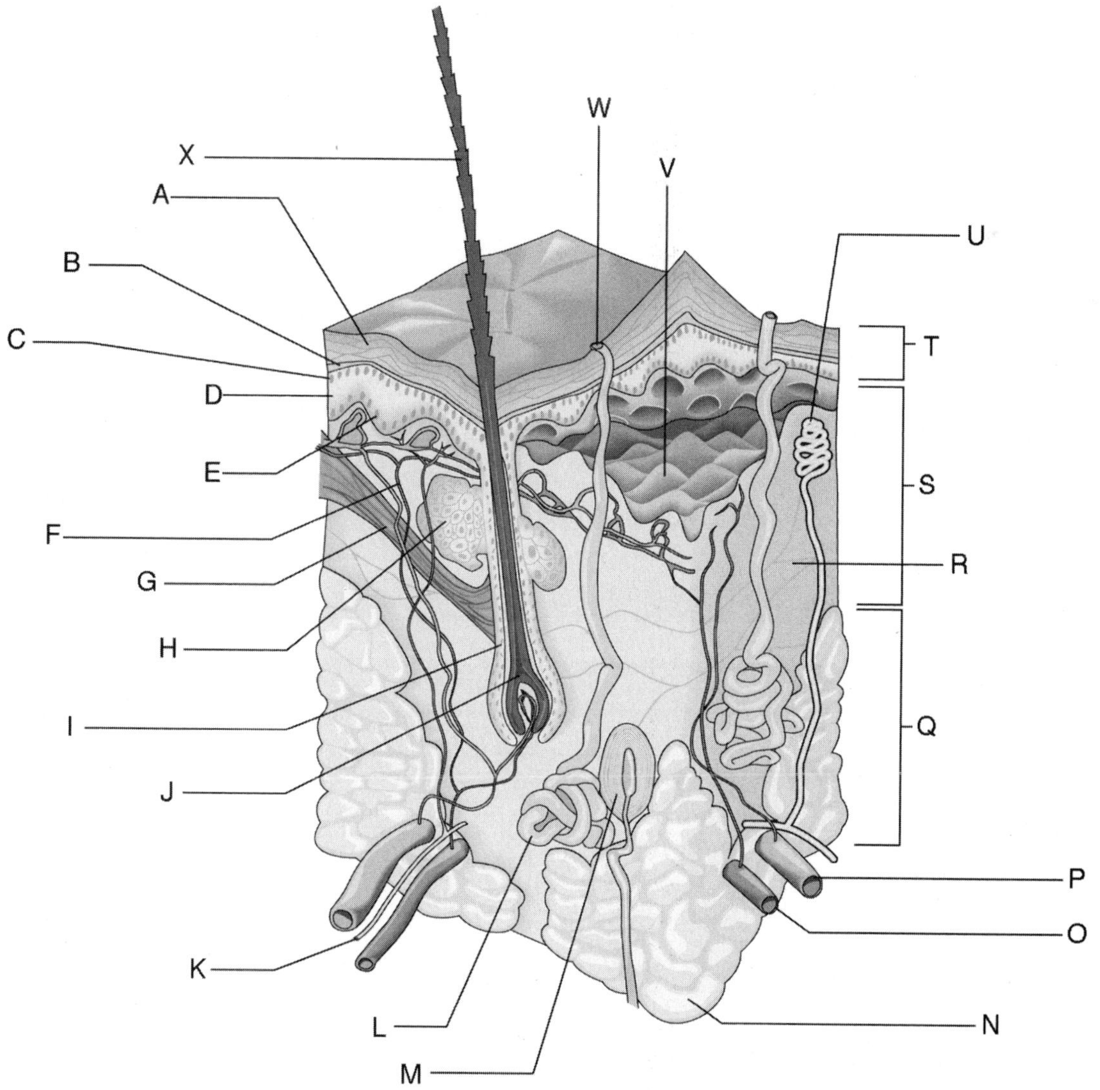

Fig. 5.5 The integumentary system (showing skin and hair).

TRUE OR FALSE: If the following statements are true, write *true* in the space provided. If they are false, replace the italicized word with one that makes the statement true.

_______________ 1. There is a fine network of blood and lymph capillaries in the *epidermis.*

_______________ 2. As people age, the *collagen* of the skin tends to lose its elasticity.

_______________ 3. Pliability of the skin depends on the elasticity of the fibers in the *subcutaneous layer.*

_______________ 4. Healthy skin possesses a slightly *acid* reaction.

_______________ 5. The color of the skin depends on the *thickness* and the blood supply.

SHORT ANSWER: Circle the term that does not belong in each of the following groups (groups flow from left to right).

stratum germinativum	reticular layer	stratum malpighian	stratum granulosum
melanin	collagen	keratin	cuticle
pacinian corpuscle	ruffini corpuscle	arrector pili	Meissner corpuscle
scar	pustule	crust	fissure
seborrhea	leukoderma	lentigines	nevus

COMPLETION: In the space(s) provided, write the word(s) that correctly complete(s) each statement.

1. There are two clearly defined divisions of the skin. The outer layer is the _______________ and the inner layer is the _______________.
2. There are two kinds of duct glands in the skin. _______________ produce sweat and _______________ glands produce oil.
3. Sweat glands are under the control of the _______________ nervous system.
4. Two appendages of the skin are _______________ and _______________.
5. The appendages of the skin referred to in the previous question are composed of _______________.

6. The ____________ muscle is connected to the base of the hair follicle.

7. When the muscle referred to in the previous question contracts, it results in a reaction commonly called ____________.

8. A structural change in the tissues caused by injury or disease is a ____________.

9. A structural change in the tissues that develops in the later stages of disease is called ____________.

10. Small masses of hardened, discolored sebum that appear most frequently on the face, shoulders, chest, and back are called ____________.

MATCHING: Match the term with the best description. Write the letter of the best description in the space provided.

_____ 1. scar

_____ 2. macule

_____ 3. pustule

_____ 4. scale

_____ 5. tumor

_____ 6. vesicle

_____ 7. bulla

_____ 8. ulcer

_____ 9. wheal

_____ 10. papule

_____ 11. crust

_____ 12. fissure

A. an accumulation of epidermal flakes such as excessive dandruff

B. an itchy, swollen lesion that lasts only a few hours

C. an open lesion on the skin accompanied by loss of skin depth

D. a small, elevated pimple in the skin

E. a crack in the skin such as in chapped hands or lips

F. the scab on a sore

G. likely to form during the healing of an injury

H. an elevation of the skin having an inflamed base and containing pus

I. an external swelling, varying in size, shape, and color

J. a small, discolored spot or patch such as freckles

K. a blister similar to but larger than a vesicle

L. a blister with clear fluid in it

COMPLETION: In the space(s) provided, write the word(s) that correctly complete(s) each statement.

1. A skin inflammation caused by outside agents or chemicals is ________________.

2. The most common type of skin cancer is ________________.

3. The most dangerous type of skin cancer is ________________.

4. A mass of connected boils is a ____________.

5. Three types of warts are ____________, ____________, and ____________.

6. Three kinds of skin cancer are ________________, ________________, and ________________.

7. The A-B-C-D-E signs for skin cancer are:

____

____

____

____

____

8. ____________ is a chronic, inflammatory skin condition characterized by round, dry patches covered with coarse, silvery scales.

9. ____________ is a highly contagious, bacterial skin infection that is most common in children.

10. Another name for furuncle is ____________.

MULTIPLE CHOICE: Carefully read each statement. Choose the word or phrase that correctly completes the meaning and write the corresponding letter in the blank provided.

1. The largest organ of the body is the ________. ________
   a) muscular system
   b) skin
   c) liver
   d) stomach

2. Protection, heat regulation, secretion, excretion, and absorption are functions of the ________. ________
   a) endocrine system
   b) skin
   c) muscles
   d) brain

3. Exposure to ultraviolet light causes the skin to darken by stimulating the production of ________. ________
   a) melanin
   b) carotene
   c) fibroblasts
   d) hemoglobin

4. Collagen, reticulum, and elastin are the fibers in the cells of the ________. ________
   a) epidermis
   b) lymph
   c) dermis
   d) blood

5. The skin gets its strength, form, and flexibility from ________. ________
   a) collagen
   b) elastin
   c) the muscles
   d) subcutaneous tissue

6. A small discolored spot on the skin is a ________. ________
   a) macule
   b) bulla
   c) tumor
   d) vesicle

7. An elevation of the skin having an inflamed base and containing pus is a ________. ________
   a) papule
   b) pimple
   c) pustule
   d) wheal

8. A crack in the skin penetrating into the dermis is called a ________. ________
   a) fissure
   b) crust
   c) scab
   d) cut

9. Skin disorders are an area that massage therapists should be able to ________. ________
   a) treat successfully
   b) use vibration on
   c) recognize and refer
   d) apply antibiotic creams to

10. A generalized term for a structural change in tissue from disease or injury is ________. ________
    a) fracture
    b) lesion
    c) hematoma
    d) laceration

11. As cells are pushed from the deeper portion of the epidermis toward the surface ________. ________
    a) they tend to die
    b) they become dermal cells
    c) they divide continually
    d) their supply of nutrients improve

12. The subcutaneous layer consists of ________. ________
    a) epithelial tissue
    b) epithelium and loose connective tissue
    c) loose connective tissue and adipose tissue
    d) adipose tissue and skeletal muscle tissue

13. A thickening in the skin caused by repeated or continued pressure is a ________. ________
    a) macule
    b) wheal
    c) bulla
    d) callus

14. An itchy swollen lesion that lasts only a few hours is a ________. ________
    a) tumor
    b) papule
    c) bulla
    d) wheal

15. Another name for skin is ________ membrane. ________
    a) synovial
    b) cutaneous
    c) mucous
    d) serous

16. "Goose bumps" are the result of ________. ________
    a) a nervous irritation
    b) contracting arrector pili muscles
    c) body heat loss
    d) oxygen depletion

17. The ________ is a semi-solid part of the skin made up of a mixture of fibers, water and 'ground substance'. ________
    a) eccrine
    b) melanin
    c) dermis
    d) epidermis

18. The ________ comprises almost a solid sheet of cells at the outermost layers of the skin. ________
    a) dermis
    b) epidermis
    c) graft
    d) subcutaneous tissue

19. When a body lies in one position too long, decreased circulation can result in ________, or '' "bedsores." ________
    a) decubitus ulcers
    b) apocrine
    c) acne rosacea
    d) hematomas

Word Review: The student is encouraged to write down the meaning of each of the following words. The list can be used as a study guide for this unit.

collagen

---

dermis

---

epidermis

---

integument

---

keratin

---

melanin

---

reticular layer

---

sebaceous

____

____

stratum germinativum

____

____

stratum granulosum

____

____

stratum spinosum

____

____

subcutaneous tissue

____

____

sudoriferous

____

____

SYSTEM TWO: THE SKELETAL SYSTEM

SHORT ANSWER: In the spaces provided, list the five main functions of the skeletal system.

1. ____

2. ____

3. ____

____

4. ____

5. ____

KEY CHOICES: Bones are classified in one of four major bone categories. Put the appropriate key letter for each of the following bone classifications in the space provided.

S = Short bones

L = Long bones

I = Irregular bones

F = Flat bones

_____ 1. tibia

_____ 2. ilium

_____ 3. phalange

_____ 4. ulna

_____ 5. occiput

_____ 6. calcaneus

_____ 7. axis

_____ 8. femur

_____ 9. talus

_____ 10. metacarpal

_____ 11. scapula

_____ 12. rib

COMPLETION: In the space(s) provided, write the word(s) that correctly complete(s) each statement.

1. The skeletal system is composed of ____________, ____________, and ____________.

2. The inorganic mineral matter of bone consists mainly of ________________ and ________________.

3. The fibrous membrane covering bone that serves as an attachment for tendons and ligaments is the ____________.

4. The spongy bone tissue in flat bones and at the ends of long bones is filled with ________________ and is the site of production for ____________.

5. The hollow chamber formed in the shaft of long bones that is filled with yellow bone marrow is the ________________.

IDENTIFICATION: Identify the structures indicated in Figure 5.6 (a diagram of a typical long bone) by writing the correct letter in the space provided.

_____ 1. proximal epiphysis

_____ 2. compact bone

_____ 3. diaphysis (shaft of bone)

_____ 4. red marrow

_____ 5. distal epiphysis

_____ 6. medullary cavity (site of yellow bone marrow in adults)

_____ 7. periosteum (covering of bone)

_____ 8. spongy bone

_____ 9. articular cartilage

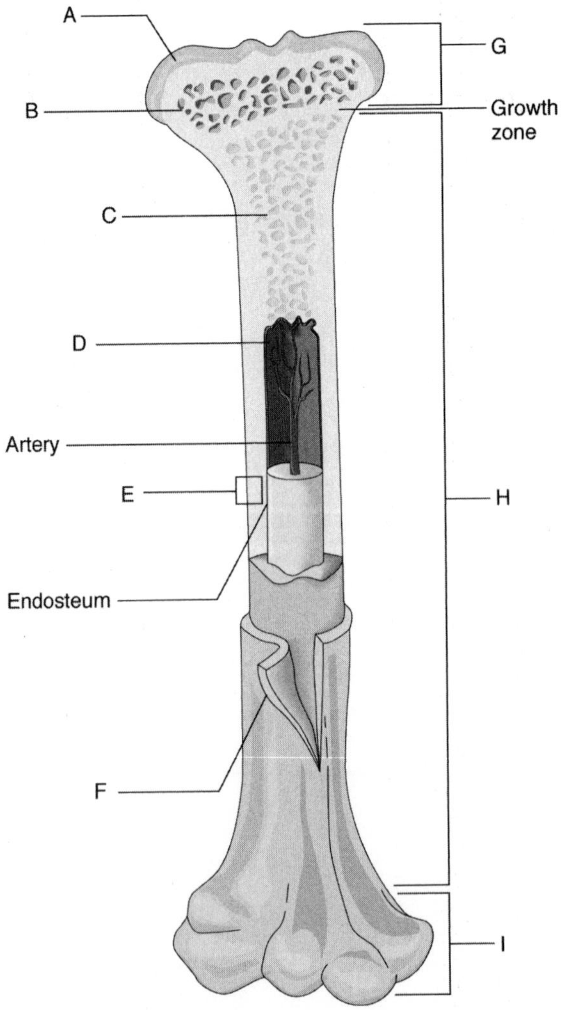

Fig. 5.6 Structure of long bone.

COMPLETION: In the space(s) provided, write the word(s) that correctly complete(s) each statement.

1. The two main parts of the skeleton are the ________________ and the ________________.

2. The bones of the skull, thorax, vertebral column, and the hyoid bone make up the ________________.

3. The bones of the shoulder, upper extremities, hips, and lower extremities make up the ________________.

4. In the human adult, the skeleton consists of _____ bones.

5. The spine consists of _____ vertebra.

6. There are _____ cervical vertebra.

7. There are _____ thoracic vertebra.

8. There are _____ lumbar vertebra.

9. There are _____ carpals in each wrist.

10. There are _____ tarsals in each ankle.

11. There are _____ phalanges in each hand.

12. The connection where two bones come together is called a ____________ or an ____________.

13. The cranium is composed of _____ bones.

14. The face is composed of _____ bones.

KEY CHOICES: Joints are classified according to their structure and their function. In the first column of spaces provided, place the appropriate key letter indicating the structural classification next to the corresponding terms. In the second column, place the appropriate key letter indicating the functional classification next to the corresponding terms.

F = fibrous joints	A = amphiarthrotic joints
C = cartilaginous joints	D = diarthrotic joints
N = synovial joints	S = synarthrotic joints

Structural Classification	Functional Classification	
________	________	1. symphysis pubis
________	________	2. glenohumeral joint
________	________	3. sagittal suture
________	________	4. elbow joint
________	________	5. bones united by fibrous connective tissue
________	________	6. hip joint
________	________	7. essentially immovable
________	________	8. sacroiliac joint
________	________	9. joint capsule with synovial fluid
________	________	10. intervertebral joints
________	________	11. articular cartilage on bones
________	________	12. joint between sphenoid and temporal bones
________	________	13. freely movable
________	________	14. allows limited movement

KEY CHOICE: Put the appropriate key letter for each of the following types of joints in the space provided. Movable joints in the body are classified descriptively.

A. pivot joints
B. ball-and-socket joints
C. hinge joints
D. gliding joints
E. saddle joints
F. condyloid ellipsoid
G. symphysis

_____ 1. joint between ulna and humerus

_____ 2. hip joint

_____ 3. knee joint

_____ 4. joint between the first metacarpal and the trapezium

_____ 5. joints between radius and carpals

_____ 6. glenohumeral joint

_____ 7. joint between axis and atlas

_____ 8. joint between radius and ulna near elbow

_____ 9. intervertebral joints

_____ 10. interphalangeal joints

_____ 11. joint between the tibia and the talus

_____ 12. between right and left pubis

IDENTIFICATION: Identify the bones in Figure 5.7 by writing the correct label in the numbered space that corresponds to the number on the figure.

1. ______________________
2. ______________________
3. ______________________
4. ______________________
5. ______________________
6. ______________________
7. ______________________
8. ______________________
9. ______________________
10. ______________________
11. ______________________
12. ______________________
13. ______________________
14. ______________________
15. ______________________
16. ______________________
17. ______________________
18. ______________________
19. ______________________
20. ______________________
21. ______________________
22. ______________________
23. ______________________
24. ______________________
25. ______________________
26. ______________________
27. ______________________
28. ______________________
29. ______________________

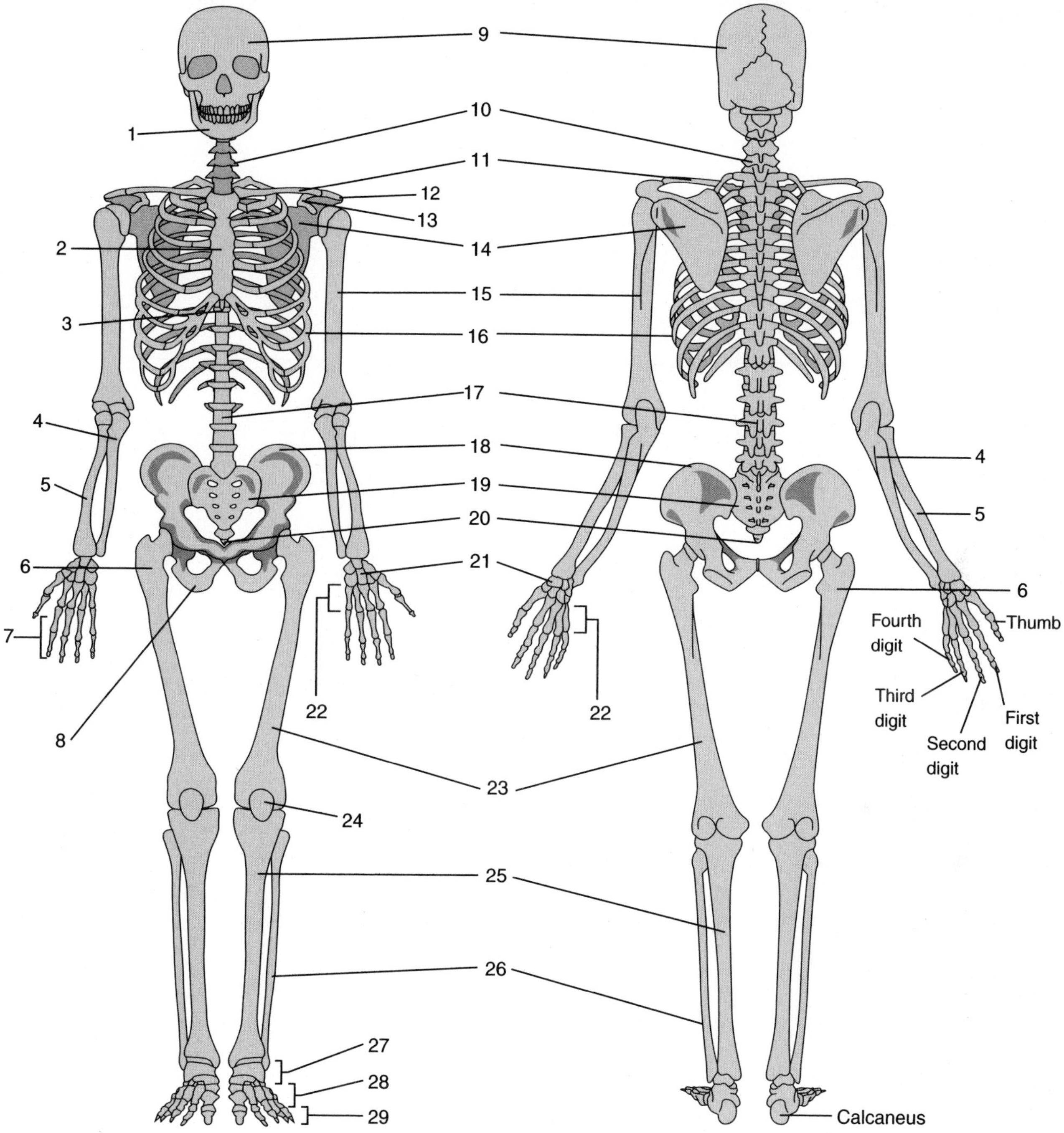

Fig. 5.7 Skeletal system, anterior view.

IDENTIFICATION: Identify the bony landmarks in Figures 5.8a and 5.8b by writing the correct name in the lettered space that corresponds to the letter in the figures.

A. ______________________

B. ______________________

C. ______________________

D. ______________________

____

E. ______________________

F. ______________________

G. ______________________

H. ______________________

I. ______________________

J. ______________________

K. ______________________

L. ______________________

M. ______________________

N. ______________________

O. ______________________

P. ______________________

Q. ______________________

R. ______________________

S. ______________________

T. ______________________

U. ______________________

V. ______________________

W. ______________________

X. ______________________

Y. ______________________

Z. ______________________

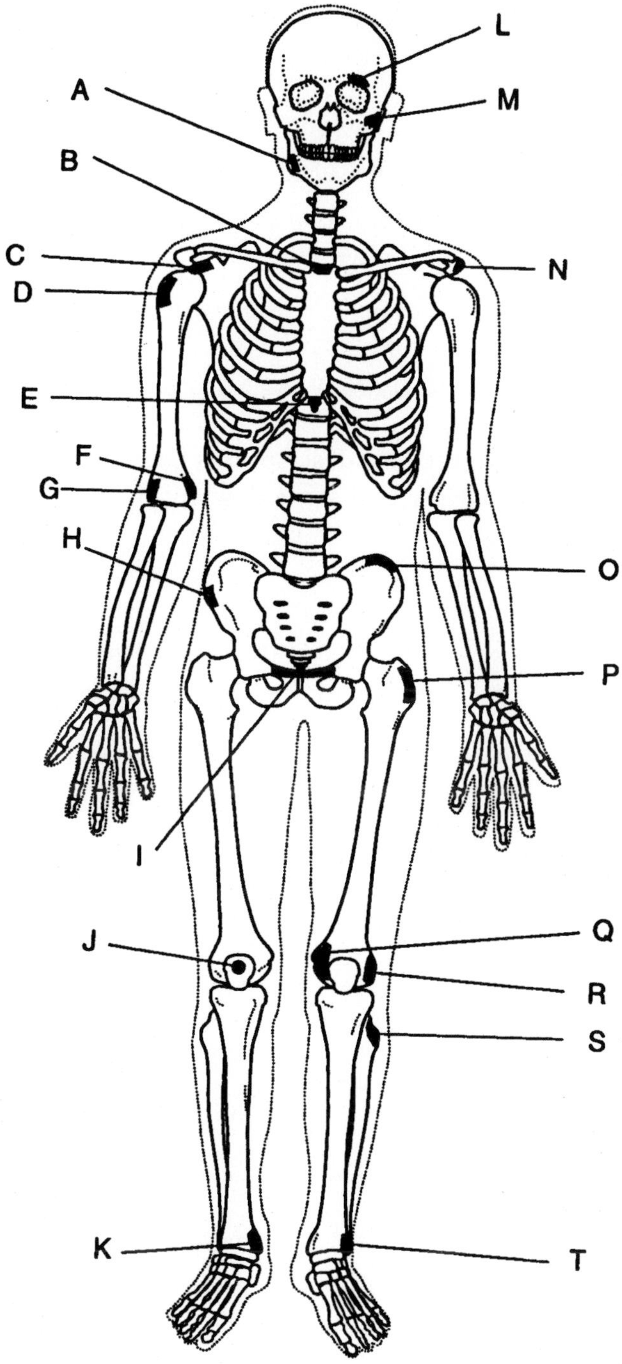

Fig. 5.8a Major bony landmarks on the body, anterior view.

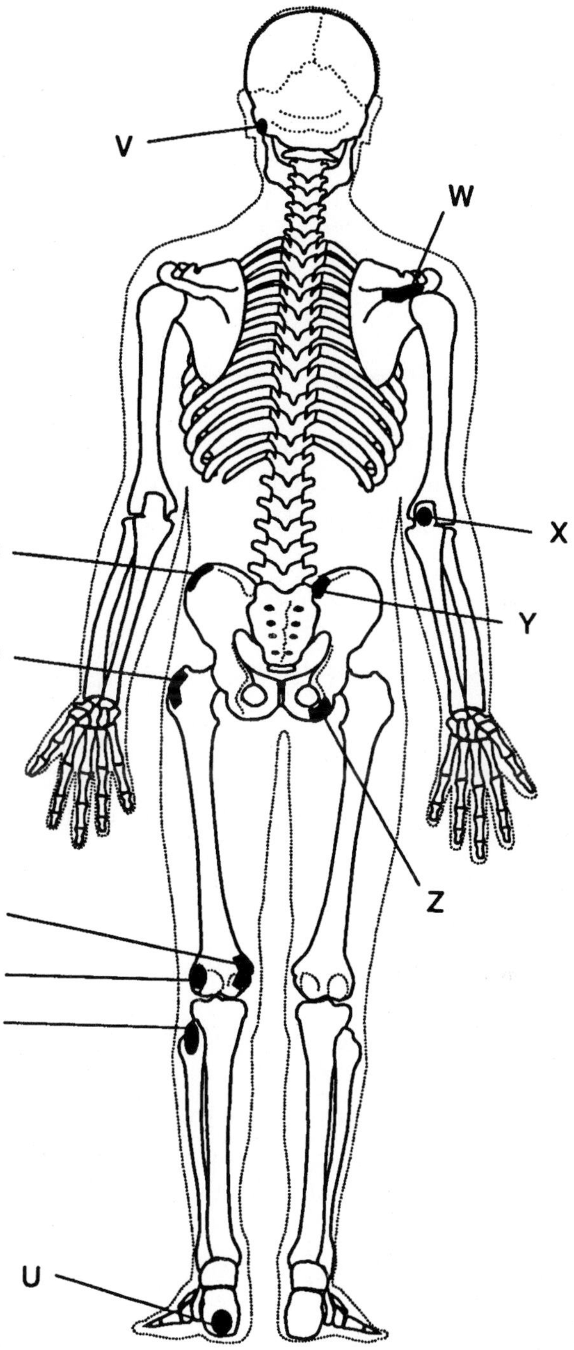

Fig. 5.8b Major bony landmarks on the body, posterior view.

IDENTIFICATION: Identify the bones and sutures in Figure 5.9 by writing the number of the bone next to the appropriate term in the space provided.

_____ A. ethmoid	_____ F. nasal	_____ K. zygomatic arch
_____ B. frontal	_____ G. occipital	_____ L. coronal suture
_____ C. lacrimal	_____ H. parietal	_____ M. lambdoidal suture
_____ D. mandible	_____ I. sphenoid	_____ N. squamosal suture
_____ E. maxilla	_____ J. temporal	

MATCHING: Match the bone names listed above with the best descriptions listed below. Write the letter of the bone name in the space provided. Note that some descriptions apply to more than one bone.

_____ 1. cheekbone

_____ 2. holds the upper teeth

_____ 3. contains the foramen magnum

_____ 4. forms the supraorbital ridge

_____ 5. four bones containing the paranasal sinuses

_____ 6. forms the sagittal suture

_____ 7. forms the coronal suture

_____ 8. forms the squamosal suture

_____ 9. forms the lambdoidal suture

_____ 10. forms the mastoid process

_____ 11. forms the chin

_____ 12. connects with all other cranial bones

_____ 13. connected to the skull with a diarthrotic joint

_____ 14. contain openings for tear ducts

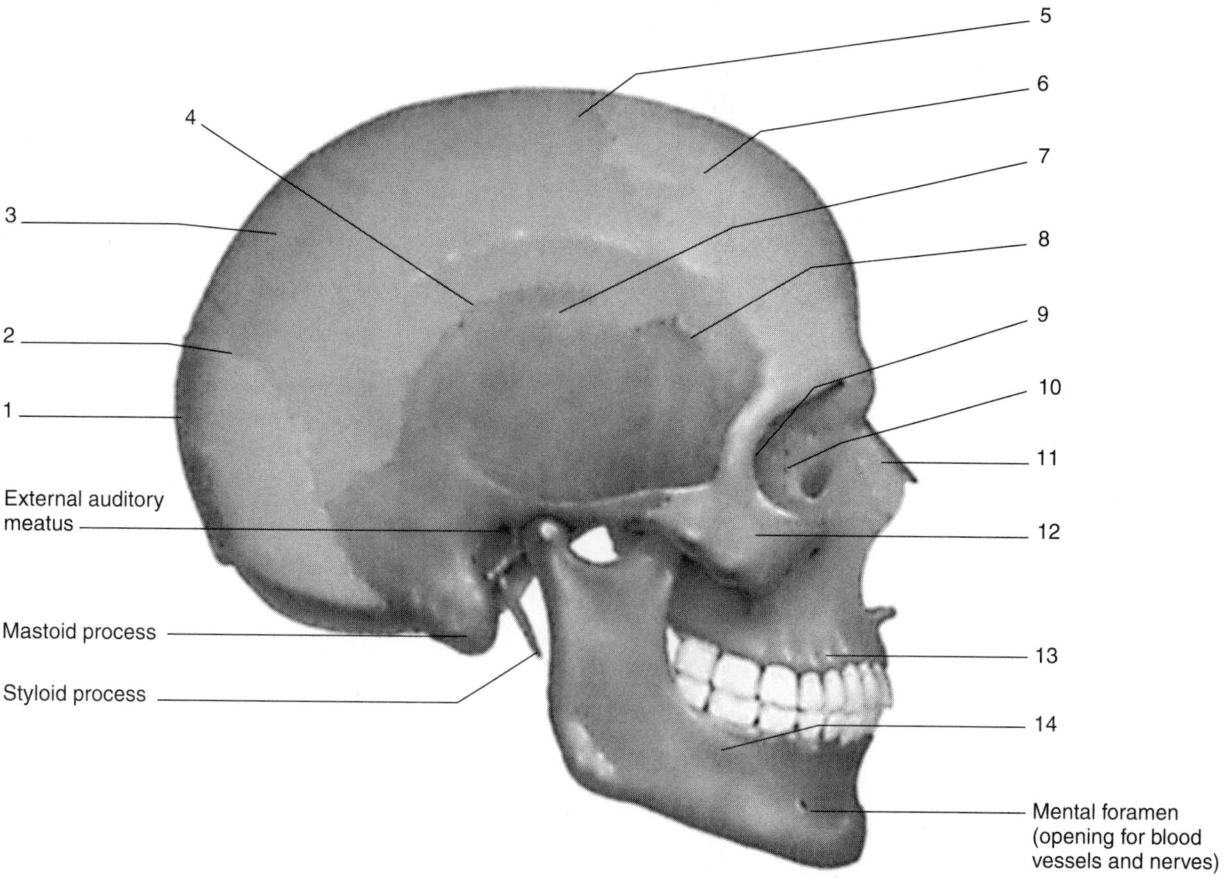

Fig. 5.9 Skeletal structures of the cranium, neck, and face.

IDENTIFICATION: Identify the parts of the spine in Figure 5.10 by writing the letter of the part next to the corresponding label in the space provided.

_____ 1. atlas, axis

_____ 2. cervical vertebrae

_____ 3. coccyx

_____ 4. lumbar vertebrae

_____ 5. sacrum

_____ 6. thoracic vertebrae

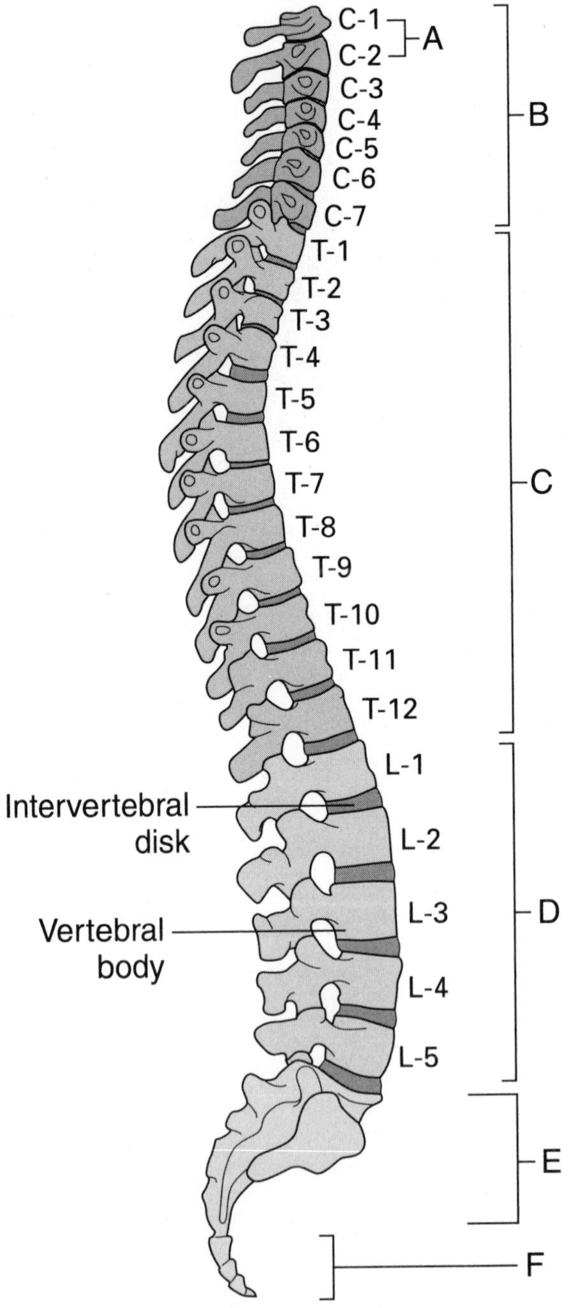

Fig. 5.10 Vertebral column.

MATCHING: Match the term with the best description. Write the letter of the best description in the space provided.

______ 1. fossa	A. a less prominent ridge of a bone than a crest
______ 2. trochanter	B. a rounded articulating process at the end of a bone
______ 3. foramen	C. a large process for muscle attachment
______ 4. sinus	D. a sharp slender projection
______ 5. process	E. a tubelike passage
______ 6. condyle	F. a depression or hollow
______ 7. line	G. a ridge
______ 8. tuberosity	H. a cavity within a bone
______ 9. meatus	I. a rounded knuckle-like prominence usually at a point of articulation
______ 10. tubercle	J. a small rounded process
______ 11. head	K. a hole
______ 12. spine	L. a large rounded process
______ 13. crest	M. a bone prominence or projection

SHORT ANSWER: Circle the term that does not belong in each of the following groups (groups flow from left to right).

tibia	patella	femur	fibula
elbow	knee	finger	hip
axis/atlas	sacroiliac	intervertebral	pubic symphysis
tubercle	fossa	tuberosity	condyle
cranium	rib	vertebra	scapula

MATCHING: Match the skeletal disorders with the best description. Write the letter of the appropriate skeletal disorder in the space provided.

A. dislocation   C. osteoarthritis   E. fracture   G. bursitis

B. sprain   D. osteoporosis   F. rheumatoid arthritis

_____ 1. an inflammation of the small fluid-filled sacs located near the joints

_____ 2. a break or rupture in a bone

_____ 3. an inflammation causing the articular cartilage to erode and the joints to calcify and eventually become immovable

_____ 4. increased porosity of the bone that causes a thinning of bone tissue

_____ 5. displacement of a bone within a joint

_____ 6. a chronic inflammatory disease, that first affects the synovial membrane lining the joints

_____ 7. stretching or tearing of ligaments

_____ 8. a chronic disease that accompanies aging, usually affecting joints that have experienced a great deal of wear and tear or trauma

IDENTIFICATION: Identify each of the spinal curves in Figure 5.11 by writing the correct label in the space provided.

A. ____________________   B. ____________________   C. ____________________

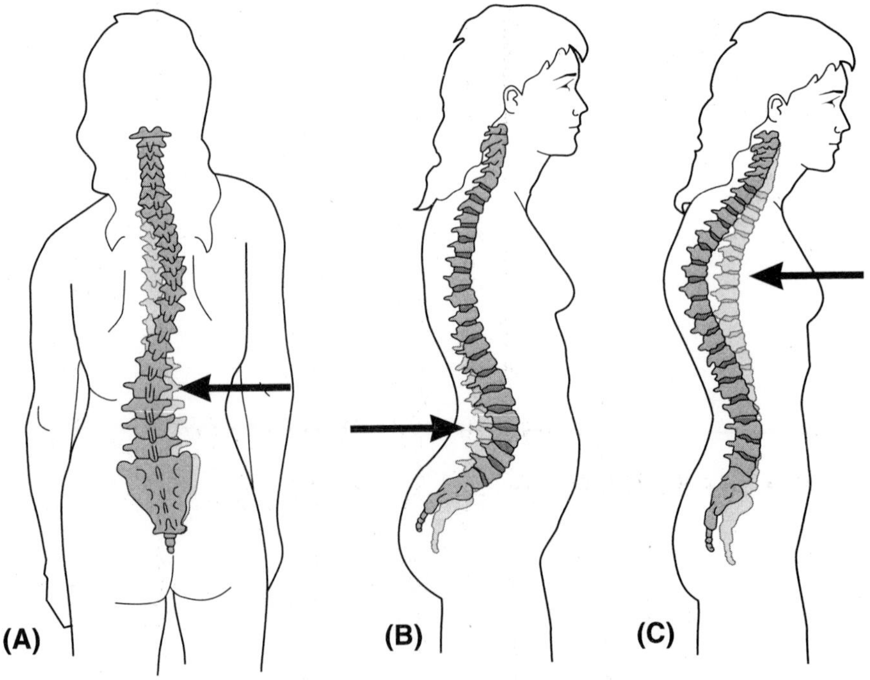

Fig. 5.11 Abnormal curvatures of the spine.

MULTIPLE CHOICE: Carefully read each statement. Choose the word or phrase that correctly completes the meaning and write the corresponding letter in the blank provided.

1. Flat bones are found in the ________. ________
   a) knee c) leg
   b) skull d) spine

2. The number of bones in the human adult skeleton is ________. ________
   a) 101 c) 310
   b) 206 d) 502

3. The bones of the upper and lower extremities form the ________. ________
   a) axial skeleton c) skull
   b) spine d) appendicular skeleton

4. White blood cells are produced by the ________. ________
   a) yellow bone marrow c) osteoclasts
   b) lymphocytes d) red bone marrow

5. A fracture in the shaft of the bone would be a break in the ________. ________
   a) epiphysis c) diaphysis
   b) epiphyseal plate d) articular cartilage

6. Muscle tendon fibers attach to bone by interlacing with ________. ________
   a) compact bone c) periosteum
   b) ligaments d) endosteum

7. Which of following is NOT a bone of the cranium? ________
   a) temporal c) zygomatic
   b) sphenoid d) parietal

8. The coracoid process is located ________. ________
   a) on the scapula c) on the pelvis
   b) behind the ear d) at the proximal end of the ulna

9. Immovable joints are called ________. ________
   a) amphiarthrotic c) synarthrotic
   b) articulations d) synovial

10. The range of motion of amphiarthrotic joints is ________. ________
    a) 360 degrees c) freely moving
    b) limited d) in a single plane

11. An example of a diarthrotic joint is ________. ________
    a) knee
    b) skull
    c) intervertebral
    d) the teeth

12. The greatest range of movement is found in ________. ________
    a) pivot joints
    b) hinge joints
    c) ball-and-socket joints
    d) saddle joints

13. A stretched ligament with some discomfort and minimal loss of function is a ________. ________
    a) Class I strain
    b) Class II sprain
    c) Class I sprain
    d) Class III sprain

14. The major purpose of the epiphyseal plate is ________. ________
    a) mending of fractures
    b) enlarging the epiphyses
    c) providing strength in long bones
    d) lengthening long bones

15. Lateral curvature of the spine is called ________. ________
    a) lordosis
    b) scoliosis
    c) convexity
    d) kyphosis

16. Degenerative joint disease is generally known as ________. ________
    a) osteoporosis
    b) rheumatoid arthritis
    c) osteoarthritis
    d) osteomyelitis

17. Which of following is NOT a part of the pelvis? ________
    a) ischium
    b) pubis
    c) zygomatic
    d) ilium

18. The part of the long bone that is soft and contains the "growth line" is referred to as the ________. ________
    a) epiphysis
    b) diaphysis
    c) bone shaft
    d) bone marrow

19. The "ankle bone" that protrudes on the inside of the leg is the ________. ________
    a) medial malleolus
    b) fibula
    c) medial epicondyle
    d) lesser trochanter

20. The knee joint is an example of a ________. ______
    a) synarthrotic joint
    b) hinge joint
    c) amphiarthrotic joint
    d) saddle joint

21. Which of the following is NOT found in the axial skeleton? ______
    a) the cranium
    b) the scapula
    c) the sacrum
    d) the sternum

22. The medial malleolus is on the ________. ______
    a) elbow
    b) wrist
    c) knee
    d) ankle

WORD REVIEW: The student is encouraged to write down the meaning of each of the following words. The list can be used as a study guide for this unit.

amphiarthrotic

____

____

appendicular skeleton

____

____

arthritis

____

____

articular cartilage

____

____

articulation

____

____

axial skeleton

bursa

cartilage

compact bone tissue

cranium

diaphysis

diarthrotic joint

epiphysis

joint capsule

kyphosis

ligament

lordosis

marrow

medullary cavity

periosteum

osteoporosis

scoliosis

sprain

synarthrotic

synovial fluid

synovial membrane

vertebra

KEY CHOICES: There are three classifications of muscles. Put the appropriate key letter(s) for each of the following muscle types in the spaces provided.

A = skeletal B = smooth C = cardiac

_____ 1. contains striations

_____ 2. shapes and contours the body

_____ 3. forms the hollow organs

_____ 4. involved with transport of materials in the body

_____ 5. found only in the heart

_____ 6. spindle shaped

_____ 7. multinucleated

_____ 8. controlled by the autonomic nervous system

_____ 9. quadrangular in shape, joined end to end

_____ 10. contracts without direct nerve action

_____ 11. referred to as the muscular system

_____ 12. coordinates activity to act as a pump

COMPLETION: In the space(s) provided, write the word(s) that correctly complete(s) each statement.

1. The main organ of the muscle system is _____________.

2. Muscle cells have the unique ability to ____________________.

3. Muscle comprises approximately _____________ percent of a person's body weight.

4. The characteristics that enable muscles to perform their functions of contraction and movement are _____________, _____________, and _____________.

5. The ability to return to its original shape after being stretched is _____________.

6. The capacity of muscles to receive and react to stimuli is _____________.

7. The ability to contract or shorten and thereby exert force is _____________.

COMPLETION: In the space(s) provided, write the word(s) that correctly complete(s) each statement.

1. The functional unit of a muscle is the ____________ or ____________.
2. The cell membrane of the muscle cell is the ____________.
3. The connective tissue covering of the muscle cell is the ____________.
4. Each muscle cell contains hundreds or even thousands of parallel ____________.
5. The interaction of ____________ and ____________ filaments gives muscle its unique contractile ability.
6. The arrangement of ____________ and ____________ gives skeletal muscles a striated or striped appearance.
7. The site where the muscle fiber and nerve fiber meet is called the ______________________ or ______________________.
8. A motor neuron and all the muscle fibers that it controls constitute a ____________.
9. When a nerve impulse reaches the end of the nerve fiber, a chemical neurotransmitter called ____________ is released.
10. The energy for muscle contraction comes from the breakdown of the ________________________________.

11. A metabolic process known as the ______________ or the ______________ takes place, resulting in the synthesis of ATP and the production of carbon dioxide, water, and energy in the form of heat.

12. When sufficient oxygen is available, ATP is synthesized through ______________ respiration.

13. When the oxygen supply is depleted, ATP is synthesized through ______________ respiration.

14. During strenuous activity, heavy breathing and accelerated heart rate are indications of ______________.

15. Rapid or prolonged muscle contractions, to the point that oxygen debt becomes extreme and the muscle ceases to respond, causes ______________.

16. The most stationary attachment of a muscle is the ______________.

17. The muscle attachment that creates the action of the structure is the ______________.

18. A(n) ______________ contraction occurs when a muscle contracts and the ends of the muscle do not move.

19. The glistening cord that connects the muscle with its attachment is a ______________.

IDENTIFICATION: Identify each skeletal muscle part in Figure 5.12 by writing the number of the part next to the appropriate term in the space provided.

_____ A. actin filament	_____ E. myofilament	_____ I. perimysium
_____ B. endomysium	_____ F. myofibril	_____ J. sarcolemma
_____ C. epimysium	_____ G. myosin filament	_____ K. sarcoplasm
_____ D. fascicle	_____ H. muscle fiber	_____ L. tendon

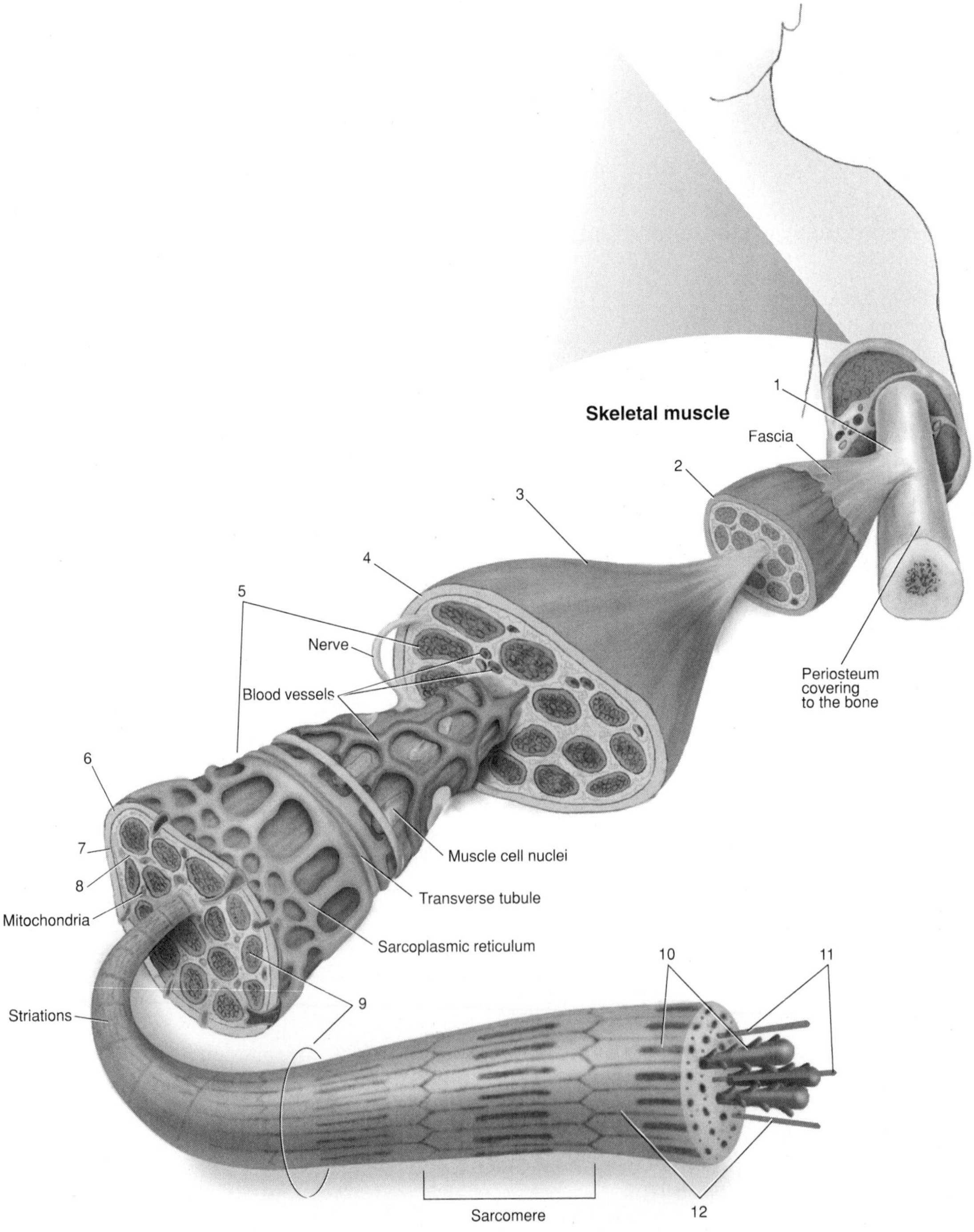

Fig. 5.12 Structure of skeletal muscle.

MATCHING: Match the skeletal muscle part listed above with the best description listed below. Write the letter of the skeletal muscle part in the space provided.

_____ 1. connective tissue projecting beyond the end of the muscle

_____ 2. connective tissue covering the entire muscle

_____ 3. separates muscles into bundles of fibers

_____ 4. connective tissue covering of each muscle cell

_____ 5. bundle of muscle fibers

_____ 6. contractile unit of muscle tissue

_____ 7. one of the microscopic threads that can be rendered visible in a muscle fiber

_____ 8. the muscle cell membrane

_____ 9. structure of the muscle cell containing actin and myosin

_____ 10. the muscle cell intercellular fluid

IDENTIFICATION: Identify each part of the muscle cell sarcomere in Figure 5.13 by writing the appropriate letter next to the correct term in the space provided.

_____ 1. A band

_____ 2. actin filament

_____ 3. H zone

_____ 4. I band

_____ 5. M line

_____ 6. myosin filament

_____ 7. sarcomere

_____ 8. Z line

_____ 9. zone of overlap

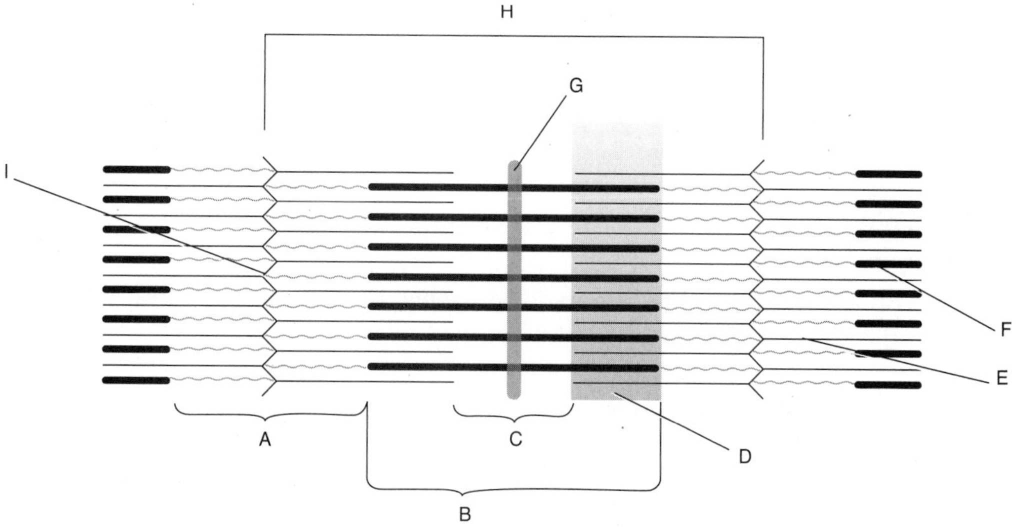

Fig. 5.13 Parts of the muscle cell.

MATCHING: Match the term with the best description. Write the letter of the appropriate term in the space provided.

A. Type I muscle fibers B. Type II muscle fibers

_____ 1. able to sustain low-level muscle contractions

_____ 2. darker red color

_____ 3. depend on anaerobic metabolism

_____ 4. fast twitch fibers

_____ 5. fatigue easily

_____ 6. have fewer mitochondria

_____ 7. high capacity to generate ATP

_____ 8. high resistance to fatigue

_____ 9. high number of mitochondria

_____ 10. larger fibers with more actin and myosin filaments

_____ 11. lighter color

_____ 12. more prominent in phasic muscles

_____ 13. more prominent in postural muscles

_____ 14. produce powerful, fast contractions

_____ 15. rich capillary supply

_____ 16. slow twitch fibers

_____ 17. tend to tighten and shorten when stressed

_____ 18. uses aerobic metabolism

_____ 19. vulnerable to muscle strains and tendonitis

IDENTIFICATION: On the following list of muscles, identify the postural muscles by placing a "P" in the space provided.

_____ 1. adductor longus and magnus

_____ 2. anterior neck flexors

_____ 3. deltoid

_____ 14. piriformis

_____ 15. quadratus lumborum

_____ 16. rectus abdominis

_____ 4. gluteals

_____ 5. iliopsoas

_____ 6. latissimus dorsi

_____ 7. levator scapulae

_____ 8. lower pectorals

_____ 9. lumbar erector spinae

_____ 10. middle and lower trapezius

_____ 11. oblique abdominals

_____ 12. pectoralis minor

_____ 13. peroneals

_____ 17. rectus femoris

_____ 18. rhomboids

_____ 19. sacrospinalis

_____ 20. scalenii

_____ 21. serratus anterior

_____ 22. sternocleidomastoid

_____ 23. tensor fascia lata

_____ 24. triceps

_____ 25. upper trapezius

_____ 26. vastus muscles

TRUE OR FALSE: If the following statements are true, write *true* in the space provided. If they are false, replace the italicized word with one that makes the statement true.

__________ 1. Muscle fibers are attached to bone by connective tissue called *ligaments.*

__________ 2. Each motor nerve attaches to *one* muscle cell.

__________ 3. The release of calcium ions by the sarcoplasmic reticulum results in a *muscle contraction.*

__________ 4. A skeletal muscle by definition has *both ends* attached to bone.

__________ 5. Only enough ATP is stored in muscle to sustain a muscle contraction for a few *minutes.*

__________ 6. ATP is produced by the *mitochondria.*

__________ 7. An eccentric contraction is an *isotonic* contraction.

COMPLETION: In the space(s) provided, write the word(s) that correctly complete(s) each statement.

1. A(n) __________ contraction occurs when a muscle is contracted and the ends of the muscle move further apart.

2. A(n) __________ contraction occurs when a muscle is contracted and the ends of the muscle move closer together.

3. Eccentric and concentric muscle contractions are both __________ contractions.

4. When an action occurs, the muscle that is responsible for that action is the

_____________________________.

5. When an action occurs, the muscle that is responsible for the opposite action is the

______________.

6. Muscles that assist the primary muscle of an action are called ______________.

7. When discussing the dynamics of the movement of the body, the three components

of motion are ____________________, ______________________, and _____________.

MATCHING: Match the term with the best description. Write the letter of the best description in the space provided.

_____	1. posterior	A. that which presses or draws down
_____	2. dilator	B. behind or in back of
_____	3. inferior	C. pertaining to the middle or center
_____	4. anguli	D. before or in front of
_____	5. levator	E. situated lower
_____	6. dorsal	F. to straighten
_____	7. superior	G. that which lifts
_____	8. medial	H. behind or in back of
_____	9. distal	I. nearer to the center or medial line
_____	10. depressor	J. at an angle
_____	11. proximal	K. farther from the center or medial line
_____	12. anterior	L. situated above
_____	13. extensor	M. that which expands or enlarges

MATCHING: Match the term with the best description. Write the letter of the appropriate term in the space provided.

_____ 1. raise the shoulders toward the ears	A. flexion
_____ 2. action of the neck when looking at the ceiling	B. extension
_____ 3. action of the hip when standing up out of a seated position	C. dorsiflexion
	D. plantar flexion
_____ 4. action of the toes when standing on tiptoes	E. adduction
_____ 5. turning the hand palm up	F. abduction
_____ 6. action of the foot when pointing toes	G. pronation
_____ 7. action of elbow during eccentric contraction of bicep	H. supination
_____ 8. bringing the knees together	I. medial rotation
_____ 9. action of knee during concentric contraction of biceps femoris	J. lateral rotation
	K. circumduction
_____ 10. turning the sole of the foot medially	L. hyperextension
_____ 11. action of the femur when turning the feet outward	M. inversion
_____ 12. action of the hip when bringing the knee toward the chest	N. eversion
_____ 13. turning the palm of the hand downward	O. elevation
_____ 14. action of the foot when pointing the toes up toward the knee	P. depression

IDENTIFICATION: Identify the muscles in Figure 5.14 by writing the correct name in the numbered space that corresponds to the number in the figure.

The Muscular System—Anterior View

1. ______________________
2. ______________________
3. ______________________
4. ______________________
5. ______________________
6. ______________________
7. ______________________
8. ______________________
9. ______________________
10. ______________________
11. ______________________
12. ______________________
13. ______________________
14. ______________________
15. ______________________
16. ______________________
17. ______________________
18. ______________________
19. ______________________
20. ______________________
21. ______________________
22. ______________________
23. ______________________
24. ______________________
25. ______________________
26. ______________________
27. ______________________

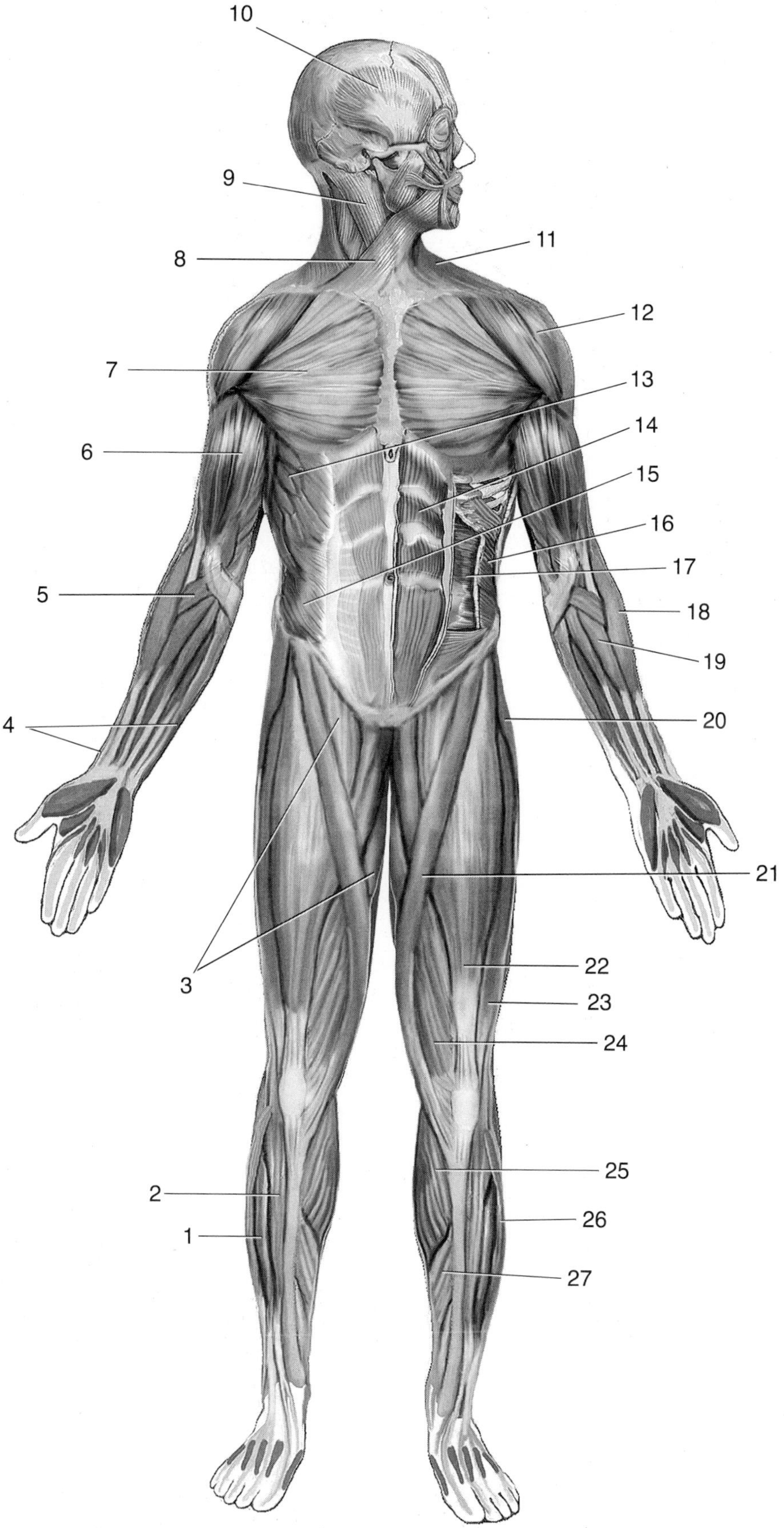

Fig. 5.14 The muscular system, anterior view.

IDENTIFICATION: Identify the muscles in Figure 5.15 by writing the correct name in the numbered space that corresponds to the number in the figure.

The Muscular System—Posterior View

1. ______________________
2. ______________________
3. ______________________
4. ______________________
5. ______________________
6. ______________________
7. ______________________
8. ______________________
9. ______________________
10. ______________________
11. ______________________
12. ______________________
13. ______________________
14. ______________________
15. ______________________
16. ______________________
17. ______________________
18. ______________________
19. ______________________
20. ______________________
21. ______________________
22. ______________________
23. ______________________
24. ______________________

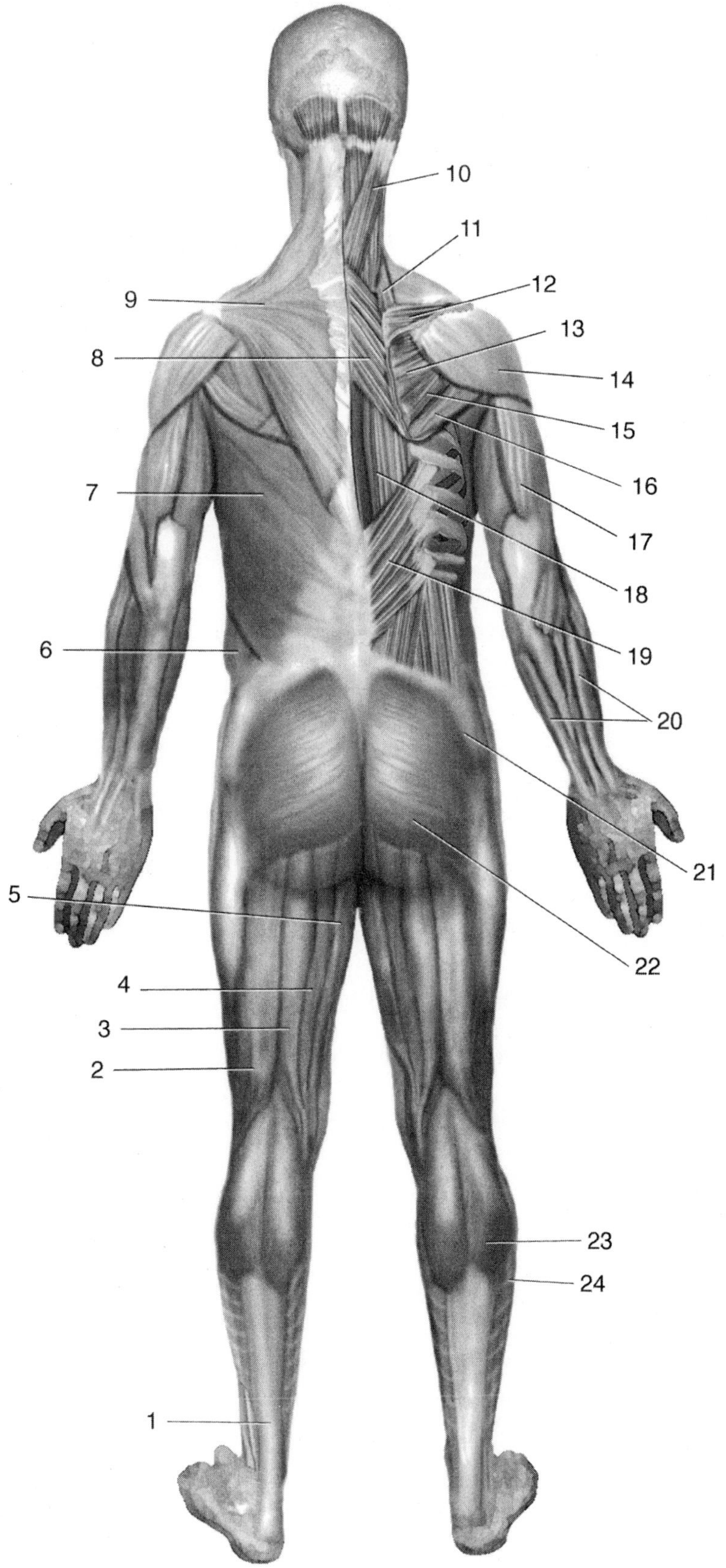

Fig. 5.15 The muscular system, posterior view.

MATCHING: In the first answer column, identify the body part the muscle acts on. Write the correct letter in the answer blank. In the second answer column, indicate the action the muscle causes when it contracts. Write the correct letter in the answer blank.

Body part	Action		
________	________	1. gluteus medius	A. Flexes
________	________	2. triceps brachii	B. Extends
________	________	3. upper trapezius	C. Adducts
________	________	4. deltoid (medial)	D. Abducts
________	________	5. gastrocnemius	E. Elevates
________	________	6. gluteus maximus	F. Plantar flexes
________	________	7. adductor magnus	G. Dorsal flexes
________	________	8. latissimus dorsi	H. Big toe
________	________	9. biceps femoris	I. Elbow
________	________	10. tibialis anterior	J. Thumb
________	________	11. peroneus longus	K. Hip
________	________	12. gracilis	L. Ankle
________	________	13. rectus femoris	M. Knee
________	________	14. vastus lateralis	N. Scapula
________	________	15. biceps brachii	O. Wrist
________	________	16. pectoralis major	P. Neck
________	________	17. sternocleidomastoid	Q. Shoulder
________	________	18. palmaris longus	R. Finger
________	________	19. sartorius	
________	________	20. tensor fascia lata	
________	________	21. abductor pollicis longus	
________	________	22. extensor hallucis longus	
________	________	23. brachioradialis	
________	________	24. extensor indicis	
________	________	25. soleus	
________	________	26. iliopsoas	
________	________	27. supraspinatus	

COMPLETION: In the space(s) provided, write the word(s) that correctly complete(s) each statement.

1. A sudden involuntary contraction of a muscle or a group of muscles is a ______________.

2. An enlargement of the breadth of a muscle as a result of repeated forceful muscle activity is called ______________.

3. When the muscle tissue degenerates and begins to waste away, the process is called ______________.

4. The process by which muscle tissue is replaced by fibrous connective tissue is ______________.

5. Two inflammatory conditions of the white fibrous tissue that cause pain and stiffness (especially the fascial tissues of the muscular system) are ______________ and ______________.

6. A group of related diseases that seems to be genetically inherited and that causes a progressive degeneration of the voluntary muscular system is ______________.

7. ______________ is characterized by pain, fatigue, and stiffness in the connective tissue of the muscles, tendons, and ligaments. It is associated with stress and poor sleep habits and is most prevalent in women.

8. An inflammation of the tendon often occurring at the musculotendinous junction is ______________.

9. An inflammation of the tendon sheath that is often accompanied by pain and swelling is called ______________.

SHORT ANSWER: Circle the term that does not belong in each of the following groups (groups flow from left to right).

brachioradialis	biceps brachii	brachialis	coracobrachialis
biceps femoris	rectus femoris	vastus medialis	vastus lateralis
supraspinatus	subscapularis	teres major	teres minor
pectineus	rectus femoris	adductor longus	gracilis
teres major	pectoralis major	subscapularis	infraspinatus

IDENTIFICATION: On the skeleton diagrams in Figures 5.16a through 5.17b, draw by shading the indicated muscles. Be as accurate as possible, paying close attention to muscle attachments. Draw the muscles on the indicated sides to minimize overlap.

Note that the right hand of all of the diagrams is supinated.

Right-hand Side

A. tibialis anterior

B. gracilis

C. adductor longus

D. pectineus

E. tensor fascia latae

F. flexor carpi ulnaris

G. external obliques

H. biceps brachii

I. serratus anterior

Left-hand Side

J. pectoralis minor

K. coracobrachialis

L. rectus abdominis

M. flexor digitorum profundus

N. adductor brevis

O. adductor magnus

P. extensor digitorum longus

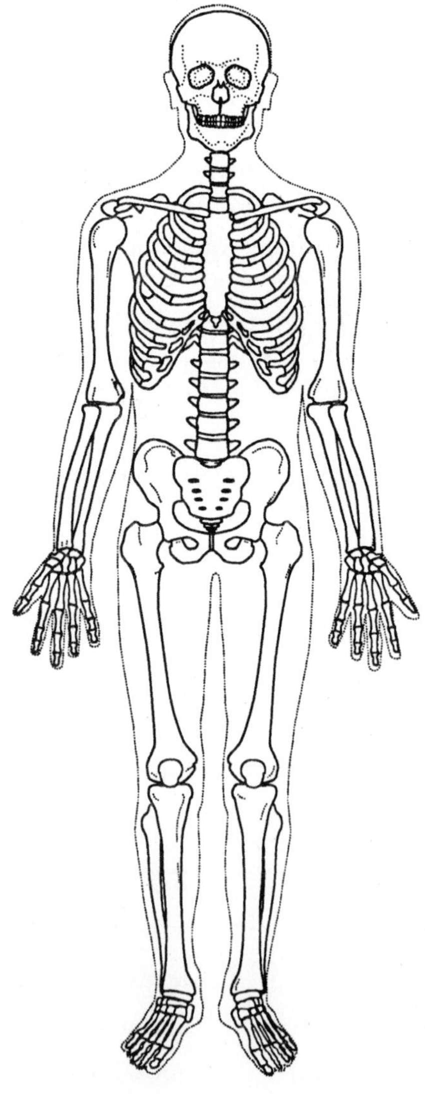

Fig. 5.16a The skeletal system, anterior view.

Right-hand Side

A. peroneus brevis
B. extensor hallucis longus
C. vastus lateralis
D. vastus medialis
E. flexor digitorum superficialis
F. iliacus
G. psoas
H. pectoralis major
I. sternocleidomastoid

Left-hand Side

J. deltoid
K. brachialis
L. quadratus lumborum
M. flexor carpi radialis
N. rectus femoris
O. peroneus longus

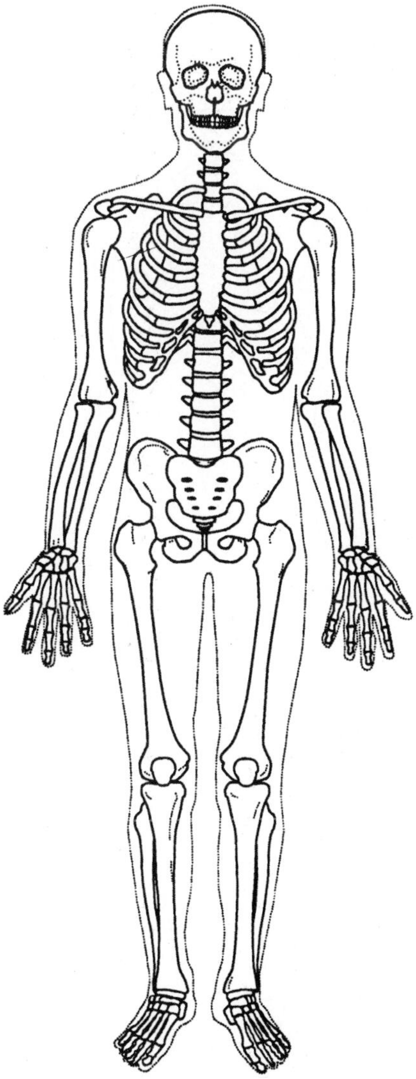

Fig. 5.16b The skeletal system, anterior view.

Left-hand Side

A. flexor digitorum longus

B. biceps femoris

C. semimembranosus

D. gluteus medius

E. brachioradialis

F. latissimus dorsi

G. rhomboids

H. levator scapulae

Right-hand Side

I. trapezius

J. teres major

K. extensor carpi radialis brevis

L. extensor carpi ulnaris

M. gluteus minimus

N. piriformis

O. semitendinosus

P. popliteus

Q. posterior tibialis

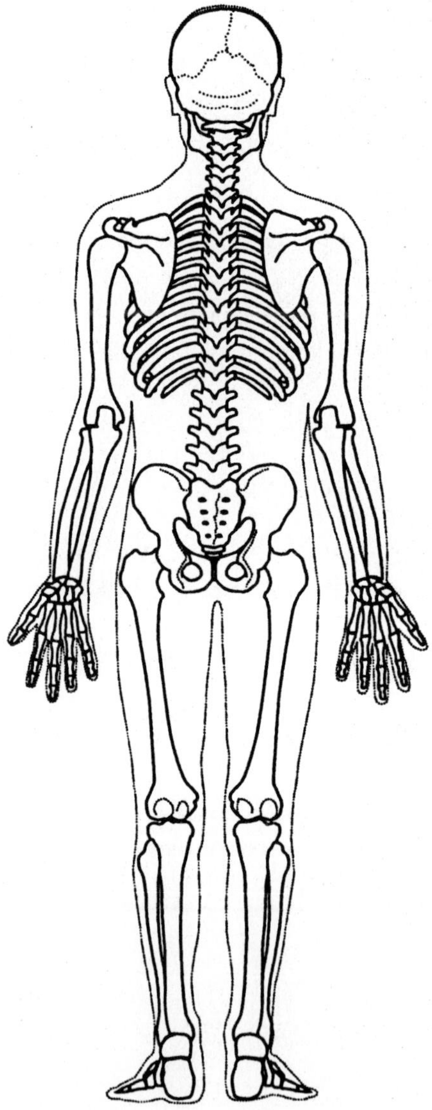

Fig. 5.17a The skeletal system, posterior view.

Left-hand Side

A. gastrocnemius

B. quadratus femoris

C. extensor carpi radialis longus

D. triceps

E. infraspinatus

F. supraspinatus

G. erector spini

Right-hand Side

H. spleneus capitis

I. teres minor

J. extensor digitorum

K. gluteus maximus

L. iliotibial band

M. soleus

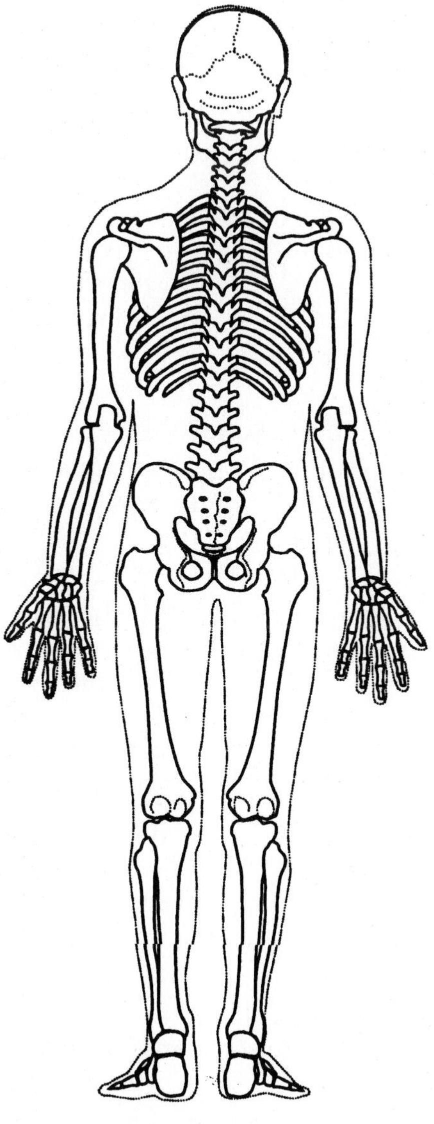

Fig. 5.17b The skeletal system, posterior view.

MULTIPLE CHOICE: Carefully read each statement. Choose the word or phrase that correctly completes the meaning and write the corresponding letter in the blank provided.

1. The ability of muscle to return to its original shape after being stretched is called ________. ________
   - a) contractility
   - b) resizing
   - c) elasticity
   - d) shortening

2. The layer of connective tissue that covers an individual muscle is called the ________. ________
   - a) fascicle
   - b) epimysium
   - c) periosteum
   - d) endomysium

3. Each muscle fiber within a fascicle is covered by tissue called ________. ________
   - a) epimysium
   - b) periosteum
   - c) endomysium
   - d) perimysium

4. Muscle's contractile ability is a result of the interaction between two filaments, myosin and ________. ________
   - a) actin
   - b) elastin
   - c) adenosine
   - d) reticulin

5. Which type of muscle tissue is found in the heart wall? ________
   - a) nonstriated
   - b) cardiac
   - c) smooth
   - d) skeletal

6. The cell membrane of a muscle fiber is called the ________. ________
   - a) endomysium
   - b) sarcolemma
   - c) sarcoplasmic reticulum
   - d) fascia

7. The striated appearance of skeletal muscles results from the ________. ________
   - a) sarcoplasmic reticulum network
   - b) transverse tubule pattern
   - c) sarcomere arrangement
   - d) aerobic conversion

8. The strength of a muscle contraction is varied by changing the ________. ________
   - a) number of motor units stimulated
   - b) strength that each individual fiber contracts
   - c) number of fibers contracting within each motor unit
   - d) the intensity of the nerve impulse

9. The transmission of the stimulus of muscle contraction is aided by ________. ________
   - a) myosin
   - b) actin
   - c) brain waves
   - d) transverse tubules

10. Energy for muscle contractions comes from ________. ________
    a) ATF
    b) CPA
    c) ADP
    d) ATP

11. ________ is found in the gap between the end of the motor nerve and the muscle fiber. ________
    a) Mitochondria
    b) Adenosine triphosphate
    c) Acetylcholine
    d) Creatine phosphate

12. The condition in which muscles cease to respond because of lack of oxygen and/or buildup of waste products is called ________. ________
    a) muscle fatigue
    b) oxygen deficiency
    c) lactic acid
    d) anaerobic respiration

13. A muscle contraction in which the body part affected by the muscle does not move is called ________. ________
    a) isotonic
    b) isometric
    c) eccentric
    d) concentric

14. A muscle contraction in which the distance between the ends of the muscle changes is called ________. ________
    a) isotonic
    b) resistant
    c) dynamic
    d) isometric

15. The muscle that originates on the coracoid process and flexes the elbow is the ________. ________
    a) brachioradialis
    b) brachialis
    c) biceps brachii
    d) coracobrachialis

16. A muscle that flexes the neck or turns the head to the opposite side is the ________. ________
    a) splenius capitus
    b) scalenus posterior
    c) sternocleidomastoid
    d) all of the above

17. A muscle strain that involves a partial tear of 10 percent to 50 percent of the muscle fibers is classified ________. ________
    a) Grade I
    b) Grade II
    c) Grade III
    d) parietal

18. A group of related genetic diseases that cause progressive degeneration of the voluntary muscular system is called ________. ________
    a) muscular dystrophy
    b) myofibrosis
    c) fibrosis
    d) atrophy

19. Aerobic cellular respiration to replenish ATP takes place in the ________.
    a) liver
    b) bloodstream
    c) mitochondria
    d) cell nucleus

WORD REVIEW: The student is encouraged to write down the meaning of each of the following words. The list can be used as a study guide for this unit.

abduction

actin

adduction

antagonist

aponeurosis

cardiac muscle

contractility

elasticity

extensibility

extension

fascia

flexion

insertion

motor neuron

motor unit

muscle belly

muscle fatigue

myofibril

myosin

origin

oxygen debt

prime mover

pronation

skeletal muscle

smooth muscle

striated

supination

synergist

tendon

COMPLETION: In the space(s) provided, write the word(s) that correctly complete(s) each statement.

1. The two divisions to the vascular system are the ______________________________ ______________ and ______________________________.
2. The double-layered membrane that covers the heart is the ______________.
3. The normal heart rate for an adult is ______________ beats per minute.
4. The blood vessels that carry blood away from the heart are the ______________ and ______________.
5. The blood vessels that carry blood back toward the heart are the ______________ and ______________.
6. The largest artery in the body is the ______________.
7. The smallest, microscopic, thin-walled blood vessels are called ______________.
8. The two circulation systems in the blood-vascular system are ______________________________ and ______________________________.

IDENTIFICATION: Identify the parts indicated in Figure 5.18 (a cross-section of a portion of the heart wall, including the pericardium) by writing the letter of the part next to the appropriate term in the space provided.

_____ 1. epicardium

_____ 2. myocardium

_____ 3. endocardium

_____ 4. parietal pericardium

_____ 5. pericardial cavity

_____ 6. visceral pericardium

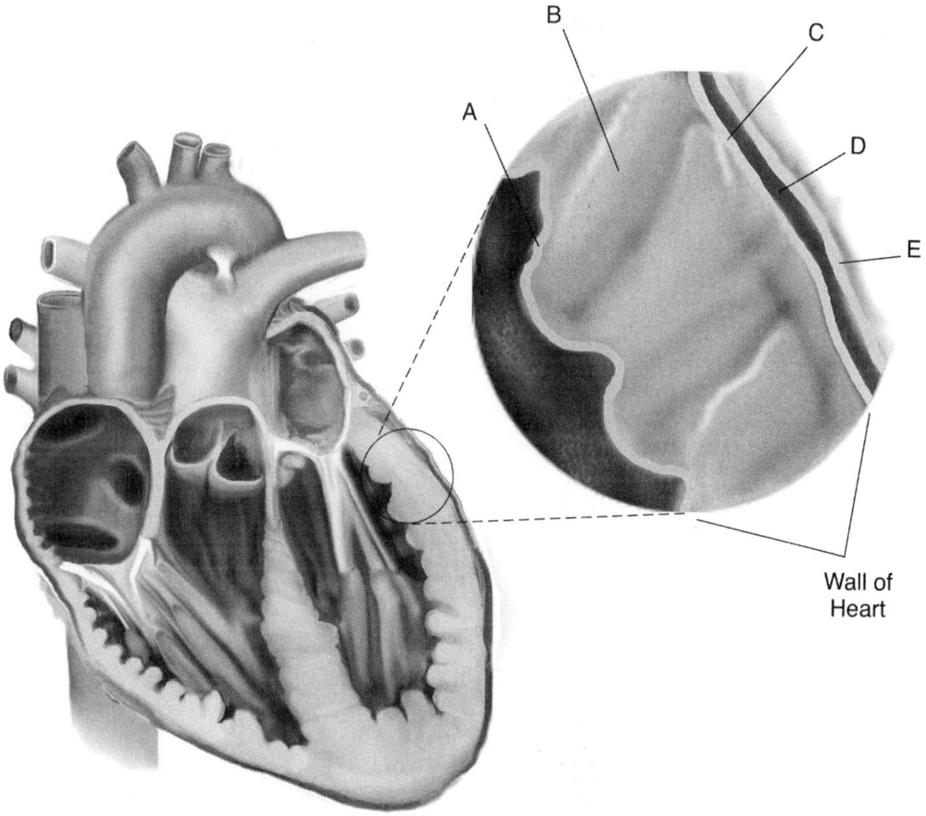

Fig. 5.18 Cross-section of wall of heart.

IDENTIFICATION: Identify the structures of the heart indicated in Figure 5.19 (a diagram of the frontal structure of the heart) by writing the letter next to the appropriate term in the space provided.

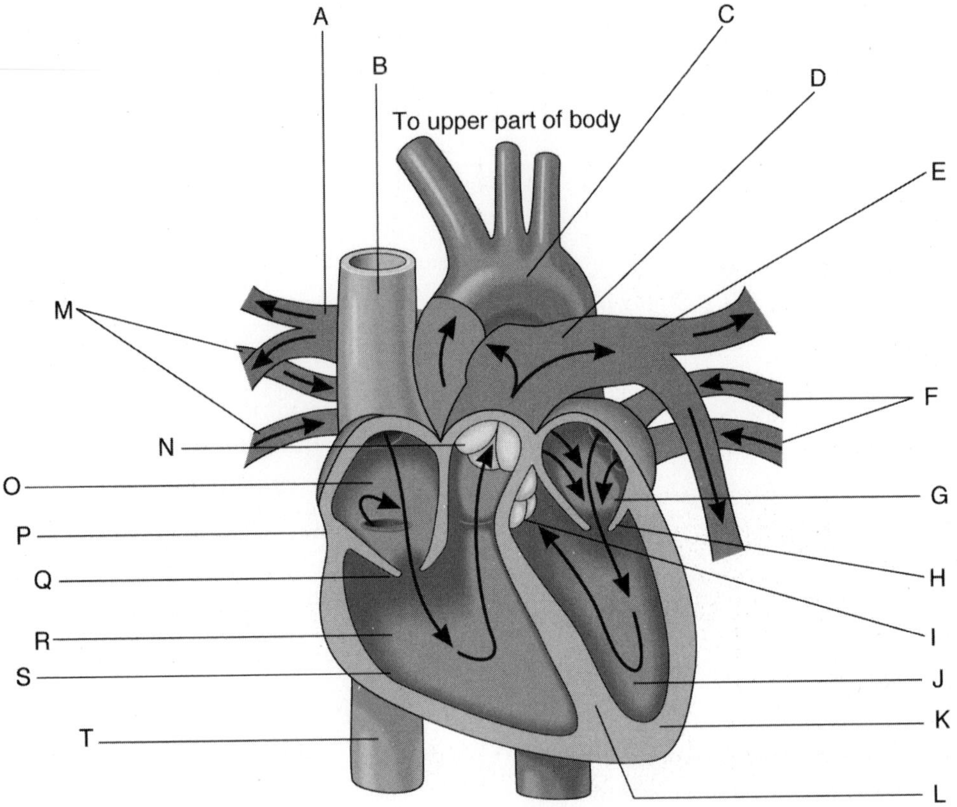

Fig. 5.19 Frontal section of the heart.

_____ 1. aorta

_____ 2. aortic semilunar valve

_____ 3. inferior vena cava

_____ 4. left atrium

_____ 5. left ventricle

_____ 6. mitral (bicuspid) valve

_____ 7. left pulmonary artery

_____ 8. pulmonary semilunar valve

_____ 9. pulmonary veins

_____ 10. right atrium

_____ 11. right ventricle

_____ 12. septum

_____ 13. superior vena cava

_____ 14. tricuspid valve

_____ 15. right pulmonary artery

_____ 16. endocardium

_____ 17. pericardium

_____ 18. pulmonary trunk

_____ 19. myocardium

TRUE OR FALSE: If the following statements are true, write *true* in the space provided. If they are false, replace the italicized word with one that makes the statement true.

_______________ 1. Impulses from the sympathetic portion of the autonomic nervous system cause *vasodilation.*

_______________ 2. Substances move through the capillary walls mostly by *osmosis.*

_______________ 3. Blood moves through the *arterioles* to the capillaries and then to the venules.

_______________ 4. *Diffusion* is a process in which substances move from an area of higher pressure to lower pressure.

_______________ 5. In *pulmonary* circulation, veins contain oxygen-rich blood.

MATCHING: Match the term with the best description. Write the letter of the appropriate term in the space provided.

A. arteriosclerosis
B. phlebitis
C. embolus
D. varicose veins
E. atherosclerosis
F. edema

_____ 1. protruding, bulbous, distended superficial veins

_____ 2. an inflammation of a vein

_____ 3. a condition of excess fluid in the interstitial spaces

_____ 4. the walls of affected arteries tend to thicken, become fibrous, and lose their elasticity

_____ 5. an accumulation of fatty deposits on the inner walls of the arteries

_____ 6. a clot that breaks loose and floats in the bloodstream

TRUE OR FALSE: If the following statements are true, write *true* in the space provided. If they are false, replace the italicized word with one that makes the statement true.

_______________ 1. The cardiovascular system of the average adult male contains about *four* liters of blood.

_______________ 2. Blood has a slightly *acid* reaction.

_______________ 3. Plasma accounts for *75* percent of the blood's volume.

_______________ 4. *White blood cells* constitute as much as 98 percent of all blood cells.

_______________ 5. Red blood cells and *white blood cells* are produced in the red bone marrow.

SHORT ANSWER: Five functions of the blood are listed below. In the spaces provided, briefly describe how the blood performs these functions.

1. Blood provides nutrients to the cells.

____

2. Blood removes wastes.

____

____

3. Blood maintains normal body temperature.

____

____

4. Blood protects against infection.

____

____

5. Blood prevents hemorrhaging.

____

COMPLETION: In the space(s) provided, write the word(s) that correctly complete(s) each statement.

1. Red blood cells are also called ______________.
2. Red blood cells are colored with an oxygen-carrying substance called ______________.
3. The process in which leukocytes actually engulf and digest harmful bacteria is called ______________.
4. The small irregularly shaped particles in the blood that play an important role in clotting are ______________ or ______________.
5. A disease characterized by extremely slow clotting of blood and excessive bleeding from even very slight cuts is ______________.
6. A condition in which there is a rapid loss or inadequate production of red blood cells is ______________.
7. A form of cancer in which there is an uncontrolled production of white blood cells is known as ______________.

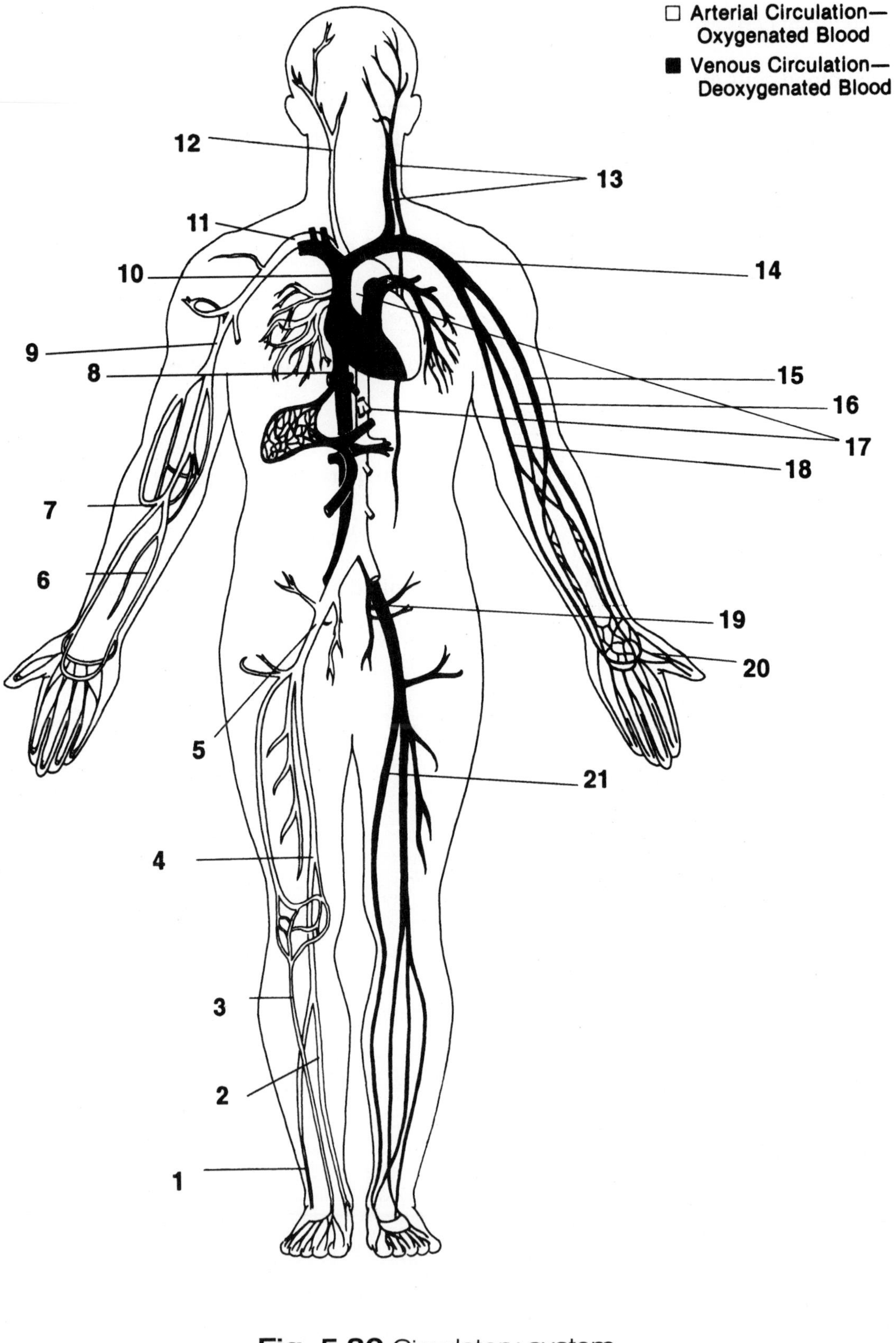

Fig. 5.20 Circulatory system.

IDENTIFICATION: Identify the numbered blood vessels in Figure 5.20 (a diagram of the major blood vessels of the body) by writing the correct term in the numbered space that corresponds to the number on the figure. (The arteries are indicated on the left side of the body as unshaded vessels. The veins are indicated on the right side of the body as shaded vessels.)

1. ______________________ 12. ______________________
2. ______________________ 13. ______________________
3. ______________________ 14. ______________________
4. ______________________ 15. ______________________
5. ______________________ 16. ______________________
6. ______________________ 17. ______________________
7. ______________________ 18. ______________________
8. ______________________ 19. ______________________
9. ______________________ 20. ______________________
10. ______________________ 21. ______________________
11. ______________________

SHORT ANSWER: Circle the term that does not belong in the following groups (groups flow from left to right).

spleen	liver	tonsils	thymus
lacteal	thoracic duct	lymphatic	venule
swelling	nausea	pain	redness
lymphocytes	monocytes	platelets	leukocytes
lymph capillaries	capillary beds	closed system	continuous flow

TRUE OR FALSE: If the following statements are true, write *true* in the space provided. If they are false, replace the italicized word with one that makes the statement true.

______________________ 1. Lymph is derived from the interstitial fluid and is *produced* by the lymph nodes.

______________________ 2. Lymphoid tissue produces a kind of white blood cell called a *lymphocyte.*

______________________ 3. All lymph eventually flows into the bloodstream.

______ 4. The right lymphatic duct collects lymph from the *right half of the body.*

______ 5. Lymph is moved through the lymph system by a pumping action of the *lymph nodes.*

COMPLETION: In the space(s) provided, write the word(s) that correctly complete(s) each statement.

1. Specialized white blood cells called ______ play a major role in the immune response.
2. White blood cells originate in ______.
3. White blood cells specialize into T-cells in the ______.
4. The agent that triggers an immune response is a(n) ______.
5. White blood cells are transported throughout the body by ______ and ______.
6. The production of antibodies is the responsibility of the ______.
7. When the immune system mistakenly attacks itself, the result is ______.
8. ______ attack and destroy antigens directly.
9. The cell that is destroyed by the HIV virus in AIDS is the ______.
10. The process of specialized cells engulfing and digesting neutralized antigens and debris is ______.

MATCHING: Match the terms with the best description. Write the letter of the appropriate term in the space provided.

A. acquired immunity	D. memory cells	G. innate immunity
B. immunity	E. vaccines	H. autoimmune diseases
C. allergen	F. allergy	

______ 1. stimulate an immune response without causing the accompanying illness

______ 2. all the physiologic mechanisms used by the body as protection against foreign substances

______ 3. is present from before birth

______ 4. allergy-causing substance

______ 5. specialized form of immunity that is the result of an encounter with a new substance

_____ 6. overreaction by the immune system to an otherwise harmless substance

_____ 7. when the body makes antibodies and T-cells directed against its own cells

_____ 8. provide immunity for years or even a lifetime

TRUE OR FALSE: If the following statements are true, write *true* in the space provided. If they are false, replace the italicized word with one that makes the statement true.

_______________ 1. Acquired immunodeficiency syndrome *(AIDS)* disease occurs when the human immunodeficiency virus (HIV) enters a person's body.

_______________ 2. An HIV-infected person is clinically said to have AIDS when their CD4+ T-cell blood count falls below *500* per cubic millimeter of blood.

_______________ 3. HIV is spread most commonly by *sexual contact* with an infected partner or through contact with infected blood.

_______________ 4. Massage *is* contraindicated for people infected with HIV or AIDS.

_______________ 5. Health care workers can reduce their risk of becoming HIV infected in their practice by following *safe sex* precautions.

MULTIPLE CHOICE: Carefully read each statement. Choose the word or phrase that correctly completes the meaning and write the corresponding letter in the blank provided.

1. Supplying the body with nutrients and carrying away waste products is the function of the ________. ________
   a) lungs
   b) circulatory system
   c) kidneys
   d) muscles

2. The two-way diffusion of substances between the blood and tissue fluids surrounding cells is the function of the ________. ________
   a) arteries
   b) veins
   c) capillaries
   d) lymph

3. Waste-laden blood returns to the heart through the ________. ________
   a) veins
   b) arteries
   c) capillaries
   d) lymphatics

4. Blood platelets are important to proper ________. ________
   a) nutrition
   b) clotting
   c) immunity
   d) circulation

5. Macrophages are large cells (WBCs) that destroy foreign bacteria by the process of ________. ________
   a) osmosis
   b) mitosis
   c) phagocytosis
   d) enzymatic action

6. The process in which substances move from an area of higher concentration to an area of lower concentration is ________. ________
   a) diffusion
   b) osmosis
   c) filtration
   d) saturation

7. Blood is supplied to the small finger side of the hand by the ________. ________
   a) ulnar artery
   b) popliteal artery
   c) parietal artery
   d) radial artery

8. The right atrium receives blood directly from ________. ________
   a) the superior and inferior vena cava
   b) the right ventricle
   c) the pulmonary veins
   d) the coronary vein

9. The liquid that surrounds tissue cells is called ________. ________
   a) lymph
   b) interstitial fluid
   c) plasma
   d) blood

10. Toxic molecules are filtered by the ________. ________
    a) lymphatic system
    b) spleen
    c) muscular system
    d) bone marrow

11. Lymph reenters the blood-vascular system through the ________. ________
    a) lymph capillaries
    b) lymph nodes
    c) spleen
    d) subclavian vein

12. Approximately how much of the fluid that leaves the blood-vascular system is absorbed by the lymph-vascular system? ________
    a) 5 percent
    b) 10 percent
    c) 20 percent
    d) 40 percent

13. A condition in which there is an inadequate population of erythrocytes is ________. ________
    a) hemophilia
    b) anemia
    c) edema
    d) leukemia

14. Which of the following is not a branch of the aorta? ________
    a) right coronary artery
    b) pulmonary artery
    c) brachiocephalic artery
    d) left subclavian artery

15. Blood from the face and scalp is drained by the ________. ________
    a) external jugular vein
    b) subclavian vein
    c) inferior vena cava
    d) cephalic veins

16. The thickest part of the heart muscle is near ________. ______
   a) the semilunar valve
   b) the right ventricle
   c) the right atrium
   d) the left ventricle

17. The inside membrane lining the heart and the valves is called ________. ______
   a) the endocardium
   b) the myocardium
   c) the pericardium
   d) the epicardium

18. The semilunar valve prevents the backflow of blood into ________. ______
   a) the lung
   b) the right atrium
   c) the right ventricle
   d) the left atrium

19. An erythrocyte ________. ______
   a) manufactures antibodies
   b) releases serotonin
   c) contains hemoglobin
   d) performs phagocytosis

20. Which of the following are white blood cells? ______
   a) leukocytes
   b) monocytes
   c) lymphocytes
   d) all of the above

21. A free-floating blood clot is called ________. ______
   a) an embolism
   b) thrombosis
   c) phlebitis
   d) an embolus

WORD REVIEW: The student is encouraged to write down the meaning of each of the following words. The list can be used as a study guide for this unit.

anemia

____

____

aorta

____

____

arteriole

____

____

arteriosclerosis

artery

atrium

auricle

blood-vascular system

capillary

cardiovascular

diffusion

edema

embolus

endocardium

epicardium

erythrocytes

filtration

hemoglobin

interstitial

lacteal

leukemia

leukocytes

lymph

lymph-vascular system

lymphatic pump

lymphatics

mitral valve

myocardium

pericardial cavity

pericardium

phagocytosis

phlebitis

plasma

platelets

pulmonary circulation

semilunar valves

serotonin

systemic circulation

thoracic duct

thrombocytes

tricuspid valve

vasoconstriction

vasodilation

vasomotor nerves

vein

vena cava

ventricle

venule

COMPLETION: In the space(s) provided, write the word(s) that correctly complete(s) each statement.

1. The major parts of the nervous system are the ____________, ____________, and ____________.
2. The structural unit of the nervous system is the ____________ or ____________.
3. There are two types of nerve fibers. ____________ connect with other neurons to receive information and a single ____________ conducts impulses away from the cell body.
4. Impulses are passed from one neuron to another at a junction called a ____________.
5. Two characteristics of a neuron are ____________ and ____________.
6. Neurons that originate in the periphery and carry information toward the central nervous system (CNS) are ____________ or ____________ neurons.
7. Neurons that carry impulses from the brain to the muscles or glands that they control are ____________ or ____________ neurons.
8. Neurons located in the brain and spinal cord that carry impulses from one neuron to another are ____________.
9. The portion of the nervous system that is surrounded by bone is the ____________, which consists of the ____________ and the ____________.
10. The CNS is covered by a special connective tissue membrane called the ____________, which has three layers: the ____________, the ____________, and the ____________.
11. The fluid that surrounds and supports the brain and spinal cord is ____________.
12. The largest portion making up the front and top of the brain is the ____________.
13. The smaller part of the brain that helps to maintain the body's balance and coordinates voluntary muscles is the ____________.
14. The three parts of the brain stem are the ____________, the ____________, and the ____________.
15. The two divisions of the peripheral nervous system are the ____________, which involves the nerves to the visceral organs, glands, and blood vessels, and the ____________, which involves the nerves to the muscles and skin.

IDENTIFICATION: Identify the structures indicated in Figure 5.21 (a diagram of a nerve cell) by writing the letter of the structure next to the correct term in the space provided.

_____ 1. axon

_____ 2. cell body

_____ 3. dendrites

_____ 4. beads of myelin

_____ 5. nucleus

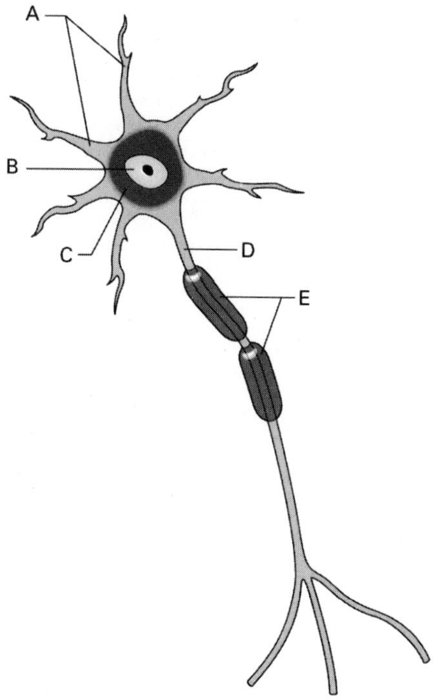

Fig. 5.21 Nerve cell.

MATCHING: Match the term with the best description. Write the letter of the appropriate term in the space provided.

A. afferent neuron	D. efferent neuron	G. nerve
B. axon	E. ganglion	H. stimuli
C. dendrite	F. interneuron	I. synapse

_____ 1. the conducting portion of a neuron

_____ 2. junction point between neurons

_____ 3. bundle of axons in the peripheral nervous system

_____ 4. collection of nerve bodies located outside the CNS

_____ 5. changes that activate the nervous system

_____ 6. receptive structure of the neuron

_____ 7. carries sensory information toward the CNS

_____ 8. transmits information from one neuron to another

TRUE OR FALSE: If the following statements are true, write *true* in the space provided. If they are false, replace the italicized word with one that makes the statement true.

_______________ 1. The spinal cord extends from the medulla oblongata to the *sacrum*.

_______________ 2. Control centers in the *pons* regulate movements of the heart and control vasoconstriction of the arteries.

_______________ 3. The *midbrain* relays impulses from the cerebrum to the cerebellum.

_______________ 4. Spinal nerves are numbered according to *the level where they exit the spine*.

_______________ 5. There are *thirty-one* pairs of spinal nerves.

_______________ 6. All of the nerves outside the brain and spinal cord are considered to be the *peripheral* nervous system.

CRANIAL NERVES

IDENTIFICATION AND MATCHING: Number the cranial nerves according to the order in which they arise from the brain. In the first column of answer blanks, write the Roman numeral that corresponds to the cranial nerve. Then, select the best description of the function of the cranial nerve from the list below the table, and write the appropriate letter in the second column of answer blanks.

Number	Function	
________	________	1. trochlear nerve
________	________	2. optic nerve
________	________	3. hypoglossal nerve
________	________	4. vagus nerve
________	________	5. accessory nerve
________	________	6. abducens nerve
________	________	7. oculomotor nerve
________	________	8. trigeminal nerve
________	________	9. auditory nerve
________	________	10. olfactory nerve
________	________	11. glossopharyngeal nerve
________	________	12. facial nerve

A. speaking, shoulder, and neck muscles

B. sensations of the face and movement of the jaw and tongue

C. moves eyeball down and out

D. sensation and movement related to talking, heart rate, breathing, and digestion

E. sense of smell

F. moves eyeball up, down, and in; constricts pupil; raises eyelid

G. tongue movement and swallowing

H. movements of the face and salivary glands

I. moves eyeball outward

J. tongue movement, swallowing, sense of taste

K. sense of sight

L. sense of hearing

SHORT ANSWER: In the spaces provided, write the answers to the following questions.

1. How many pairs of cervical nerves are there? ______

2. How many pairs of thoracic nerves are there? ______

3. How many pairs of lumbar nerves are there? ______

4. How many pairs of sacral nerves are there? ______

MATCHING: Match the term with the best description. Write the letter of the appropriate term in the space provided.

A. mechanoreceptors
B. thermoreceptors
C. photoreceptors
D. chemoreceptors
E. nociceptors

______ 1. detect heat and cold

______ 2. detect light

______ 3. detect pain

______ 4. proprioceptors

______ 5. respond to tissue damage and extreme stimuli

______ 6. Ruffini end organs and Merkel disks

______ 7. rods and cones in the retina

______ 8. sense pressure, vibration

______ 9. sense smell and taste

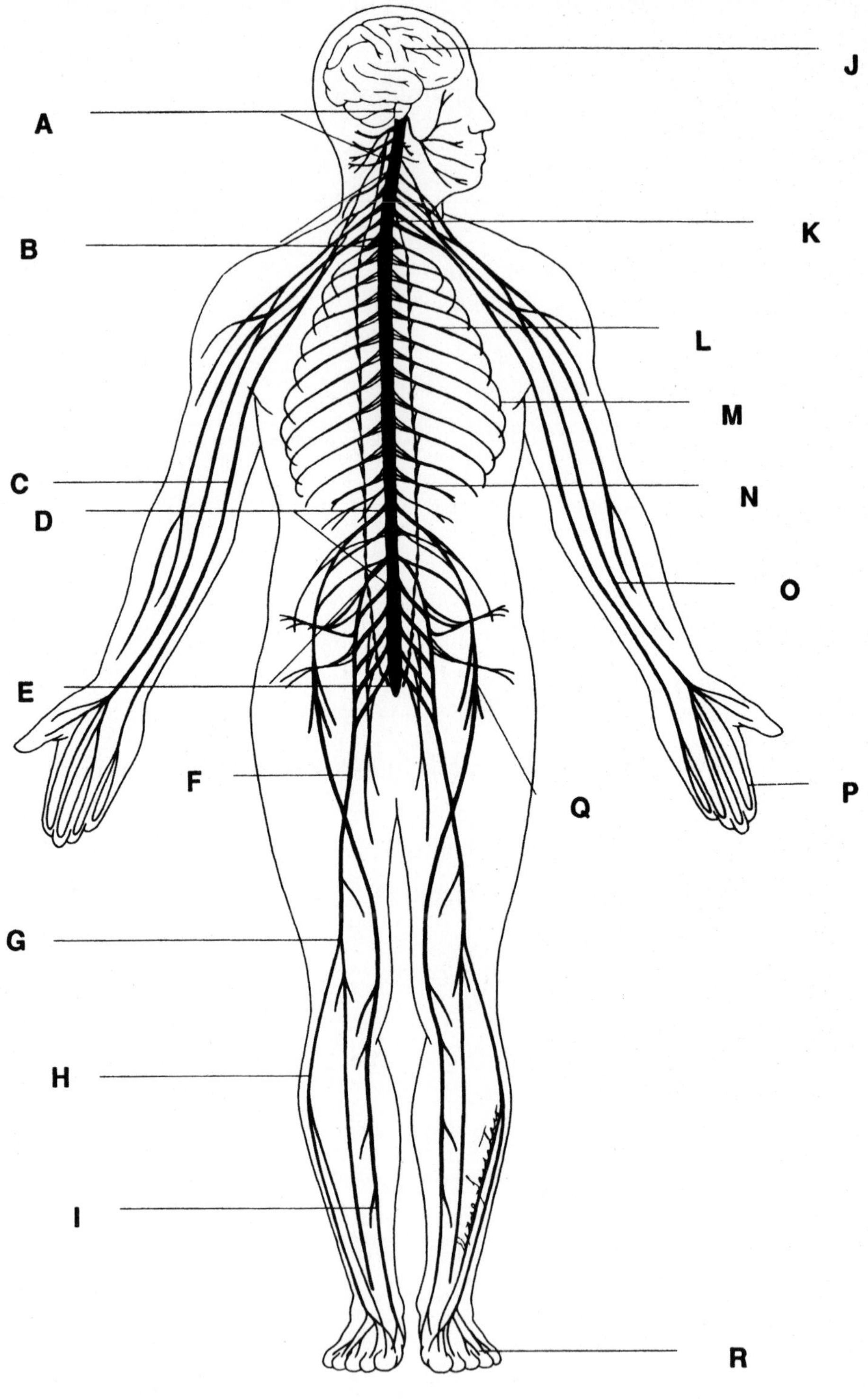

Fig. 5.22 The nervous system.

IDENTIFICATION: Identify the major parts of the nervous system in Figure 5.22 by writing the letter of the part next to the appropriate term in the space provided.

_____ 1. autonomic chain of ganglia

_____ 2. brachial plexus

_____ 3. brain

_____ 10. peroneal nerve

_____ 11. radial nerve

_____ 12. sacral plexus

_____ 4. cervical plexus

_____ 5. femoral nerve

_____ 6. intercostal nerve

_____ 7. lumbar plexus

_____ 8. median nerve

_____ 9. plantar nerve

_____ 13. saphenous nerve

_____ 14. sciatic nerve

_____ 15. spinal cord

_____ 16. tibial nerve

_____ 17. ulnar nerve

_____ 18. spinal nerve

MATCHING: Match the term with the best description. Write the letter of the term in the space provided.

A. central nervous system
B. peripheral nervous system
C. somatic nervous system
D. autonomic nervous system
E. sympathetic nervous system
F. parasympathetic nervous system

_____ 1. Stimulation causes increased respiration, dilated pupils, increased heart rate, and cardiac output.

_____ 2. Consists of motor nerves, sensory nerves, and mixed nerves.

_____ 3. Is completely housed and protected in a bony covering.

_____ 4. General function is to conserve energy.

_____ 5. Is composed of the sympathetic and parasympathetic nervous system.

_____ 6. Includes the autonomic and somatic nervous system.

_____ 7. Nerve fibers arise from the second, third, and fourth sacral spinal nerves and the III, VII, IX, and X (vagus nerve) cranial nerves.

_____ 8. Is composed of cranial nerves, spinal nerves, and nerve ganglia.

_____ 9. Is composed of the brain and spinal cord.

_____ 10. Prepares the organism for energy-expending, stressful, or emergency situations.

_____ 11. Regulates smooth muscle, the heart, and other involuntary functions.

_____ 12. Interprets incoming information and issues orders.

_____ 13. Carries information to and from all parts of the body.

_____ 14. Carries information to and from the skeletal muscles and skin.

_____ 15. Involves a chain of ganglia located along the spine.

COMPLETION: In the space(s) provided, write the word(s) that correctly complete(s) each statement.

1. The simplest form of nervous activity that includes a sensory and motor nerve and few, if any, interneurons is called a ____________.

2. The nerve pathway of the simplest form of nervous activity is called a ____________.

IDENTIFICATION: Identify the structures indicated in Figure 5.23 (a diagram of a simple reflex arc) by writing the letter of the structure next to the appropriate term in the space provided. (Note the arrows that indicate the direction of the nerve impulse.)

_____ 1. sensory neuron

_____ 2. dorsal root

_____ 3. motor neuron

_____ 4. connecting neuron

_____ 5. sensory nerve receptor

_____ 6. spinal cord

_____ 7. spinal ganglion

_____ 8. ventral root

_____ 9. muscle (effector)

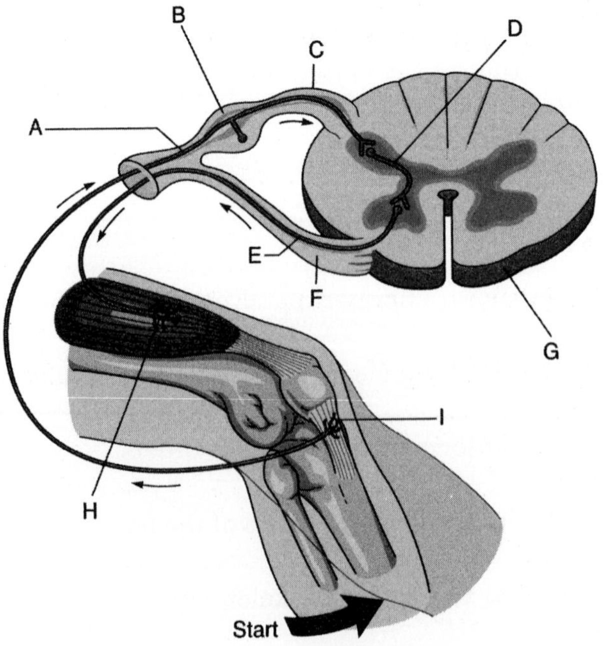

Fig. 5.23 Simple reflex arc.

COMPLETION: In the space(s) provided, write the word(s) that correctly complete(s) each statement.

1. Sensory nerves that record conscious sensations such as heat, cold, pain, and pressure are termed ______________.

2. Sensory nerves that respond to the unconscious inner sense of position and movement of the body are termed ______________.

3. The system of sensory and motor nerve activity that provides information as to the position and rate of movement of different body parts is ______________.

4. ______________ sense the length and stretch of the muscle as well as how far and fast the muscle is moving.

5. ______________ consist of intrafusal muscle fibers, annulospiral, and flower-type nerve receptors.

6. ____________________ are multibranched sensory nerve endings located in tendons in the area where muscle fibers attach to tendon tissue.

7. ____________________ measure the amount of tension produced in muscle cells that occurs as a result of the muscle's stretching and contracting.

MATCHING: Match the term with the best description. Write the letter of the appropriate term in the space provided.

A. amyotrophic lateral sclerosis
B. encephalitis
C. epilepsy
D. hemiplegia
E. meningitis
F. multiple sclerosis
G. nerve compression
H. nerve entrapment
I. neuritis
J. paraplegia
K. Parkinson's disease
L. poliomyelitis
M. quadriplegia
N. shingles
O. spinal cord injury
P. stroke

_____ 1. the result of the breakdown of the myelin sheath, which inhibits nerve conduction

_____ 2. characterized by tremors and shaking, especially in the hands

_____ 3. a degenerative neurologic condition affecting the motor nerves of the brain, causing weakness, spasticity, and atrophy of the voluntary muscles

_____ 4. an acute inflammation of a nerve trunk and the dendrites at the end of the sensory neurons, caused by the herpes zoster virus

_____ 5. paralysis of the lower part of the body

_____ 6. paralysis affecting the arms and the legs

_____ 7. paralysis affecting one side of the body

_____ 8. the inflammation of a nerve that is usually a symptom of some other condition

_____ 9. the result of a blood clot or ruptured blood vessel in or around the brain

_____ 10. abnormal electrical activity in the CNS characterized by seizures

_____ 11. caused by soft tissue, such as muscle, fascia, tendon, or ligament, that puts pressure against a nerve

_____ 12. a crippling or even deadly disease that affects the motor neurons of the medulla oblongata and spinal cord, resulting in paralysis

_____ 13. caused by disease or trauma to the vertebral column, resulting in loss of sensation and movement to the body below the site of injury

_____ 14. a viral disease causing inflammation of the brain and meninges

_____ 15. an acute inflammation of the pia and arachnoid mater around the brain and spinal cord

_____ 16. caused by bone or cartilage pressing against the nerve

MULTIPLE CHOICE: Carefully read each statement. Choose the word or phrase that correctly completes the meaning and write the corresponding letter in the blank provided.

1. The junction at which impulses are passed from one neuron to another is called a/an ________. _____
   a) axon
   b) neuromuscular junction
   c) synapse
   d) dendrite

2. The central nervous system consists of the spinal cord and the ________. _____
   a) motor neurons
   b) afferent nerves
   c) mixed nerves
   d) brain

3. A motor neuron is also called a/an ________. _____
   a) efferent neuron
   b) interneuron
   c) nerve cell
   d) afferent neuron

4. The three types of neurons are ________. _____
   a) sympathetic, parasympathetic, peripheral
   b) afferent, efferent, connecting
   c) sensory, motor, interneuron
   d) receptors, effectors, conductors

5. Body balance and voluntary muscle movement are controlled by the ________. ________
   a) cerebellum
   b) cerebrum
   c) brain stem
   d) midbrain

6. The spinal cord has ________ pairs of spinal nerves: ________
   a) 25
   b) 31
   c) 42
   d) 36

7. Movement of head, neck, and shoulders is controlled by the ________. ________
   a) cervical plexus
   b) somatic system
   c) brachial plexus
   d) cranial nerves

8. All thought, association, and judgment take place in the ________. ________
   a) cerebellum
   b) thalamus
   c) cerebral cortex
   d) medulla oblongata

9. The largest and longest nerve in the body is the ________ nerve. ________
   a) brachial
   b) vagus
   c) lumbar
   d) sciatic

10. Damage to the ________ nerve could cause inability of the diaphragm to function. ________
    a) phrenic
    b) axillary
    c) hypoglossal
    d) pneumogastric

11. Nerves from the fifth, sixth, and seventh cervical vertebrae form the ________. ________
    a) radial nerve
    b) cervical plexus
    c) brachial plexus
    d) ulnar nerve

12. Specialized nerve endings that sense the amount of tension produced in muscle cells are called ________. ________
    a) spindle cells
    b) Golgi tendon organs
    c) exteroceptors
    d) Ruffini end organs

13. Which of the following are considered peripheral nerves? ________
    a) cranial nerves
    b) spinal nerves
    c) sympathetic nerves
    d) all of the above

14. The parasympathetic and sympathetic nervous systems constitute the ________. ________
    a) central nervous system
    b) peripheral nervous system
    c) autonomic nervous system
    d) none of the above

15. The axon is a nerve fiber ________. ________
    a) carrying the impulse toward the cell body
    b) that is the body's communication center
    c) carrying the impulse away from the cell body
    d) with sensory function only

16. Annulospiral receptors and Golgi tendon organs are parts of the ________. ________
    a) proprioceptors
    b) autonomic nervous system
    c) exteroceptors
    d) central nervous system

17. The three brain coverings are collectively known as the ________. ________
    a) thalamus
    b) motor cortex
    c) meninges
    d) convolutions

18. The pons, midbrain, and medulla oblongata form the ________. ________
    a) cerebral hemispheres
    b) cerebellum
    c) brain stem
    d) cerebral cortex

19. ________ serves as the insulating sheath covering the axon. ________
    a) cerebrospinal fluid
    b) myelin
    c) pia mater
    d) meninges

20. A condition in which there is an inflammation of one or more peripheral nerves is ________. ________
    a) meningitis
    b) neuritis
    c) neuralgia
    d) encephalitis

21. Often a stroke causes a type of paralysis called ________. ________
    a) cerebrovascular accident
    b) paraplegia
    c) quadriplegia
    d) hemiplegia

WORD REVIEW: The student is encouraged to write down the meaning of each of the following words. The list can be used as a study guide for this unit.

afferent nerve

afferent neuron

arachnoid mater

autonomic nervous system

axon

brachial plexus

brain

brain stem

central nervous system

cerebellum

cerebrospinal fluid

cerebrovascular accident

cerebrum

cervical plexus

cranial nerves

dendrite

dura mater

efferent nerve

efferent neuron

epilepsy

ganglia

Golgi tendon organs

hemiplegia

interneuron

kinesthesia

lumbar plexus

medulla oblongata

meninges

mixed nerve

motor nerve

motor neuron

muscle spindle cells

nerve

nerve cell

nerve fibers

neuralgia

neuritis

neuron

neurotransmitter

paraplegia

____

____

parasympathetic nervous system

____

____

peripheral nervous system

____

____

pia mater

____

____

pons

____

____

proprioception

____

____

proprioceptors

____

____

quadriplegia

____

____

reflex

reflex arc

sacral plexus

sciatic nerve

sciatica

sensory nerve

sensory neuron

somatic nervous system

spinal cord

spinal cord injury

stroke

sympathetic nervous system

synapse

COMPLETION: In the space(s) provided, write the word(s) that correctly complete(s) each statement.

1. Glands that have tubes or ducts that carry their secretions to a particular part of the body are ____________ or ____________.
2. Glands that depend on the blood and lymph to carry their secretions to various affected tissues are ____________ glands.
3. The chemical substances manufactured by the endocrine glands are known as ____________.

IDENTIFICATION: Identify the hormone-producing organs in Figure 5.24 by writing the correct term in the numbered space that corresponds to the number on the figure. Also name the hormone-producing organs described in numbers 10, 11, and 12.

A.

1. ____________________ 6. ____________________

2. ____________________ 7. ____________________

3. ____________________ 8. ____________________

4. ____________________ 9. ____________________

5. ____________________

B.

____________ 10. The posterior and anterior pituitaries hang from the bottom of this hormone-producing organ.

____________ 11. This is present only in pregnant women.

____________ 12. These are the four small glands attached to the thyroid.

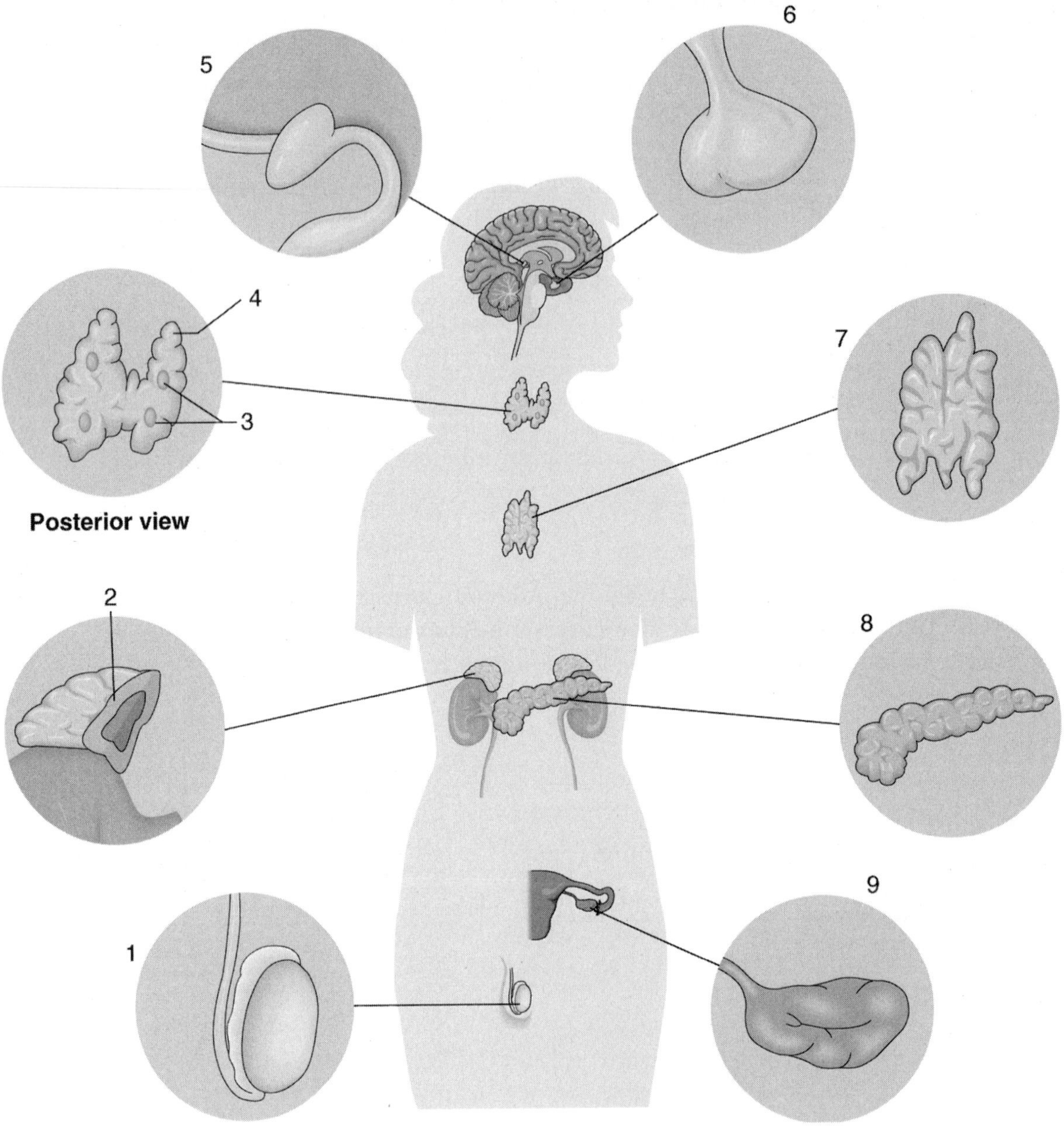

Fig. 5.24 The endocrine system.

MATCHING: Using the following list of organs, match the organ with the hormone(s) that it produces or releases. Write the letter of the organ(s) in the space provided.

A. adrenal gland (cortex)
B. adrenal gland (medulla)
C. pituitary (anterior lobe)
D. pituitary (posterior lobe)
E. ovaries
F. testes
G. pancreas
H. thymus
I. thyroid
J. parathyroid
K. pineal

Hormones

_____ 1. prolactin

_____ 2. aldosterone

_____ 3. insulin

_____ 4. thyroxin

_____ 5. estrogen

_____ 6. cortisol

_____ 7. calcitonin

_____ 8. parathormone

_____ 9. adrenocorticotropic hormone (ACTH)

_____ 10. hydrocortisone

_____ 11. gonadotropic hormones

_____ 12. glucagon

_____ 13. triiodothyronine

_____ 14. oxytocin

_____ 15. progesterone

_____ 16. mineralocorticoids

_____ 17. epinephrine

_____ 18. thyroid-stimulating hormone (TSH)

_____ 19. testosterone

_____ 20. norepinephrine

_____ 21. growth hormone

_____ 22. corticosteroids

_____ 23. antidiuretic hormone

MATCHING: Match the term with the best description. Write the letter of the appropriate term in the space provided.

A. adrenocorticotropin
B. aldosterone
C. calcitonin
D. cortisol
E. estrogens
F. follicle-stimulating hormone
G. glucagon
H. insulin
I. lactogenic hormone
J. luteinizing hormone
K. oxytocin
L. parathormone
M. progesterone
N. TSH

_____ 1. antagonistic to insulin, produced by the same gland

_____ 2. promotes the lining of the uterus to thicken in preparation for fertilization

_____ 3. anterior pituitary hormones that regulate the female cycle

_____ 4. stimulates development of secretory parts of mammary glands

_____ 5. directly regulate the menstrual cycle

_____ 6. stimulates thyroid to produce thyroxin

_____ 7. decreases calcium in the blood

_____ 8. increases calcium level in the blood

_____ 9. stimulates mammary glands to secrete milk

_____ 10. helps protect the body during stress; stimulates the adrenal cortex

_____ 11. necessary for glucose to be taken up by cells

IDENTIFICATION: The following list of conditions are usually the result of hyper- or hypoactivity of an endrocine gland's production of a particular hormone. In the first answer column, indicate whether the condition is caused by to hyper- or hypoactivity. In the second answer column, write the name of the hormone involved.

Activity	Hormone	
_____	__________________	1. giantism
_____	__________________	2. Addison's disease
_____	__________________	3. Graves' disease
_____	__________________	4. masculinization; abnormal hairiness
_____	__________________	5. tetany

_______ ____________________ 6. slow heart rate, sluggish physical and mental activity

_______ ____________________ 7. spontaneous abortion

_______ ____________________ 8. acromegaly in an adult

_______ ____________________ 9. decalcification of bones, making them brittle and prone to fracture

_______ ____________________ 10. high blood glucose; glucose in the urine

_______ ____________________ 11. Cushing's syndrome

_______ ____________________ 12. dwarfed stature and mental retardation (cretinism)

_______ ____________________ 13. failure of the reproductive organs to mature

MULTIPLE CHOICE: Carefully read each statement. Choose the word or phrase that correctly completes the meaning and write the corresponding letter in the blank provided.

1. Various skin and intestinal glands belong to the ________. _______
   a) endocrine group
   b) exocrine group
   c) dermis
   d) digestive system

2. Glands that depend on blood and lymph to carry their secretions belong to the ________. _______
   a) endocrine group
   b) exocrine group
   c) neuron group
   d) messenger group

3. Insulin causes ________. _______
   a) a decrease in the level of blood glucose
   b) an increase in the production of glucose from glycogen
   c) a decrease in the permeability of cell membranes to glucose
   d) none of the above

4. Endocrine glands secrete chemicals called ________. _______
   a) lymph
   b) neurotransmitters
   c) hormones
   d) enzymes

5. The gland that has both exocrine and endocrine qualities is the ________. _______
   a) thyroid
   b) pancreas
   c) adrenal gland
   d) kidney

6. The body's metabolism is regulated by the ________ gland. ________
   a) thyroid
   b) pituitary
   c) thymus
   d) adrenal

7. The hormone that represses or resolves conditions of inflammation is ________. ________
   a) estrogen
   b) thyroxin
   c) adrenaline
   d) cortisol

8. The pituitary gland is called the master gland because it ________. ________
   a) maintains the blood pressure
   b) is situated at the base of the brain
   c) maintains the body's fluid balance
   d) regulates and coordinates the functions of all other glands

9. It is known that the action of the thymus hormone is related to ________. ________
   a) ovulation
   b) antibody production
   c) carbohydrate metabolism
   d) distribution of hair over the body

10. A deficiency in the hormone from the parathyroid gland will produce ________. ________
    a) dwarfism
    b) cretinism
    c) decrease of potassium in the blood
    d) imbalance in the calcium level of the body

11. A person having an increase in the production of thyroxin would be most likely to have ________. ________
    a) an increase in the level of blood sugar
    b) a decrease in blood pressure
    c) an increase in metabolic rate
    d) an increase in physical growth and a decrease in mental ability

12. The two hormones secreted by the ovaries are important in the ________. ________
    a) regulation of the metabolic rate
    b) transmission of sex-linked genetic traits
    c) maintenance of water balance in the body
    d) development of secondary sex characteristics and normal menstruation

13. As a rule, most hormone concentrations in the blood are controlled by ________. ________
    a) nerve impulses
    b) cellular demands
    c) positive feedback mechanisms
    d) negative feedback mechanisms

14. There are four small ________ located on the back of the thyroid gland. ________
    a) adrenal glands
    b) islets of Langerhans
    c) parathyroid glands
    d) follicles

15. The anterior pituitary produces ATCH, which in turn stimulates the ________. ________
    a) adrenal glands
    b) thyroid gland
    c) heart
    d) sex glands

16. ________ are hormones that are secreted from the outer layer of the adrenal cortex. ________
    a) Mineralocorticoids
    b) Glucocorticoids
    c) Sex hormones
    d) Growth hormones

17. The thyroid gland has the ability to remove ________ from the blood, which is used in the synthesis of thyroxin and triiodothyronine. ________
    a) glucagons
    b) iodine
    c) cortisol
    d) glucose

18. One category of the steroids, called mineralocorticoids, ________. ________
    a) constrict the superficial blood vessels
    b) depress kidney action
    c) regulate fluid and electrolyte balance
    d) relax the smooth muscles of the intestines

19. The female counterpart to testosterone is ________. ________
    a) prolactin
    b) progesterone
    c) estrogen
    d) luteinizing hormone

20. A person born without a functioning thyroid gland will suffer from ________. ________
    a) giantism
    b) dwarfism
    c) diabetes
    d) cretinism

WORD REVIEW: The student is encouraged to write down the meaning of each of the following words. The list can be used as a study guide for this unit.

adrenal glands

ACTH

aldosterone

antidiuretic hormone (ADH)

calcitonin

cortisol

diabetes mellitus

ducts

endocrine glands

epinephrine

estrogen

exocrine glands

glucagon

glucocorticoids

goiter

gonadotropic hormones

gonads

growth hormone

hormones

hyperactive

hypoactive

insulin

islets of Langerhans

master gland

mineralocorticoids

norepinephrine

ovaries

oxytocin

pancreas

parathormone

parathyroid glands

pituitary gland

prolactin

target organs

testes

testosterone

tetany

thyroid gland

TSH

thyroxin

triiodothyronine

IDENTIFICATION: Identify the structures indicated in Figure 5.25 by writing the letter of the structure next to the appropriate term in the space provided.

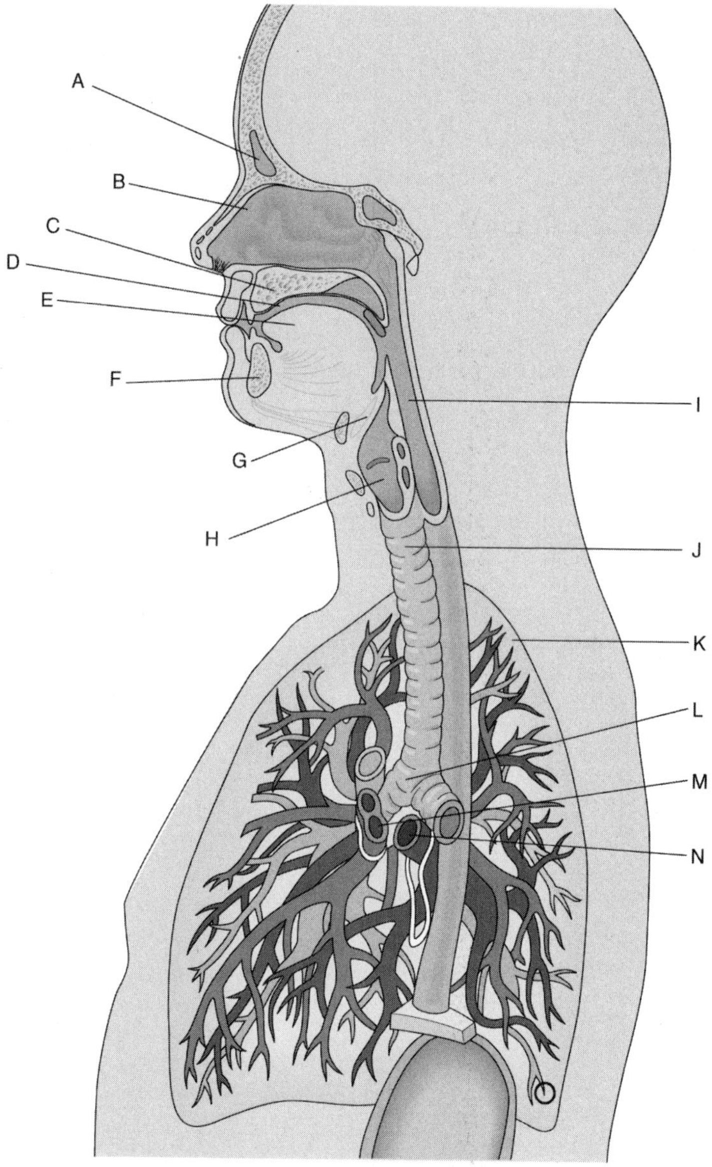

Fig. 5.25 Respiratory organs and structures.

_____ 1. bronchus

_____ 2. roof of mouth

_____ 3. lower jawbone

_____ 4. epiglottis

_____ 5. larynx

_____ 6. lung

_____ 7. nasal passage

_____ 8. oral cavity

_____ 9. tongue

_____ 10. pulmonary vein

_____ 11. sinuses

_____ 12. pharynx

_____ 13. pulmonary artery

_____ 14. trachea

COMPLETION: In the space(s) provided, write the word(s) that correctly complete(s) each statement.

1. The exchange of oxygen and carbon dioxide that takes place in the body is called ____________.
2. The exchange between the external environment and the blood that takes place in the lungs is termed ____________.
3. The gaseous exchange between the blood and the cells of the body is termed ____________.
4. The oxidation that occurs within the cell is termed ____________.
5. Air enters the nasal cavity through the ____________.
6. The function of the mucosa of the nasal cavity is to ____________, ____________, and ____________ the air.
7. The passageway common to the digestive system and the respiratory system that is also referred to as the throat is called the ____________.
8. The air passes through the voice box or the ____________.
9. In the chest, the windpipe or ____________ divides into two ____________.
10. The entire system of multibranched air passages is called the ____________.
11. The air passages terminate in clusters of air sacs called ____________.
12. The act of ventilation is accomplished by ____________.

TRUE OR FALSE: If the following statements are true, write *true* in the space provided. If they are false, replace the italicized word with one that makes the statement true.

____________ 1. The blood in the pulmonary arteries has a high concentration of *oxygen*.

____________ 2. Oxygen moves from the lungs to the blood by *diffusion*.

____________ 3. The by-products of *internal respiration* are water, carbon dioxide, and energy.

____________ 4. *Carbon dioxide* is carried by the red blood cells in the blood.

____________ 5. When the diaphragm contracts, it causes a person to *exhale*.

MULTIPLE CHOICE: Carefully read each statement. Choose the word or phrase that correctly completes the meaning and write the corresponding letter in the blank provided.

1. Exchange of carbon dioxide and oxygen is called ________. ______
   a) respiration
   b) relaxation
   c) oxidation
   d) ventilation

2. Internal respiration occurs between the blood and the ________. ______
   a) cells
   b) air
   c) lymph
   d) lungs

3. Oxygen is carried from the lungs to body cells by linking (chemically bonding) with ________. ______
   a) carbaminohemoglobin
   b) hydrogen ions
   c) hemoglobin
   d) carbonic acid

4. Normal adult respiration occurs this many times per minute: ______
   a) 10 to 15
   b) 25 to 30
   c) 14 to 20
   d) 40 to 50

5. The largest respiratory muscle/muscles is/are the ________. ______
   a) diaphragm
   b) intercostals
   c) scalenus
   d) posterior serratus

6. The functions of the nose include ________. ______
   a) assisting in speech
   b) serving as the organ of smell
   c) filtering, warming, and moistening the incoming air
   d) all of the above

7. The walls of the alveoli are composed of ________. ______
   a) ciliated epithelium cells
   b) single epithelium cells
   c) stratified epithelium
   d) loose connective tissue

8. When the diaphragm contracts, it ________. ______
   a) pushes upward against the lungs and causes them to deflate
   b) flattens out, allowing the lungs to expand and fill with air
   c) causes the intercostal muscles to relax and expand the chest wall
   d) pushes downward and inward, causing the lungs to deflate and expel air

9. Which of the following describes the bronchi? ________
   a) resemble the trachea in structure
   b) are structured into two primary air ways
   c) furnish a passageway by which air can reach the lungs
   d) all of the above

10. The cartilaginous structure at the base of the tongue that helps to prevent food and liquid from entering the trachea is the ________. ________
    a) pharynx
    b) uvula
    c) epiglottis
    d) soft palate

11. The layer of serous membrane that is firmly attached to the surface of a lung is called ________. ________
    a) visceral pleura
    b) mucosa
    c) parietal pleura
    d) cilia

12. A flexible cylindrical tube, the ________ , is supported by C-shaped pieces of hyaline cartilage arranged one above the other. ________
    a) larynx
    b) trachea
    c) pharynx
    d) bronchioles

13. The functions of the pharynx include ________. ________
    a) aiding in phonation
    b) furnishing open passageway for air going to and from the lungs.
    c) serving the digestive tracts as a passageway
    d) all of the above

14. The ________ is /are soft, spongy, cone shaped organ(s) located in the thoracic cavity. ________
    a) pharynx
    b) larynx
    c) the trachea
    d) lungs

15. Also commonly called the throat, the ________ is located behind the mouth cavity and between the nasal cavity and the larynx. Part of its function is to provide a passageway for food traveling from the oral cavity to the esophagus. ________
    a) glottis
    b) mucous membrane
    c) soft palate
    d) pharynx

16. A ________ lines the nasal cavity and includes an extensive network of blood vessels. Heat leaves the blood and warms the incoming air as it passes over this. ________
    a) bronchial tree
    b) glottis
    c) mucous membrane
    d) bronchi

17. Although the ________ function(s) mainly to reduce the weight of the skull, it/they also serve(s) as a resonant chamber that affects the quality of the voice. ________
    a) nasal cavity
    b) pharynx
    c) nose
    d) sinuses

18. The ________ is an enlargement in the airway at the top of the trachea that serves as a passageway for air moving in and out of the trachea, as well as providing a mechanism for sound production. ________
    a) larynx
    b) pharynx
    c) epiglottis
    d) bronchi

19. The main way in which gas exchange happens through the respiratory membrane is by ________. ________
    a) infusion
    b) evaporation
    c) diffusion
    d) radiation

20. A by-product of cellular respiration is ________. ________
    a) carbon dioxide
    b) heat
    c) water
    d) all of the above

WORD REVIEW: The student is encouraged to write down the meaning of each of the following words. The list can be used as a study guide for this unit.

alveoli

____

____

cellular respiration

____

____

diaphragm

____

____

exhalation

____

____

external respiration

inhalation

internal respiration

larynx

nasal cavity

pharynx

respiration

trachea

ventilation

COMPLETION: In the space(s) provided, write the word(s) that correctly complete(s) each statement.

1. The process of converting food into substances capable of nourishing cells is ______________.

2. The process in which the digested nutrients are transferred from the intestines to the blood or lymph vessels to be transported to the cells is ______________.

3. The muscular tube that goes from the lips to the anus is the ______________ or the ______________.

4. Organs that aid digestion but are located outside the digestive tract are known as ______________ digestive organs.

5. The physical activity of digestion that takes place in the mouth is called ______________.

6. The chemical digestive activity that takes place in the mouth is from secretions by the ______________.

7. The physical or mechanical activity in the alimentary canal is from the action of the ______________.

IDENTIFICATION: Identify the structures indicated in Figure 5.26 by writing the correct terms in the numbered space that corresponds to the number on the figure.

1. ____________________
2. ____________________
3. ____________________
4. ____________________
5. ____________________
6. ____________________
7. ____________________
8. ____________________
9. ____________________
10. ____________________
11. ____________________
12. ____________________

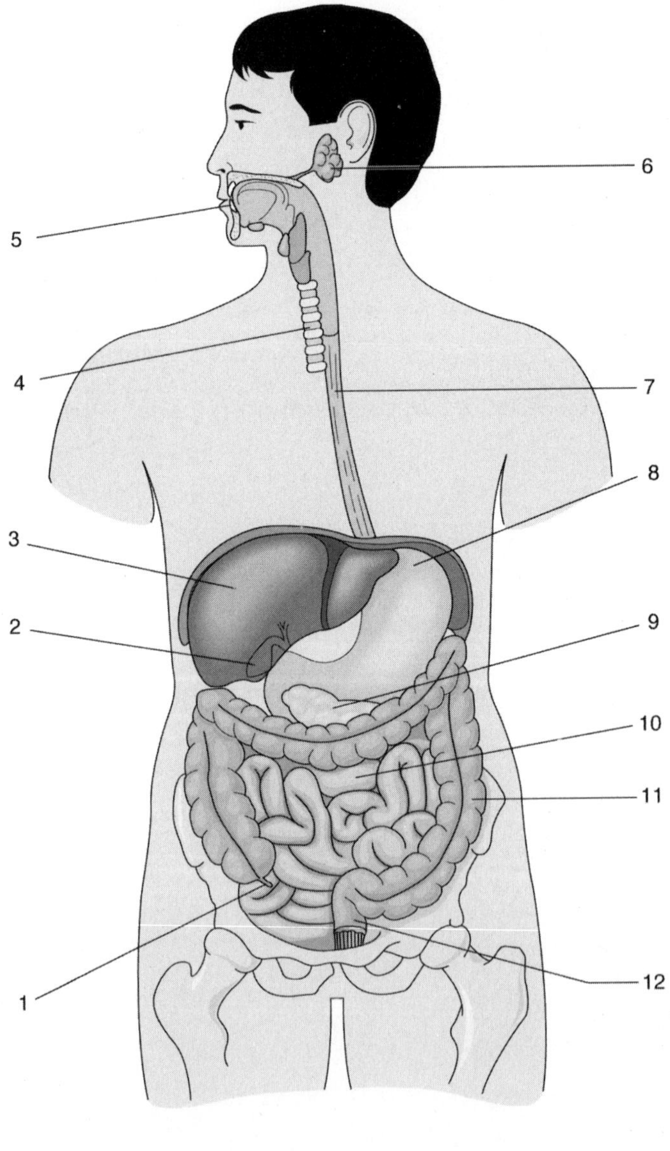

Fig. 5.26 The digestive system.

MATCHING: Match the term with the best description. Write the letter of the appropriate term in the space provided.

A. bolus
B. cardiac sphincter
C. cecum
D. chyme
E. colon
F. duodenum
G. ileocecal valve
H. ileum
I. lacteals
J. mucosa
K. oral cavity
L. peristalsis
M. pyloric valve
N. rectum
O. saliva
P. serous layer
Q. submucosa
R. villa

_____ 1. beginning of the large intestine

_____ 2. contains enzymes that begin to break down carbohydrates

_____ 3. a mixture of digestive juices, mucus, and food material

_____ 4. a soft food ball that is swallowed

_____ 5. prevents movement from the large intestine to the small intestine

_____ 6. outer covering of the intestine that is continuous with the peritoneum lining the abdominal cavity

_____ 7. rhythmic, wavelike, muscular motion

_____ 8. opening at the top of the stomach

_____ 9. temporary storage of solid waste

_____ 10. opening at the end of the stomach

_____ 11. a membrane made up of epithelial cells that carry on secretion and absorption

_____ 12. where food is masticated

_____ 13. plays an important role in determining how long food is held in the stomach

_____ 14. first section of the small intestine

_____ 15. stores, forms, and excretes waste products; regulates the body's water balance

_____ 16. finger-like projections that increase the surface area of small intestines

_____ 17. organ that receives bile and pancreatic juices

_____ 18. lymph capillaries in the small intestine

_____ 19. serves to nourish the surrounding tissues and carry away the absorbed material

_____ 20. last section of the small intestine

_____ 21. organ responsible for water absorption and feces formation

MULTIPLE CHOICE: Carefully read each statement. Choose the word or phrase that correctly completes the meaning and write the corresponding letter in the blank provided.

1. The alimentary canal includes (not counting any accessory organs) ________. ________
   a) mouth, teeth, throat, stomach, and large intestines
   b) mouth, throat, pancreas, gallbladder, and large intestines
   c) mouth, pharynx, esophagus, stomach, small and large intestines
   d) mouth, pharynx, pancreas, vermiform appendix, small and large intestines

2. Transfer of nutrients from the intestines to the blood or lymph is called ________. ________
   a) absorption
   b) digestion
   c) nutrition
   d) osmosis

3. Metabolism is a series of chemical reactions that take place in the tissue cells. These reactions are necessary for ________. ________
   a) building tissue and storing fat
   b) using nutritive elements to provide energy
   c) providing for elimination of waste products
   d) building and repairing tissue and releasing heat and energy

4. The small intestine consists of three parts that, beginning at the stomach, appear in the following order: ________
   a) ileum, duodenum, jejunum
   b) duodenum, jejunum, ileum
   c) jejunum, ileum, duodenum
   d) duodenum, ileum, jejunum

5. The total length of the adult alimentary canal is about ________. ________
   a) five yards
   b) 25 to 30 feet
   c) 50 feet
   d) twice as long as a person's height

6. The wavelike muscular movement that propels material through the alimentary canal is ________. ________
   a) initiated by swallowing
   b) a reflexive action caused by the presence of material in the canal
   c) called peristalsis
   d) all of the above

7. The complete process of digestion changes sugars and starches to ________. ________
   a) maltose
   b) glucose
   c) glycogen
   d) glycerol

8. Bile is important in digestion because it ________. ________
   a) digests simple fats
   b) changes complex sugars to glucose
   c) dissolves meat fibers and makes them easiest to digest
   d) breaks down fat globules so that they can be more easily digested by enzymes

9. The functions of the gallbladder include ________. ________
   a) filtering bile from the blood
   b) the manufacture of bile
   c) beta cells secreting important enzymes used to control metabolism
   d) contracting and ejecting bile into the duodenum while digestion is going on in the stomach and intestines

10. The sphincter between the esophagus and the stomach is called the ________. ________
    a) pyloric sphincter
    b) cardiac sphincter
    c) ileocecal sphincter
    d) anal sphincter

11. The structure at the junction of the large and small intestines that controls the passage of feces is the ________. ________
    a) jejunum
    b) appendix
    c) pylorus sphincter
    d) ileocecal valve

12. From which part of the intestines does the appendix arise? ________
    a) the cecum
    b) the jejunum
    c) the sigmoid flexure
    d) the ascending colon

13. The structures in the small intestine that are chiefly responsible for the absorption of digested food are called ________. ________
    a) villi
    b) rugae
    c) caries
    d) ampullae

14. The walls of the digestive system are composed of ________. ________
    a) cardiac muscle
    b) skeletal muscle
    c) smooth muscle
    d) sphincter muscle

15. Food is broken down into its chemical components by the action of ________. ________
    a) enzymes
    b) hormones
    c) peristalsis
    d) sphincter muscles

16. The organ in which protein digestion begins is the ________. ________
    a) mouth
    b) stomach
    c) duodeneum
    d) jejunum

17. At each end of the stomach are muscles that relax to form an opening and contract to close the opening. These muscles are known as ________. ________
    a) smooth muscles
    b) skeletal muscles
    c) cardiac muscles
    d) sphincter muscles

18. Enzymes are secreted by the ________. ________
    a) villi
    b) epiglottis
    c) liver and gallbladder
    d) linings of the stomach and intestines

19. The epiglottis serves to prevent food from ________. ________
    a) being absorbed too rapidly
    b) being aspirated into the trachea
    c) moving along the intestines too rapidly
    d) backing up from the stomach into the esophagus

20. The colon functions mainly to ________. ________
    a) digest fats
    b) secrete enzymes
    c) absorb water from the waste materials of digestion
    d) absorb digested food materials into the circulating fluids

21. Simple sugar is normally stored in the liver in the form of ________. ________
    a) lactose
    b) lactase
    c) glucose
    d) glycogen

22. Salivary glands are found in all the following locations except ________. ________
    a) in the nasopharynx
    b) in front of and below the ear
    c) under the back part of tongue
    d) under the front part of the tongue

23. The sigmoid colon empties into the ________. ________
    a) rectum
    b) transverse colon
    c) anal canal
    d) descending colon

24. The gallbladder functions to ________. ________
    a) store bile between meals
    b) concentrate bile by reabsorbing water
    c) release bile when stimulated by a hormone from the small intestine
    d) all of the above

25. The parts of the colon in order, from proximal to distal, are ________.
   a) descending, transverse, ascending, sigmoid
   b) ascending, transverse, descending, sigmoid
   c) ascending, descending, transverse, sigmoid
   d) transverse, ascending, descending, sigmoid

WORD REVIEW: The student is encouraged to write down the meaning of each of the following words. The list can be used as a study guide for this unit.

absorption

____

____

accessory digestive organs

____

____

alimentary canal

____

____

anal canal

____

____

ascending colon

____

____

bile

____

____

bolus

cardiac sphincter

cecum

chyme

colon

common bile duct

descending colon

digestion

duodenum

feces

hydrochloric acid

ileum

ileocecal valve

jejunum

lacteals

oral cavity

pancreatic duct

pancreatic fluid

peristalsis

pyloric sphincter

rectum

saliva

salivary glands

sigmoid colon

small intestine

transverse colon

villi

MATCHING: Match the term with the best description. Write the letter or letters of the appropriate excretory organ next to the term describing what that organ eliminates.

A. kidneys
B. large intestine
C. liver
D. lungs
E. skin

_______ 1. urine

_______ 2. food wastes

_______ 3. expiration

_______ 4. bile

_______ 5. uric acid

_______ 6. feces

_______ 7. urea

_______ 8. heat

_______ 9. carbon dioxide

_______ 10. perspiration

_______ 11. water

COMPLETION: In the space(s) provided, write the word(s) that correctly complete(s) each statement.

1. The functional unit of the kidney is the _____________.
2. The tubes that carry urine from the kidneys to the bladder are called _____________.
3. A hormone produced in the kidneys that acts to regulate blood pressure is _____________.

TRUE OR FALSE: If the following statements are true, write *true* in the space provided. If they are false, replace the italicized word with one that makes the statement true.

_____________ 1. The kidneys normally filter 40 to 50 *gallons* of blood plasma a day.

_____________ 2. When a person urinates, *voluntary* muscles in the walls of the bladder contract, forcing the urine out of the body.

IDENTIFICATION: Identify the structures indicated in Figure 5.27 by writing the correct term in the numbered space that corresponds to the number on the figure.

1. ____________________
2. ____________________
3. ____________________
4. ____________________
5. ____________________
6. ____________________
7. ____________________
8. ____________________
9. ____________________

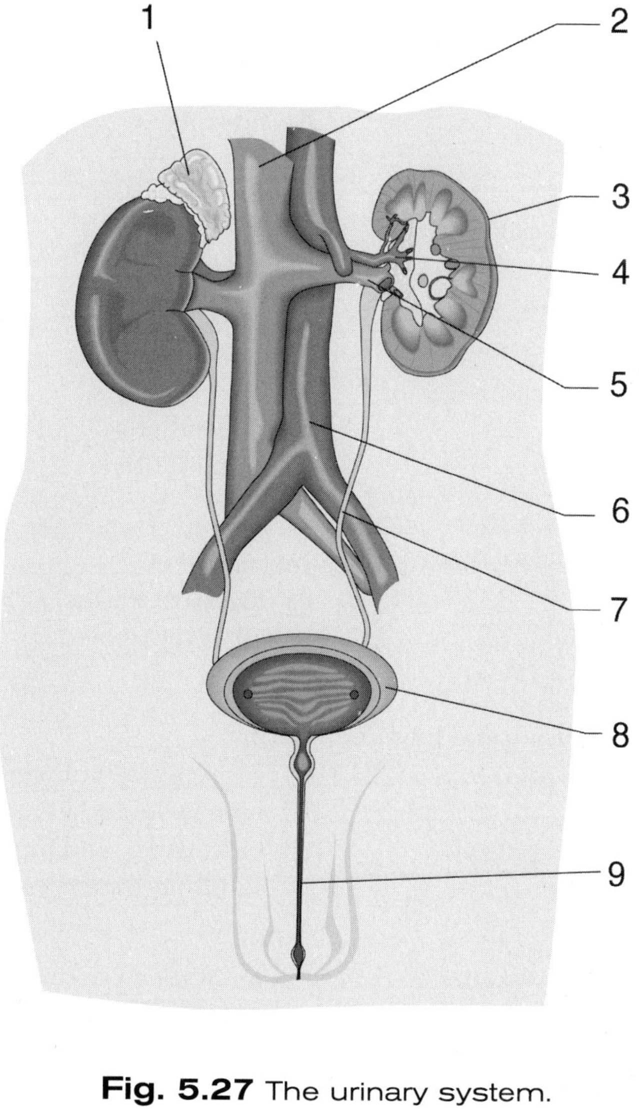

Fig. 5.27 The urinary system.

MULTIPLE CHOICE: Carefully read each statement. Choose the word or phrase that correctly completes the meaning and write the corresponding letter in the blank provided.

1. Urine is produced in and eliminated from the organs of the urinary system in the following order: ________
   a) cortex, urethra, bladder, ureter
   b) kidney, urethra, bladder, ureter
   c) kidney, pelvis, ureter, bladder
   d) kidney, ureter, bladder, urethra

2. The opening between the bladder and the urethra is controlled by a ________. ________
   a) flaplike valve
   b) sphincter muscle
   c) band of cartilage
   d) fold of membranous tissue

3. The excretory function of the lungs is the elimination of ________. ________
   a) oxygen
   b) heat
   c) carbon dioxide
   d) mucous

4. Materials for the production of urine come from the ________. ________
   a) kidney
   b) bladder
   c) bloodstream
   d) lymph system

5. The wall of the bladder is composed of ________. ________
   a) cartilage
   b) smooth muscle
   c) skeletal muscle
   d) adipose tissue

6. The excretory function of the colon is the elimination of ________. ________
   a) water
   b) heat
   c) digestive wastes
   d) all of the above

7. The basic constituents of normal human urine are ________. ________
   a) electrolytes, albumin, and water
   b) water, salts, sugar, and protein
   c) gases, water, coloring materials, and glucose
   d) salts, water, and organic substances such as urea

8. Which of the following is not considered an organ of the excretory system? ________
   a) the lungs
   b) the kidneys
   c) the colon
   d) the nose

9. Nephrons consist of ________. ________
   a) glomerulus and tubules
   b) arterioles and lymph nodes
   c) capillaries and islet cells
   d) mucous membrane and synapses

10. The glomerulus, encased in a capsule, contains a network of ________. ________
    a) fascia
    b) capillaries
    c) nervous tissue
    d) smooth muscles

11. The outer portion of the kidney is the ________. ________
    a) medulla
    b) Bowman's capsule
    c) loop of Henle
    d) cortex

12. The ________ surrounds the glomerulus. ________
    a) renal artery
    b) proximal tubule
    c) Bowman's capsule
    d) trigone in the bladder

13. The urge to void usually begins when the normal bladder contains approximately how much urine? ________
    a) four to eight drams (15 to 30 cc)
    b) one to two quarts (1000 to 2000 cc)
    c) two to four quarts (2000 to 4000 cc)
    d) one-half to two-thirds pint (250-350 cc)

14. The inner portion of the kidney is the ________. ________
    a) medulla
    b) ureter
    c) renal pelvis
    d) cortex

15. The blood supply to the kidney is carried by the ________. ________
    a) renal artery
    b) loop of Henle
    c) renal vein
    d) proximal tubule

16. A cluster of capillary loops is the ________. ________
    a) renal artery
    b) proximal tubule
    c) renal vein
    d) glomerulus

17. The functional unit of the kidney is the ________. ________
    a) cell
    b) nephron
    c) glomerulus
    d) loop of Henle

18. The liver produces ________, which is excreted by the kidneys. ________
    a) bile
    b) uric acid
    c) glucose
    d) urea

19. Fluid is carried from the kidneys to the bladder by the ________. ________
    a) renal vein
    b) renal artery
    c) ureters
    d) urethra

20. Of the amount of plasma that is filtered through the kidneys, approximately how much is excreted as urine? ________
    a) 0.1%
    b) 1%
    c) 5%
    d) 10%

WORD REVIEW: The student is encouraged to write down the meaning of each of the following words. The list can be used as a study guide for this unit.

bile

____

____

bladder

____

____

excretion

____

____

metabolic wastes

____

____

nephron

____

____

renin

____

____

ureters

____

____

urethra

____

____

urinary system

____

____

SYSTEM TEN: THE HUMAN REPRODUCTIVE SYSTEM

COMPLETION: In the space(s) provided, write the word(s) that correctly complete(s) each statement.

1. One-celled organisms that do not need a partner to reproduce do so by nonsexual means called ____________ reproduction.
2. The term used to describe a reproductive cell that can unite with another reproductive cell to form the cell that develops into a new individual is called a ____________.
3. In men, the reproductive cells are called ____________.
4. In women, the reproductive cells are called ____________.
5. The cell formed by the union of the male and female reproductive cells is called a ____________.
6. The gland in the female that produces the reproductive cell is the ____________.
7. The gland in the male that produces the reproductive cell is the ____________.

SHORT ANSWER: Number the following terms from 1 to 5 in the order that sperm would travel from the time it is produced until it leaves the body.

_____ vas deferens

_____ urethra

_____ epididymis

_____ seminiferous tubules

_____ ejaculatory ducts

MATCHING: Match the term with the best description. Write the letter of the appropriate term in the space provided.

A. Cowper's glands
B. epididymis
C. prostate gland
D. seminal vesicles
E. testes
F. urethra
G. vas deferens

_____ 1. conveys both urine and sperm out of the body

_____ 2. two convoluted, glandular tubes located on each side of the prostate gland

_____ 3. stores the sperm until it becomes fully mature

_____ 4. forms the male hormone testosterone

_____ 5. mucus-producing glands that serve to lubricate the urethra

_____ 6. contains specialized cells that produce the spermatozoa

_____ 7. surrounds the first part of the urethra

_____ 8. two pea-sized glands located beneath the prostate gland

_____ 9. secretes an alkaline fluid that neutralizes the acidic vaginal secretions

_____ 10. secretions contain simple sugars, mucus, and prostaglandin

_____ 11. two small, egg-shaped glands made up of minute convoluted tubules

_____ 12. sperm collects here until it is expelled from the body

_____ 13. located in the scrotum; receives sperm from the testes

IDENTIFICATION: Identify the structures indicated in Figure 5.28 by writing the letter of the structure next to the appropriate term in the space provided.

_____ 1. bulbourethral gland

_____ 2. urethra

_____ 3. epididymis

_____ 4. erectile tissue

_____ 5. glans penis

_____ 6. prepuce

_____ 7. prostate gland

_____ 8. scrotum

_____ 9. seminal vesicle

_____ 10. testis

_____ 11. urinary bladder

_____ 12. vas deferens

_____ 13. spine

_____ 14. rectum

_____ 15. anal opening

_____ 16. ureter

_____ 17. symphysis pubis

_____ 18. spermatic cord

_____ 19. ejaculatory duct

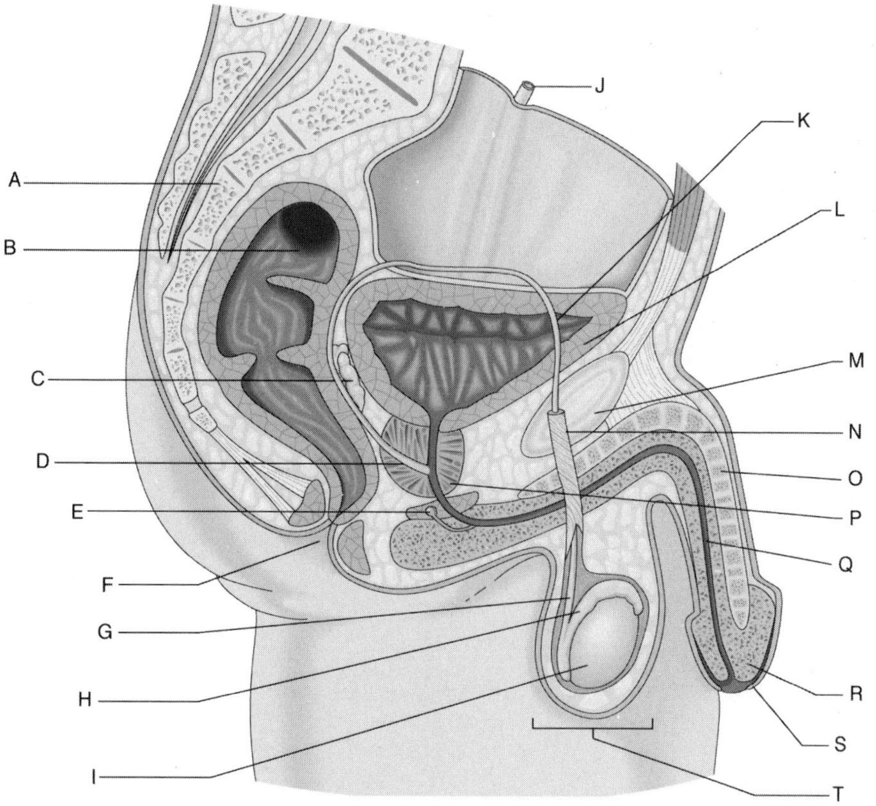

Fig. 5.28 The male reproductive system.

COMPLETION: In the space(s) provided, write the word(s) that correctly complete(s) each statement.

1. The external part of the female reproductive system that includes the labia majora and the labia minora is termed the ____________.
2. The muscular tube or canal that is the lower part of the birth canal is called the ____________.
3. The chamber that houses the developing fetus is the ____________.
4. The egg-carrying tubes of the female reproductive system are the ____________.
5. The glands that produce estrogen and progesterone are the ____________.
6. The egg cell capable of being fertilized by a spermatozoon is the ____________.

MATCHING: Match the term with the best description. Write the letter of the appropriate term in the space provided.

A. corpus luteum	C. gestation	E. menstruation
B. estrogen	D. menopause	F. ovulation

_____ 1. controls the development of secondary female sexual characteristics

_____ 2. the release of the egg cell from the ovary

_____ 3. ovarian site of estrogen and progesterone production

_____ 4. occurs from the time an ovum is fertilized until childbirth

_____ 5. the cyclic uterine bleeding that normally occurs at approximately 4-week intervals

_____ 6. follicle transformed by luteinizing hormone

_____ 7. the physiologic cessation of the menstrual cycle

IDENTIFICATION: Identify the structures indicated in Figure 5.29 by writing the letter of the structure next to the appropriate term in the space provided.

_____ 1. anal opening

_____ 2. cervix

_____ 3. fallopian tube

_____ 4. labia minora

_____ 5. labia majora

_____ 6. ovary

_____ 7. spine

_____ 8. rectum

_____ 9. symphysis pubis

_____ 10. urethra

_____ 11. urinary bladder

_____ 12. uterus

_____ 13. vagina

_____ 14. urinary opening

_____ 15. fundus of uterus

_____ 16. ureter

_____ 17. sacral promontory

_____ 18. clitoris

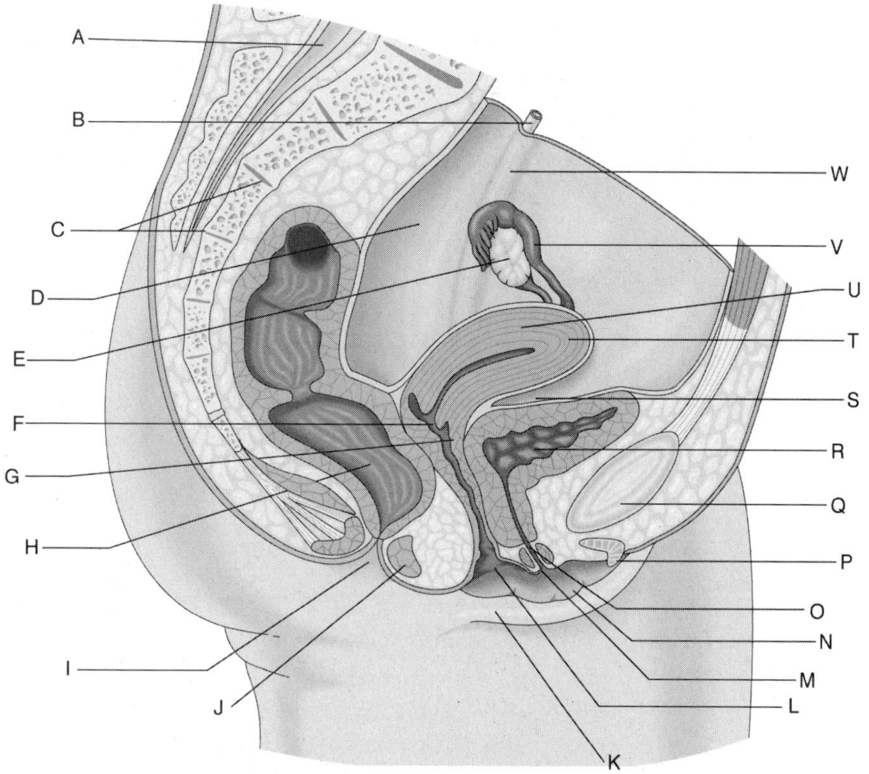

Fig. 5.29 The female reproductive system.

MULTIPLE CHOICE: Carefully read each statement. Choose the word or phrase that correctly completes the meaning and write the corresponding letter in the blank provided.

1. Sperm cells are stored primarily in the ________. ________
   a) epididymis
   b) vas deferens
   c) seminal vesicles
   d) ejaculatory ducts

2. The hormone responsible for the development and maintenance of male secondary sexual characteristics is ________. ________
   a) ACTH
   b) FSH
   c) testosterone
   d) gonadotropin-releasing hormone

3. The upper openings of the uterine cavity join with the ________. ________
   a) fimbriae
   b) ovaries
   c) cervical canal
   d) fallopian tubes

4. Which of the following are canals or tubes through which the sperm pass as they are transported to the outside of the body? ________
   a) urethra
   b) epididymis
   c) vas deferens
   d) all of these

5. The number of spermatozoa that penetrate, and thereby fertilize, the ovum is ________. ________
   a) only one
   b) about 100
   c) at least 3
   d) about 1 million

6. Once the sperm enters the female reproductive tract, it is capable of fertilizing the ovum for ________. ________
   a) a month
   b) hours or days
   c) less than an hour
   d) more than a week

7. The ejaculatory ducts empty into the ________. ________
   a) vas deferens
   b) scrotum
   c) urethra
   d) epididymis

8. The penis is composed of what type of tissue? ________
   a) fatty
   b) muscular
   c) erectile
   d) cartilaginous

9. The hormone mainly responsible for the development and maintenance of female secondary sexual characteristics is ________. ________
   a) androgen
   b) estrogen
   c) progesterone
   d) luteinizing hormone

10. The labia minora ________.
    a) compose the middle portion of the uterus
    b) function chiefly as the female organs of sexual sensation
    c) are two liplike folds situated on either side of external opening of the vagina
    d) form a membranous fold that encircles the vaginal orifice

11. The tubular portion of the uterus that extends downward into the upper part of the vagina is the ________. ________
    a) cervix
    b) perimetrium
    c) endometrium
    d) ostium uteri

12. The inner lining of the uterus is known as the ________. ________
    a) hymen
    b) epididymis
    c) myometrium
    d) endometrium

13. The free ends of the fallopian tubes ________. ________
    a) encircle the uterus
    b) are closed, finger-like processes
    c) form a solid mass over each ovary
    d) are open-ended, with finger-like fimbriae

14. The physiologic cessation of the menstrual cycle is ________. ________
    a) menarche
    b) menopause
    c) a period
    d) virginity

15. Fertilization of an ovum usually takes place in the ________. ________
    a) uterus
    b) cervix
    c) fallopian tubes
    d) vagina

16. The secretions of the various glandular tissues of the male reproductive system combine to form ________. ________
    a) semen
    b) testosterone
    c) mucous
    d) sperm

17. The pathway that the sperm travel from the testes out of the body is ________. ________
    a) urethra, seminiferous tubule, epididymis, vas deferens
    b) seminiferous tubule, epididymis, vas deferens, urethra
    c) epididymis, seminiferous tubule, vas deferens, urethra
    d) vas deferens, epididymis, seminiferous tubule, urethra

18. A cell formed by the unification of a male and female reproductive cell is a ________. ________
    a) gamate
    b) fetus
    c) zygote
    d) embryo

19. The ________ produces an alkaline fluid that is part of the semen. ________
   a) Cowper's gland
   b) testes
   c) seminal vesicle
   d) prostate gland

20. Which of the following organs do not contribute to the formation of semen? ________
   a) seminal vesicles
   b) testes
   c) vas deferens
   d) prostate gland

WORD REVIEW: The student is encouraged to write down the meaning of each of the following words. The list can be used as a study guide for this unit.

asexual reproduction

____

____

bulbourethral glands

____

____

cervix

____

____

corpus luteum

____

____

ejaculatory ducts

____

____

epididymis

____

____

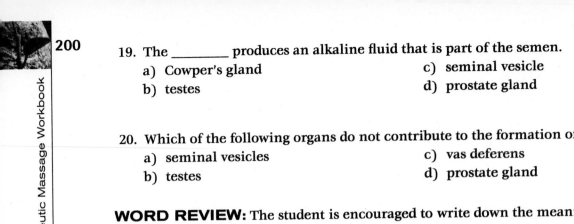

estrogen

fallopian tubes

fertilization

fetus

gamete

gestation

gonad

labia majora

labia minora

luteinizing hormone

menopause

menstrual cycle

menstruation

penis

pregnancy

ovary

oviducts

ovulation

ovum

progesterone

prostate gland

scrotum

semen

seminal fluid

seminal vesicles

spermatozoa

testes

testosterone

urethra

uterus

vagina

vas deferens

vulva

zygote

Part 3

Massage Practice

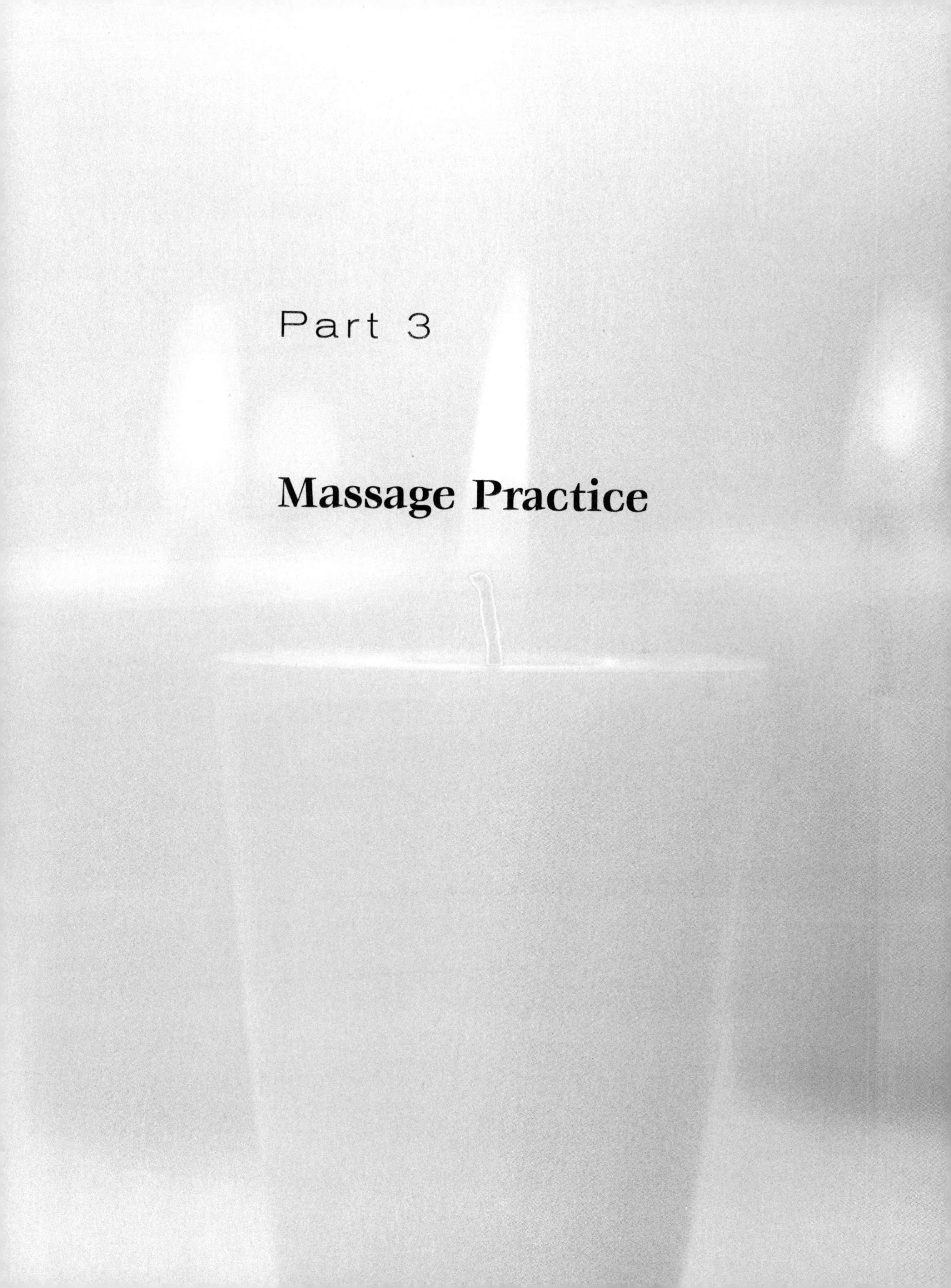

Effects, Benefits, Indications, and Contraindications of Massage

CHAPTER 6

COMPLETION: In the space(s) provided, write the word(s) that correctly complete(s) each statement.

1. A massage should not be given when ________________ are present.
2. Direct physical effects of the massage techniques on the tissues are considered to be ____________ effects.
3. Indirect responses to touch that affect body functions and tissues through the nervous or energy systems are termed ____________ effects.
4. Effects of massage on the structures of the body are considered ______________ effects.
5. Mental and emotional effects of massage are ______________ effects.
6. Any physical, emotional, or mental condition that might cause a particular massage treatment to be unsafe or detrimental to the client's well-being is a ________________.

TRUE OR FALSE: If the following statements are true, write *true* in the space provided. If they are false, replace the italicized word with one that makes the statement true.

____________ 1. Kneading and compression help to increase *strength* in muscles.

____________ 2. *Active joint movements* increase strength, flexibility, and circulation.

_______ 3. A *conditional* contraindication prohibits administering massage to only a local part of the body, such as local contagious conditions, open wounds, or arthritis, but massaging other areas is fine.

MATCHING: Match the massage techniques listed below with the best description. Write the letter(s) of the appropriate massage technique in the space provided.

A. active joint movements	D. friction	G. passive joint movement
B. compression	E. kneading	H. percussion
C. deep stroking	F. light stroking	I. vibration

_____ 1. prevents and reduces excessive scarring following trauma

_____ 2. rotation of joints through their range of motion with no resistance or assistance by muscular activity on the part of the client

_____ 3. relaxes and lengthens the muscles

_____ 4. prevents and reduces the development of adhesions

_____ 5. contraction of voluntary muscles by the client that are either resisted or assisted by the therapist

_____ 6. helps to firm and strengthen muscles

_____ 7. produces calming sedative effects

_____ 8. directed toward the heart in the direction of venous blood flow

_____ 9. increases the permeability of the capillary beds and produces an increased flow of interstitial fluid

_____ 10. produces hyperemia in the muscle tissue

MATCHING: Match the hypothetical situations with the best treatment choice(s). Write the letter(s) of the appropriate choice(s) in the space provided.

A. Avoid the affected area.

B. Consult with the client's physician before proceeding.

C. Do not perform the massage at this time.

D. Massage specifically on the affected area.

E. Proceed with a light noninvasive, soothing massage.

F. Proceed with the massage as usual.

G. Refer the client to a doctor.

_____ 1. Miss Harris is 26 years old and has been in to see you on a monthly basis. When she comes in for her regular appointment, she complains of a general achiness, she is slightly flushed, and she has a temperature of 101.5 degrees.

_____ 2. Mrs. Clements asks for you to come to her home to give her a massage. She says she would come to your office except that she has the flu.

_____ 3. Mr. James's wrist is red, swollen, and warm to the touch. He has come in for a general massage and asks you to pay particular attention to his wrist.

_____ 4. Mrs. Annest has come in for a massage. As she is getting on the table, you notice a red, flaky area on the inside of her elbow and another one on the back of her shoulder. When you ask, she says that they are "just some itchy patches she has had for a couple of weeks."

_____ 5. When Mr. Inkles lies face down on the table, you notice a number of inflamed bumps and pimples between his shoulder blades and on his shoulders.

_____ 6. Mr. Johnson, 40 years old, indicates that he is under a doctor's care for a condition that has caused a severe decalcification of the bones.

_____ 7. An 83-year-old woman with noticeably stooped shoulders and somewhat deformed hands wants to start getting massages to help recover from a fractured hip she suffered 3 months earlier.

_____ 8. A 35-year-old mother of three comes in for relief of sore feet and an achy lower back. When giving her a massage, you notice several bulging bluish masses on her legs.

_____ 9. A 28-year-old man comes into the clinic for a massage. He says that he was thrown from a horse 2 days earlier and has a lot of discomfort in his hip and thigh. When he gets on the table, you note a large black and blue area around his hip. He says that he has gone to the doctor and X-rays have determined there were no broken bones.

_____ 10. A 35-year-old woman comes in for a massage. One week earlier she was in a car accident. No bones were broken, but she was shaken up pretty badly. She has large bruises on her upper arm and thigh that are still somewhat discolored.

_____ 11. A woman who is 7 months' pregnant comes in and wants a massage because she is "stressed out." You notice that her hands and feet are somewhat swollen. When you press a finger into her ankle, it leaves a slight impression.

_____ 12. Mr. Hill is 54 years old and is under a physician's care for high blood pressure. His physician has recommended massage as part of his treatment. You take his blood pressure when he comes for his massage and it is 170 over 130.

_____ 13. Mrs. Baird is 44 years old and is in the middle of a series of chemotherapy treatments after having a malignant growth removed from her colon. She is seeking massage for relief from stress and "to be good to herself."

_____ 14. A 48-year-old female executive is under a doctor's care for chronic fatigue and mental exhaustion. The doctor has recommended massage as part of her treatment.

COMPLETION: In the space(s) provided, write the word(s) that correctly complete(s) each statement.

1. Short, invigorating massage stimulates the _______________ nervous system.

2. Longer, relaxing massage sedates the _______________ nervous system and stimulates the _______________ nervous system.

3. Research has shown that an hour-long, rhythmic massage encourages relaxation and reduces the blood levels of _______________ and _______________.

4. The positive effects of relaxing massage interrupt the transmission of pain sensations from entering the central nervous system because of what is known as the _______________.

5. The classic signs of inflammation are _____________, _____________, _____________, and _____________.

MULTIPLE CHOICE: Carefully read each statement. Choose the word or phrase that correctly completes the meaning and write the corresponding letter in the blank provided.

1. Adhesion development and excessive scarring following trauma can be prevented or reduced with _____
   a) gliding movements
   b) petrissage
   c) friction massage
   d) percussion movements

2. In Swedish massage, movements should generally be _____
   a) toward the heart
   b) relaxing
   c) away from the heart
   d) invigorating

3. A contraindication of massage is ______
   a) mild high blood pressure
   b) AIDS
   c) muscle spasm
   d) fever

4. Inflammation of a vein is called ______
   a) thrombosis
   b) phlebitis
   c) embolism
   d) aneurysm (aneurosa)

5. If a client comes for a massage and has a low-grade fever (100.5° F), the practitioner should ______
   a) have him drink plenty of water before and after the massage
   b) give them a very light massage
   c) refer him to a doctor
   d) make him an appointment for another time and send them home

6. A piece of a blood clot floating in the blood is called ______
   a) varicose
   b) phlebitis
   c) embolus
   d) aneurysm (aneurosa)

7. A mass of blood trapped in tissue or a body cavity as a result of internal bleeding is called ______
   a) hematoma
   b) phlebitis
   c) contusion
   d) edema

8. Cancer is a disease that is often spread through ______
   a) the genes
   b) the lymphatic system
   c) an open wound
   d) the digestive system

9. Massage during pregnancy is ______
   a) contraindicated
   b) usually beneficial
   c) done only with a doctor's approval
   d) avoided except under special conditions

10. Body areas where caution should be used to avoid damaging underlying anatomic structures are called ______
    a) contraindications
    b) endangerment sites
    c) untouchable
    d) landmarks

11. Stimulation of the parasympathetic nervous system causes ______
    a) a fight-or-flight response
    b) increased circulation to the internal organs
    c) increased blood flow to the muscles
    d) all of the above

12. Conditions that require the practitioner to adjust the massage when there are health concerns for which certain massage techniques might cause discomfort or have adverse effects are ______
    a) conditional contraindications
    b) regional contraindications
    c) absolute contraindications
    d) to be referred to a doctor

13. Reduced anxiety, an enhanced sense of relaxation, and renewed energy are ______
    a) indications for massage
    b) contraindications for massage
    c) physiologic benefits of massage
    d) psychological benefits of massage

14. Indirect responses to massage techniques that affect body functions or tissues are ______
    a) mechanical effects of massage
    b) to be avoided
    c) psychological effects
    d) reflex effects

15. The method in which the client's arm is moved through its range of motion by the therapist while the client remains relaxed is ______
    a) passive joint movement
    b) active joint movement
    c) assisted joint movement
    d) contraindicated in muscle injuries

16. Massage strokes that affect the venous blood flow should ______
    a) be light and continuous
    b) be directed toward the heart
    c) be directed toward the extremities
    d) continue from one end of the body part to the other

17. Hyperemia is ______
    a) a contraindication for massage
    b) a condition in which the body produces too much blood
    c) an increase in the amount of blood stored in muscle tissue
    d) an undesirable side effect of improper or excessive massage

18. Massage that increases lymph flow should not be done on persons with ______
    a) high blood pressure
    b) arthritis
    c) lymphoma
    d) diabetes

19. If a client has bulging bluish veins on their lower legs, the practitioner should ________
   a) avoid all but the most superficial strokes on those areas
   b) not massage the legs or feet
   c) consult the client's doctor before the massage
   d) proceed with a normal massage and refer the client to a specialist

20. A man in his late twenties comes for a massage. When he is face down you notice red bumps and pimples on his upper back and shoulders. You proceed by ________
   a) asking him to shower and especially clean the affected area
   b) continuing with the massage but avoid the area
   c) continuing the massage but using no oil on the affected area
   d) discontinuing the massage

21. A woman well into the second trimester comes for a massage. She complains of fatigue and swelling in her legs and arms. You should ________
   a) position her comfortably with plenty of pillows and perform a gentle full-body massage
   b) give a prenatal massage and send her to a doctor
   c) recommend that she see her doctor before the massage
   d) position her on her side with plenty of support and massage only her back

22. The first and foremost rule of massage is ________
   a) do no harm
   b) refer to a doctor when in doubt
   c) perform a consultation before the massage
   d) get the client's permission before proceeding

WORD REVIEW: The student is encouraged to write down the meaning of each of the following words. The list can be used as a study guide for this unit.

active joint movement

____

____

aneurosa

____

____

aneurysm

cancer

central nervous system

contraindication

contusion

dopamine

edema

elasticity

embolus

endangerment site

epinephrine

gate control theory

hematoma

homeostasis

inflammation

lymphedema

mechanical effects

osteoporosis

parasympathetic nervous system

passive joint movement

peripheral nervous system

phlebitis

pitting edema

reflex effects

serotonin

____

____

sympathetic nervous system

____

____

thrombophlebitis

____

____

varicose veins

____

____

CHAPTER 7

Equipment and Products

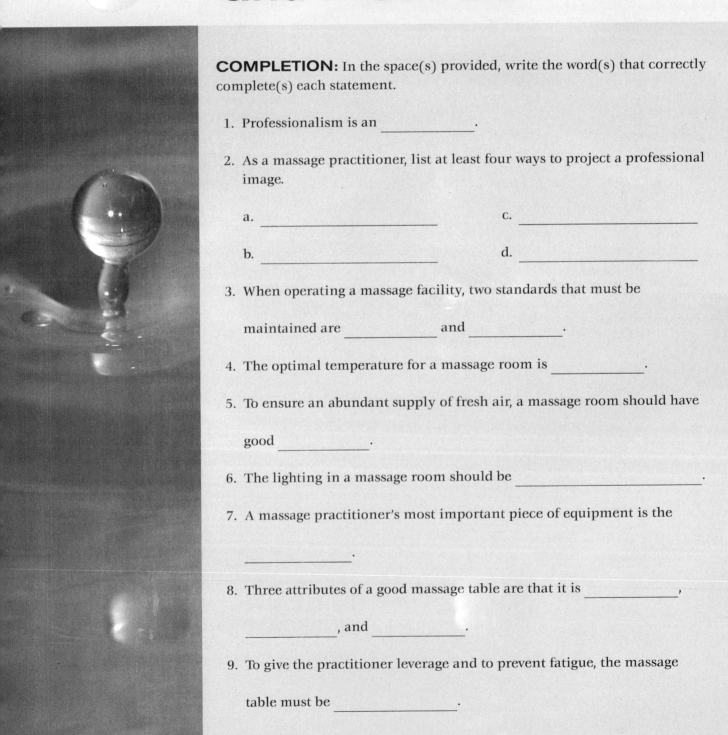

COMPLETION: In the space(s) provided, write the word(s) that correctly complete(s) each statement.

1. Professionalism is an ______________.

2. As a massage practitioner, list at least four ways to project a professional image.

   a. ______________________ c. ______________________

   b. ______________________ d. ______________________

3. When operating a massage facility, two standards that must be maintained are ______________ and ______________.

4. The optimal temperature for a massage room is ______________.

5. To ensure an abundant supply of fresh air, a massage room should have good ______________.

6. The lighting in a massage room should be ______________________.

7. A massage practitioner's most important piece of equipment is the ______________.

8. Three attributes of a good massage table are that it is ______________, ______________, and ______________.

9. To give the practitioner leverage and to prevent fatigue, the massage table must be ________________.

10. A good width for a massage table is ____________.

11. A good length for a massage table is ____________.

12. One of a massage practitioner's most important supplies is the ____________ that they use on their clients.

13. If there is reason to believe that the client is sensitive or allergic to a product or oil, the practitioner can perform a ____________.

14. The three main areas of a massage business operation are the ____________, the ____________, and the ____________.

15. To position a client comfortably, the therapist can use a variety of supportive devises called ____________.

16. Besides sheets and towels, the practitioner should have ____________________ on hand to prevent a client from becoming chilled.

MULTIPLE CHOICE: Carefully read each statement. Choose the word or phrase that correctly completes the meaning and write the corresponding letter in the blank provided.

1. The size of a massage room should be at least ______
   a) 5 feet by 6 feet
   b) 10 feet by 12 feet
   c) 5 feet by 9 feet
   d) 15 feet by 20 feet

2. The ideal Fahrenheit temperature for a massage room is ______
   a) 75°
   b) 65°
   c) 80°
   d) 85°

3. Matching massage movements to the tempo of the music is ______
   a) desirable
   b) unprofessional
   c) not desirable
   d) professional

4. The height of a massage table is determined by the ______
   a) height of the client
   b) weight of the client
   c) practitioner's height
   d) size of the room

5. The best covering for a massage table is ______
   a) velvet
   b) suede
   c) vinyl
   d) cotton

6. If oil has an unpleasant odor but is not rancid, add a few drops of
   a) lemon juice
   b) essential oil
   c) vinegar
   d) Lysol

7. The primary purpose for a good massage lubricant is
   a) to moisten the practitioner's hands
   b) to moisturize the client's skin
   c) to reduce the friction between the client's skin and practitioner's hands
   d) to add a pleasant aroma to the massage experience

8. The time to determine product allergies is
   a) during consultation
   b) at the beginning of massage
   c) at the end of massage
   d) during the second visit

9. The purpose of linens is
   a) to keep the vinyl from touching the clients skin
   b) to provide warmth to the client
   c) to provide modest covering for the client
   d) all of the above

Sanitary and Safety Practices

CHAPTER 8

COMPLETION: In the space(s) provided, write the word(s) that correctly complete(s) each statement.

1. In personal care services, the three levels of decontamination are ____________, ____________, and ____________.
2. The removal of all living organisms on an object or surface, including bacterial spores, is called ____________.
3. Any item that comes in contact with the client must be clean and ____________.
4. A massage practitioner's hands can be sanitized by ________________________.
5. Minute, unicellular microorganisms exhibiting both plant and animal characteristics are called ____________.
6. Beneficial and harmless bacteria that perform useful functions are termed ____________.
7. Bacteria that cause or produce disease are termed ____________.
8. Three general forms of pathogenic bacteria are ____________, ____________, and ____________.
9. The body's natural ability to resist infection is ____________.

10. The body's most important defense against invasion of harmful bacteria is the

    ______________.

11. Proteins that are produced in the body in response to contact with an invading bacteria

    are ______________.

12. Submicroscopic pathogenic agents that invade living cells and are capable of transmitting

    disease are called ______________.

13. The primary precaution in infection control is thorough ______________.

14. An acceptable way to sanitize linens is to wash them in hot, soapy water and add

    one-half to one cup of ______________.

15. Floors, sinks, and restrooms can be cleaned and sanitized with a solution of

    ______________.

16. A common disinfectant used to clean surfaces and implements is a ______________ percent chlorine bleach solution.

17. If there is suspicion of bacterial contamination, the hands can be rinsed with

    ______________.

SHORT ANSWER: In the spaces provided, write short answers to the following questions.

1. If a client has an infection or contagious disease, what are two things that the massage practitioner should do?

    a. ______________________________

    b. ______________________________

2. When should the massage practitioner wash her hands?

    ____

3. List three acceptable means of sanitizing implements.

    a. ______________________________

    b. ______________________________

    c. ______________________________

4. List two agents that can be used to disinfect implements.

   a. ______________________________

   b. ______________________________

5. The primary precaution for infection control in the massage practice is

   ____

MATCHING: Match the procedure for disinfecting or sterilizing with the given situation. Write the letter or letters of the appropriate procedure in the space provided.

A. boiling in water
B. chlorine bleach
C. cresol or Lysol
D. immersing in quats
E. rinsing with alcohol solution
F. soap and hot water
G. wiping with alcohol

_____ 1. massage table surface with normal use

_____ 2. massage table face cradle

_____ 3. practitioner's hands before a massage

_____ 4. practitioner's hands after a massage

_____ 5. practitioner's hands after working on client with possible contagious skin condition

_____ 6. bathroom sink

_____ 7. bathroom floor

_____ 8. shower stall

_____ 9. linens after normal use

_____ 10. linens after use on clients with possible contagious conditions

_____ 11. brushes and combs kept for client use

_____ 12. towels used for wraps and hydrotherapy

MULTIPLE CHOICE: Carefully read each statement. Choose the word or phrase that correctly completes the meaning and write the corresponding letter in the blank provided.

1. Every state protects the public health through _____
   a) commissions
   b) laws
   c) sanitation
   d) inspections

2. Disease-producing bacteria are termed
   a) nonpathogenic
   b) pathogenic
   c) viruses
   d) antibodies

3. The mode of decontamination that destroys microorganisms, including bacterial spores, is
   a) antiseptics
   b) sanitation
   c) disinfecting
   d) sterilization

4. The practitioner's hands should be washed before client contact using
   a) disinfectant
   b) antibacterial soap
   c) alcohol
   d) detergent

5. One of the body's most important defenses against the invasion of harmful bacteria is
   a) healthy skin
   b) good teeth
   c) clean hands
   d) drinking liquids

6. A sign that the body is working to destroy harmful microorganisms is
   a) infection
   b) fluid retention
   c) immunity
   d) inflammation

7. Which level of decontamination is achieved by immersing implements in a 10 percent bleach solution for 10 minutes?
   a) no decontamination will take place
   b) sanitizing
   c) disinfecting
   d) sterilizing

8. To disinfect linens, add to wash water one cup of
   a) chlorine bleach
   b) ammonia
   c) detergent
   d) Lysol

9. Hands can be sanitized with
   a) quats
   b) soap and water
   c) disinfectant
   d) bleach

10. Sheets and towels with a rancid odor should be
   a) discarded
   b) bleached
   c) softened
   d) washed

11. Using proper lifting techniques when moving equipment or clients is an example of ________
   a) first aid
   b) product liability
   c) equipment safety
   d) personal safety

12. When going on an outcall, you should always ______
    a) bring extra towels
    b) tell someone your destination
    c) wear warm clothes
    d) drive yourself

13. Which level of cleanliness is recommended for the hands before giving a massage? ______
    a) disinfecting
    b) sanitizing
    c) sterilizing
    d) none of the above

14. One of the primary ways to prevent the spread of disease is ______
    a) use a good air-filtering system
    b) use disposable cups
    c) regularly wash hands with soap and water
    d) rinse your hands with alcohol

15. Pathogens enter the body in varied ways that can be called paths of ______
    a) arrival
    b) manifestation
    c) reproduction
    d) transmission

16. If you suspect that your linens have been contaminated by a client with an infectious condition, you should ______ ______
    a) launder them in hot water and detergent
    b) add one cup bleach to the wash
    c) dry them in a hot dryer
    d) all of the above

17. The practitioner's hands should be washed after working on an HIV-infected person with ______
    a) a germicidal soap
    b) chlorine bleach
    c) a sterilizing agent
    d) all of the above

18. A class of proteins that serve to protect the body against invading bacteria are called ______
    a) antigens
    b) antibodies
    c) pathogens
    d) lymphocytes

19. The proper concentration of chlorine bleach for disinfecting implements and surfaces is ______
    a) full strength
    b) one part bleach to two parts water
    c) one part bleach to five parts water
    d) one part bleach to nine parts water

20. When removing a cream or a salve from an open container to use on a client, the practitioner should ______
    a) first wash their hands
    b) discard the remaining product or give it to the client
    c) use a spatula or other implement
    d) immediately replace the cover to prevent contamination

WORD REVIEW: The student is encouraged to write down the meaning of each of the following words. The list can be used as a study guide for this unit.

antibodies

antigen

bacteria

body mechanics

congenital

contagious

contaminate

disinfection

fomite

fungi

immunity

infection

infectious agent

path of transmission

pathogen

sanitation

sodium hypochlorite

sterilization

universal precaution

virus

Consultation and Documentation

CHAPTER 9

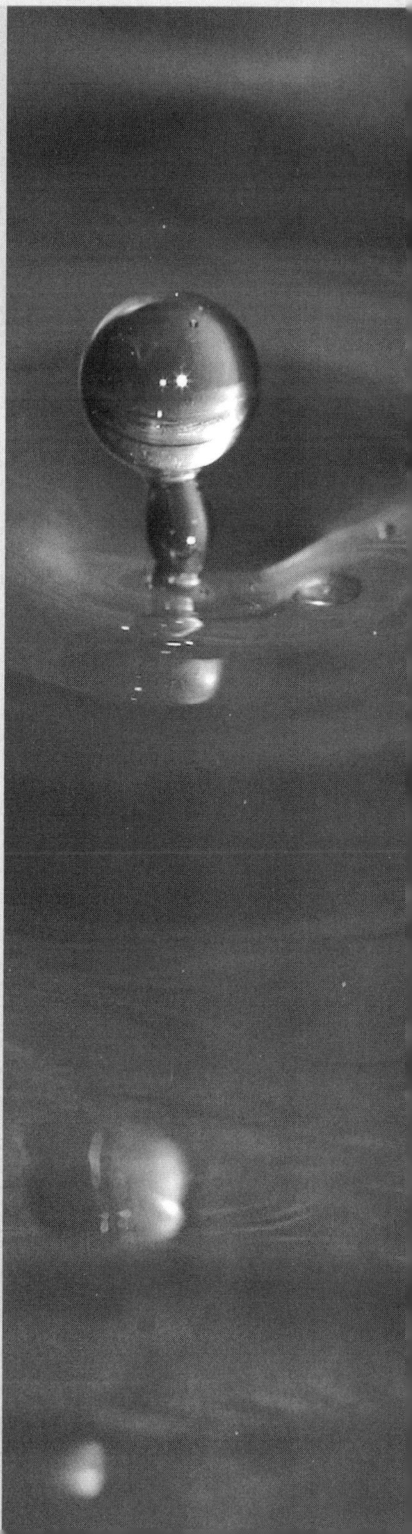

COMPLETION: In the space(s) provided, write the word(s) that correctly complete(s) each statement.

1. A meeting between the prospective client and the practitioner, in which views are discussed and valuable information is exchanged is called a

   ______________.

2. For a consultation to be effective, there must be clear ______________ between the client and the practitioner.

3. The two most effective ways for the practitioner to ask questions

   of the client are ______________ and ______________.

SHORT ANSWER: In the spaces provided, write short answers to the following questions.

1. List seven things that the therapist can accomplish during the consultation.

   a. ____

   b. ____

   c. ____

   d. ____

   e. ____

   f. ____

   g. ____

2. When making a first appointment with a prospective client, what are three questions that can be asked for screening?

a. ___

b. ___

c. ___

3. List four areas that a practitioner may include in a policy statement.

a. ___

b. ___

c. ___

d. ___

4. List three reasons to perform a preliminary assessment.

a. ___

b. ___

c. ___

5. List five topics that should be included in the massage policies and procedures.

a. ___

b. ___

c. ___

d. ___

e. ___

6. List six topics that should be included as business policies.

   a. ______________________

   b. ______________________

   c. ______________________

   d. ______________________

   e. ______________________

   f. ______________________

   ____

7. List four topics of disclosure that the therapist must provide to obtain informed consent from the client.

   a. ______________________

   b. ______________________

   c. ______________________

   d. ______________________

COMPLETION: In the space(s) provided, write the word(s) that correctly complete(s) each statement.

1. To help to disclose problems and the physiologic basis for the client's complaints, an assessment includes ____________, ____________, and ____________.

2. Information gained from intake and medical history forms, answers to questions, and descriptions the client offers are the basis for the ____________.

3. Noticing how clients hold their bodies, how they move, and how they react to questions or manipulative tests are part of ____________.

4. Various manipulative and verbal tests that help to determine more precisely the tissues or conditions involved are part of the ____________.

5. The outline that a practitioner develops and follows when giving massage treatments is termed a ____________.

SHORT ANSWER: In the spaces provided, write short answers to the following questions.

1. List four sources of information used when formulating a treatment plan.

   a. ______________________________

   b. ______________________________

   c. ______________________________

   d. ______________________________

2. List four types of information that are kept in the client files.

   a. ______________________________

   b. ______________________________

   c. ______________________________

   d. ______________________________

3. Which four types of information does a practitioner record in a treatment record?

   a. ______________________________

   b. ______________________________

   c. ______________________________

   d. ______________________________

4. What are the four sections of a SOAP chart and what does each section contain?

   a. ______________________________

   b. ______________________________

   c. ______________________________

   d. ______________________________

5. What can the practitioner do to maintain client confidentiality?

   a. ______________________________

   b. ______________________________

   c. ______________________________

   d. ______________________________

MULTIPLE CHOICE: Carefully read each statement. Choose the word or phrase that correctly completes the meaning and write the corresponding letter in the blank provided.

1. The process of clarifying the appropriateness of an appointment is called ______
   a) consultation
   b) screening
   c) selecting
   d) discrimination

2. Client information can be obtained by ______
   a) consulting with a doctor
   b) personal history forms
   c) client interviews
   d) all of the above

3. A thorough preliminary client assessment includes a ______
   a) client history
   b) client observation
   c) client examination
   d) all the above

4. Noticing how the client holds his body and how he moves is called ______
   a) body mechanics
   b) observation
   c) personology
   d) subjective assessment

5. An outline that the practitioner can follow for giving treatments is called a ______
   a) treatment plan
   b) client history
   c) recipe
   d) client file

6. Work performed on a client is documented in the ______
   a) treatment plan
   b) client history
   c) SOAP notes
   d) billing records

7. Accurate records of a client's treatment help the therapist to ______
   a) achieve better results
   b) abide by state laws
   c) compare progress with other clients
   d) charge higher fees

8. All client information should be considered ______
   a) before calling their physician
   b) research material
   c) when diagnosing their condition
   d) confidential

9. When should the practitioner obtain informed consent from the client? ______
   a) at the end of the consultation, after adequate information has been exchanged
   b) when a treatment plan has been agreed on
   c) when there are changes in the course of treatment
   d) all of the above

10. Downcast eyes, slouching shoulders, a bright smile, and fidgeting hands are all examples of ________
    a) emotional insecurity
    b) body mechanics
    c) body language
    d) nervousness

11. Which of the following is not part of an initial consultation? ________
    a) review outcomes related to desired goals
    b) determine client's expectations and needs
    c) provide information to client about credentials and training
    d) obtain informed consent

WORD REVIEW: The student is encouraged to write down the meaning of each of the following words. The list can be used as a study guide for this unit.

body language

____

____

client file

____

____

confidentiality

____

____

consultation

____

____

informed consent

____

____

____

medical history

____

____

nonverbal communication

policies and procedures

preliminary assessment

rapport

SOAP notes

treatment plan

CHAPTER 10 Classical Massage Movements

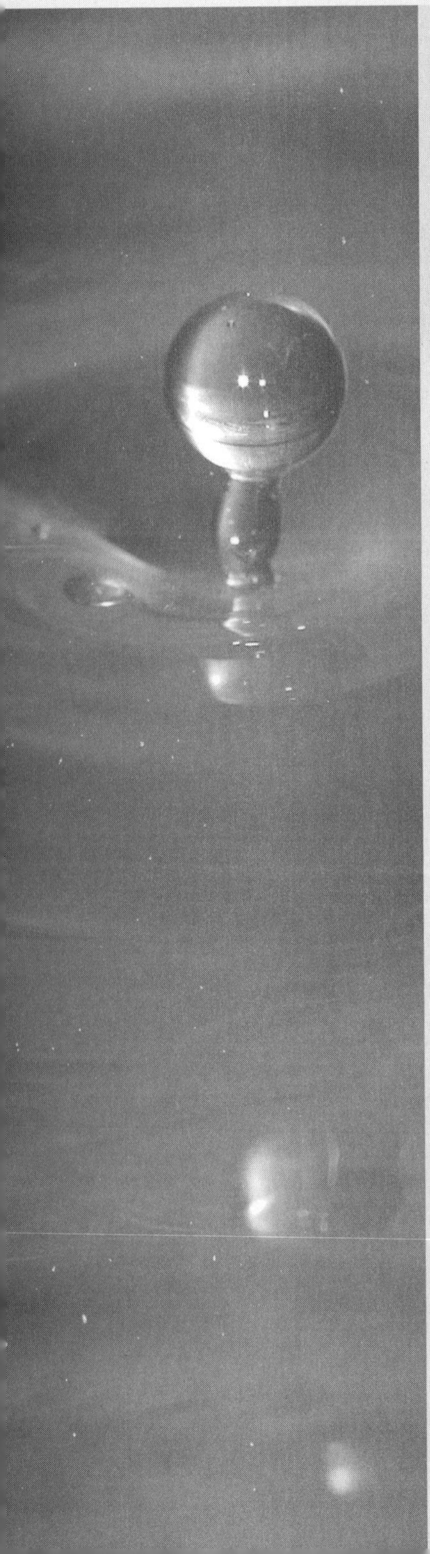

COMPLETION: In the space(s) provided, write the word(s) that correctly complete(s) each statement.

1. Three physical factors that control the results of a manipulation are the ____________, ____________, and ____________ of the movement.

2. Another important factor that affects the outcome of a technique or massage is the ____________ with which it is given.

3. In Swedish massage, most movements are directed ____________ the heart.

4. Massage strokes are directed toward the heart to affect the flow of ____________ and ____________.

5. The six major categories of massage movements are ____________, ________________, ________________, ________________, ________________, and ________________.

IDENTIFICATION: Identify the classification of massage manipulation described in each statement by writing the classification next to the appropriate description in the space provided.

________________ 1. applied in the direction of the venous and lymphatic flow

________________ 2. lifts, squeezes, and presses the tissues

________________ 3. used to distribute any lubricant and to prepare the area for other techniques

_______________ 4. manipulation of the articulations of the client

_______________ 5. generally the first and last contact the practitioner has with the client

_______________ 6. placing of the practitioner's hand or fingers on the client without movement in any direction

_______________ 7. rapid striking motion against the surface of the client's body

_______________ 8. moving more superficial layers of flesh against the deeper tissues

_______________ 9. moving a body part through a range of motion

_______________ 10. the stationary contact of the practitioner's hand and the client's body

_______________ 11. moving the hand over some portion of the client's body with varying amounts of pressure

_______________ 12. used to assist a client to restore mobility or increase flexibility in a joint

_______________ 13. raising tissues from their ordinary position and then squeezing, rolling, or pinching with firm pressure

_______________ 14. manipulating one layer of tissue over or against another

MATCHING: Match the touch and gliding techniques listed below with the best clinical situation. Write the letter or letters of the appropriate technique(s) in the space provided.

A. superficial touch
B. deep touch
C. superficial gliding
D. deep gliding

_____ 1. Client has moderately high blood pressure.

_____ 2. Client is nervous and irritated.

_____ 3. Client is in pain from severe arthritis.

_____ 4. Client is healthy and has thick, heavy musculature.

_____ 5. Client has trigger points in the neck and shoulders.

_____ 6. Client is critically ill with lymphoma.

_____ 7. Client has stress points in the tendons around the elbow and knee.

_____ 8. Client complains of insomnia.

_____ 9. This is the main technique used in foot reflexology.

_____ 10. This technique is used when applying oil to the body.

_____ 11. Client requests a deep relaxing massage.

_____ 12. This is the main technique used in shiatsu.

_____ 13. Client is generally tired.

_____ 14. Client is visibly nervous and tense.

MATCHING: Match the term in the first column with the best description in the second column. Write the letter of the best description in the space provided.

_____ 1. hacking

_____ 2. skin rolling

_____ 3. aura stroking

_____ 4. active, assistive joint movements

_____ 5. superficial gliding

_____ 6. cross-fiber friction

_____ 7. kneading

_____ 8. friction

_____ 9. superficial touch

_____ 10. circular friction

_____ 11. tapping

_____ 12. active, resistive joint movements

_____ 13. feather stroking

_____ 14. compression

_____ 15. deep touch

_____ 16. passive joint movements

_____ 17. deep gliding

_____ 18. vibration

A. rhythmic pumping action directed into the muscle perpendicular to the body part

B. a stroke with enough pressure to have a mechanical effect

C. applied in a transverse direction across the muscle, tendon, or ligament fibers

D. the natural weight of the practitioner's finger, fingers, or hand held on a given area of the client's body

E. quick, striking manipulations with the ulnar border of the hand

F. help from the practitioner as the client moves a limb

G. moving the skin in a circular pattern over the deeper tissues

H. a continuous shaking or trembling movement transmitted from the practitioner's hand or an electrical appliance

I. very light fingertip pressure with long, flowing strokes

J. moving more superficial layers of flesh against deeper tissues

K. applying pressure with no other movement

L. picking the skin and subcutaneous tissue up between the thumbs and fingers and rolling it

M. moving a flexible, firm hand lightly over an extended area of the body

N. raising the skin and muscular tissues from their ordinary position and squeezing with a firm pressure, usually in a circular direction

O. quick, striking manipulations with the tips of the fingers

P. moving a client's joint while his muscles are relaxed

Q. the practitioner's resistance of a client's movement

R. hands gliding over a body part without touching

TRUE OR FALSE: If the following statements are true, write *true* in the space provided. If they are false, replace the italicized word with one that makes the statement true.

_______________ 1. Massage strokes directed away from the heart are termed *centripetal.*

_______________ 2. To have a *sedating* effect, the rhythm of the massage must be steady and slightly faster than the client's natural rhythm.

_______________ 3. A primary indication of tension and dysfunction in soft tissue is *numbness.*

_______________ 4. The pressure used with a massage technique should start out light, then increase, and, finally, end as *light pressure.*

_______________ 5. Deep massage techniques that cause a client to react in pain must be *avoided.*

MULTIPLE CHOICE: Carefully read each statement. Choose the word or phrase that correctly completes the meaning and write the corresponding letter in the blank provided.

1. Most current massage styles are based on _______
   a) Swedish movements
   b) Swiss movements
   c) German movements
   d) Chinese movements

2. When a practitioner recognizes the purposes and effects of movements and adapts the treatment to the client, the massage practice has become _______
   a) manipulative
   b) scientific
   c) therapeutic
   d) resourceful

3. A massage practitioner's main mode of communication _______
   a) is touch
   b) is during the consultation
   c) is conversation during the treatment
   d) takes place after the session

4. A massage movement directed away from the heart is called _______
   a) clockwise
   b) centripetal
   c) contraindicated
   d) centrifugal

5. In massage, placing the hand, finger, or forearm on the client without movement is called _______
   a) touch
   b) gliding
   c) intrusive
   d) friction

6. Sliding the hand over some portion of the client's body with varying amounts of pressure is called ______
   a) friction
   b) kneading
   c) gliding
   d) vibration

7. Rapidly striking the hands against the surface of the client's body is called ______
   a) percussion
   b) friction
   c) petrissage
   d) joint movement

8. When calming, stimulating, or anesthetizing effects are desired, the practitioner should use ______
   a) friction
   b) percussion
   c) deep touch
   d) vibration

9. A type of gliding wherein the practitioner's hands glide the length of the client's entire body or body part without actually touching is called ______
   a) gliding
   b) aura stroking
   c) contraindicated
   d) feather stroking

10. Effleurage over small areas such as the face is usually performed with the ______
    a) fingers
    b) palm of hand
    c) heel of hand
    d) elbow

11. Which of the following is not a factor in determining the depth of a deep, gliding movement? ______
    a) pressure exerted
    b) part of hand used
    c) weight of client
    d) intention of application

12. Kneading helps to reduce ______
    a) blood pressure
    b) adhesions
    c) stretch marks
    d) arm strain

13. Moving a superficial layer of tissue against a deeper layer of tissue is called ______
    a) cupping
    b) kneading
    c) friction
    d) deep pressure

14. A technique that causes an increase in the amount of blood in an area or hyperemia is ______
    a) percussion
    b) skin rolling
    c) deep gliding
    d) compression

15. Heat makes the connective tissues around muscles ______
    a) stronger
    b) more pliable
    c) stiffer
    d) longer

16. The preferred technique to reduce fibrosis and the formation of scar tissue at the site of a soft tissue injury is ________
    a) deep touch
    b) deep gliding
    c) active joint movements
    d) transverse friction massage

17. A mechanical vibrator that has a back-and-forth movement is called ________
    a) orbital
    b) oscillating
    c) vertical
    d) horizontal

18. A mechanical vibrator that has a circular movement is called ________
    a) oscillating
    b) round
    c) orbital
    d) global

19. When doing passive joint movements, the change in the quality of movement as the limb reaches the extent of its possible range is termed ________
    a) range of movement
    b) stretch
    c) end feel
    d) pathologic barrier

20. ________ is classified as a friction movement in Swedish massage. ________
    a) Fulling
    b) Hacking
    c) Compression
    d) Gliding

21. The technique of lifting and squeezing a part of the body is considered ________
    a) kneading
    b) friction
    c) compression
    d) deep gliding

22. The first technique in developing a therapeutic relationship between a massage therapist and a client is ________
    a) superficial gliding strokes
    b) the consultation
    c) introducing yourself
    d) touch

23. The intention with which a manipulation is applied influences its ________
    a) pressure
    b) duration
    c) effect
    d) all of the above

24. A rhythmic, perpendicular pumping action to the muscle body describes ________
    a) lymphatic pump
    b) compression
    c) hacking
    d) beating

25. A technique often used to relieve muscle spasms, stress points, and trigger points is ________
    a) light touch
    b) superficial gliding
    c) deep touch
    d) cross-fiber friction

26. Beating, slapping, and tapping are all examples of which type of massage movement? ________
    a) friction
    b) gliding
    c) percussion
    d) touch

27. The preferred technique to reduce fibrosis and the formation of scar tissue at the site of a soft tissue injury is ________
    a) deep touch
    b) deep gliding
    c) active joint movements
    d) transverse friction massage

28. The movement of a joint from one extreme of the articulation to the other is ________
    a) range of motion
    b) active joint movement
    c) passive joint movement
    d) stretching

29. The primary indication of tension or dysfunction in muscle or soft tissue is ________
    a) pain
    b) fibrous bands of tissue
    c) trigger points
    d) all of the above

30. ________ is/are done centrifugally with only the fingertips. ________
    a) Tappotement
    b) Superficial touch
    c) Aura strokes
    d) Feather strokes

WORD REVIEW: The student is encouraged to write down the meaning of each of the following words. The list can be used as a study guide for this unit.

active joint movements

____

____

anatomic barrier

____

____

aura stroking

____

____

beating

chucking

circular friction

compression

cross-fiber friction

cupping

effleurage

end feel

feather strokes

friction

gliding

hacking

jostling

kneading

passive joint movements

pathologic barrier

percussion

____

____

petrissage

____

____

physiologic barrier

____

____

range of motion

____

____

rocking

____

____

rolling

____

____

shaking

____

____

skin rolling

____

____

slapping

superficial gliding

tapping

touch

vibration

wringing

CHAPTER 11

Application of Massage Technique

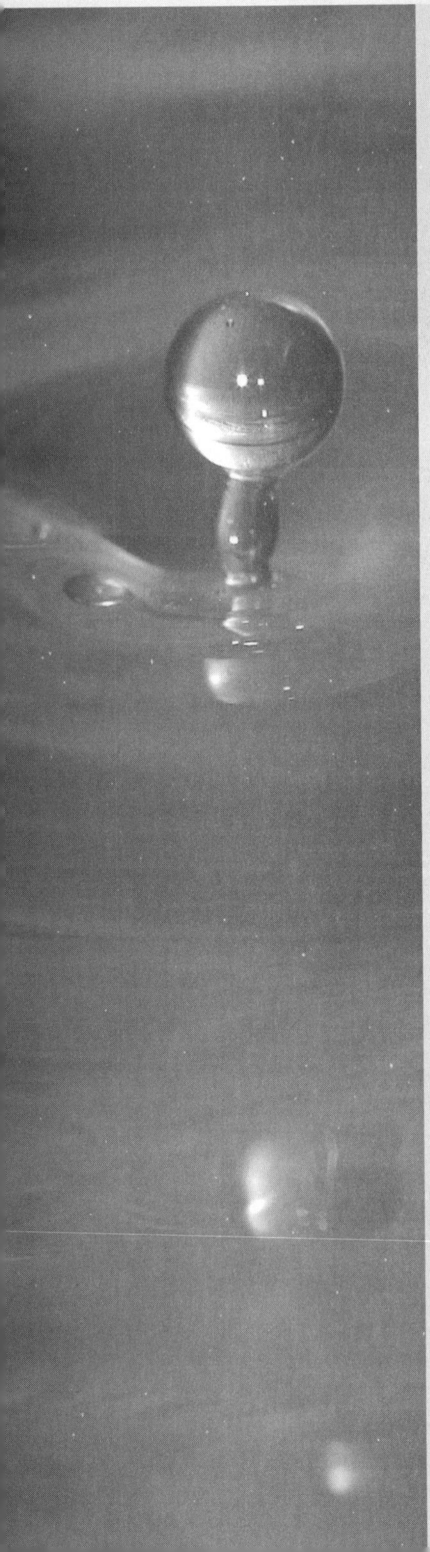

COMPLETION: In the space(s) provided, write the word(s) that correctly complete(s) each statement.

1. The primary tools that the practitioner uses when giving a massage are the ____________.

2. The practitioner conserves energy and increases power in massage movements by using his ____________.

3. The observation of body postures in relation to safe and efficient body movement is called ____________.

4. To increase strength and power and at the same time reduce the chance of fatigue and injury, the practitioner must use ____________.

5. The risk of injury to the body is directly proportional to the amount of stress and the amount of ____________.

6. The Chinese term for the body's geographic center is the ____________.

7. The state of self-assurance, balance, and emotional stability is often referred to as being ____________.

8. The concept that the practitioner functions as a conduit or conductor, allowing negative energies to pass out of the client and positive energies to flow in, is known as

_____________.

9. The most common stances for the practitioner while performing a massage are called

_____________________________.

10. The stance in which both feet are placed in line with the edge of the table is called the

_____________.

11. The most commonly used stance is _________________.

12. An exercise that helps the practitioner to reach the full length of a client's body part while shifting weight on the feet and maintaining good posture and balance is called

_______________.

13. An exercise in which one imagines turning a large wheel is called _____________.

14. An exercise that involves a powerful forward movement followed by a controlled withdrawal is called ______________________.

15. The exercise that emphasizes the importance of posture, concentration, centering, grounding, and correct breathing is called _____________.

SHORT ANSWER: In the spaces provided, write short answers to the following questions.

1. When practicing most massage techniques, where should the practitioner's hands be?

____

2. In which way does the practitioner apply deeper pressure or more force to a movement?

____

____

3. Why is it important to the practitioner not to raise and tighten the shoulders when giving a massage?

____

4. List seven advantages of using good body mechanics and proper stances when giving massages.

   a. ______________________________

   ____

   b. ______________________________

   c. ______________________________

   ____

   d. ______________________________

   e. ______________________________

   ____

   f. ______________________________

   ____

   g. ______________________________

SHORT ANSWER: In the spaces provided, write short answers to the following questions.

1. When should the practitioner wash his hands?

   ____

2. List four ways to avoid chilling the client.

   a. ______________________________

   b. ______________________________

   c. ______________________________

   d. ______________________________

   ____

3. In which direction should gliding movements be given?

   ____

4. Why should extremely heavy or jarring movements be avoided?

   ____

MULTIPLE CHOICE: Carefully read each statement. Choose the word or phrase that correctly completes the meaning and write the corresponding letter in the blank provided.

1. The proper application of massage technique uses the practitioner's ______
   a) palms
   b) entire body
   c) shoulders
   d) fingers

2. The most important tools used by a massage practitioner are the ______
   a) hands
   b) vibrators
   c) massage tables
   d) lotions

3. The first rule in massage and bodywork is to ______
   a) greet the client in a friendly manner
   b) always refer to other health practitioners when indicated
   c) determine indications and contraindications before starting the massage
   d) do no harm

4. The observation of body postures in relation to safe and efficient movement in daily living activities is called ______
   a) physical boundaries
   b) body language
   c) assessment techniques
   d) body mechanics

5. To increase power and conserve energy when giving massages, the practitioner should ______
   a) lift weights
   b) exercise daily
   c) use their entire body
   d) breathe deeply and concentrate

6. Preventing backaches and conserving strength is achieved through ______
   a) exercise
   b) correct posture
   c) weight lifting
   d) diet

7. The degree of misalignment of the supporting structures of the body is termed ______
   a) body mechanics
   b) joint angle
   c) range of motion
   d) biomechanical deviation

8. The concept that you have a geographic center in your body is called ______
   a) centering
   b) *chi*
   c) channeling
   d) grounding

9. The concept that you have a connection with the client and can help her to release unwanted tension and stress is called ______
   a) channeling
   b) centering
   c) grounding
   d) counseling

10. The pattern or design of a massage is called ______
    a) touch
    b) stroke
    c) sequence
    d) plan

11. A Chinese term for a geographic and energetic center of the body is the ______
    a) tai chi
    b) chi
    c) tan tein
    d) Lao Tzu

12. The practitioner can increase the depth of a manipulation by ______
    a) leaning into it
    b) squeezing harder
    c) using two hands
    d) breathing into it

13. Using good body mechanics when practicing massage increases strength and power as it reduces ______
    a) the length of the massage
    b) the client's heart rate
    c) injury risk
    d) pressure and stress

14. When performing most massage movements, the practitioner's hands should be ______
    a) relatively close to the center of the practitioners body
    b) on the same side of the client's body
    c) close together
    d) on the opposite sides of the body part being massaged

WORD REVIEW: The student is encouraged to write down the meaning of each of the following words. The list can be used as a study guide for this unit.

archer stance

____

____

body mechanics

____

____

centering

grounding

horse stance

tan tein

CHAPTER 12

Procedures for Complete Body Massages

SHORT ANSWER: In the spaces provided, write short answers to the following questions.

1. What is the purpose of explaining your general procedures to clients on their first visit?

   a. ______________________________

   b. ______________________________

2. Ideally, which clothing should a client wear when getting a massage?

   ____

3. How can the practitioner dispel anxiety that the client might have about nudity?

   ____

   ____

4. Why should the practitioner assist the client on and off of the table?

   ____

5. How can the practitioner ensure that the client assumes the correct position on the table?

   ____

6. What is the most suitable position for a woman who is seven months pregnant to receive a massage?

   ____

7. What can be done if a client cannot lie down for a massage?

____

COMPLETION: In the space(s) provided, write the word(s) that correctly complete(s) each statement.

1. The procedure used to ensure a client's warmth and sense of modesty is called _______________.

2. The implement used to support a client who cannot comfortably lie flat on the table is a _______________.

3. The process of using linens to keep a client covered while performing a massage is called _______________.

SHORT ANSWER: In the spaces provided, write short answers to the following questions.

1. What are three advantages of draping to clients?

   a. _______________

   b. _______________

   c. _______________

2. Which advantage does draping offer the practitioner?

____

____

3. What is a good temperature for a massage room?

____

4. For those times when the massage room is slightly cool, name two things the practitioner can use to ensure the client's warmth.

   a. ______________________________

   b. ______________________________

5. When using proper draping procedures, which part of the client's body is uncovered?

   ____

6. List two types of draping and the linens required for each.

   a. ______________________________

   b. ______________________________

   ____

SHORT ANSWER: In the spaces provided, write short answers to the following questions.

1. To get from the dressing area or hydrotherapy area to the massage table, which covering does the client use to maintain modesty:

   a. when using top cover draping?

   ____

   b. when using full sheet draping?

   ____

2. The client uses a wrap or towel to get from the dressing area to the massage table. Which size should it be?

   ____

   ____

3. Where should the opening on the wrap be located?

   ____

4. List three reasons it is important to maintain contact with the client once it is established.

   a. ______________________________

   ____

   b. ______________________________

   ____

   c. ______________________________

   ____

5. What are two important objectives of a good massage sequence?

   a. ______________________________

   b. ______________________________

   ____

6. When a therapist is considering a sequence for a full body massage, what are two primary considerations?

   a. ______________________________

   b. ______________________________

SEQUENCING: In the following exercises, arrange the body parts into a massage sequence by numbering the body parts, beginning with (1), in the order in which they would be massaged.

1. Arrange the following body parts into a sequence for a full-body massage. Begin with the right hand and successively number the body parts in the order in which they would be massaged.

_____ back

_____ face

_____ left arm

_____ left foot

_____ left hand

_____ left leg (back)

_____ left leg (front)

_____ neck (face up)

_____ right arm

_____ right foot

_____ right hand

_____ right leg (back)

_____ right leg (front)

_____ torso

2. Arrange the following body parts into a sequence for a massage. Begin with the left foot and successively number the body parts in the order in which they would be massaged.

_____ back	_____ right hand
_____ left arm	_____ right arm
_____ left foot	_____ right foot
_____ left hand	_____ right leg (back)
_____ left leg (back)	_____ right leg (front)
_____ left leg (front)	_____ torso
_____ neck (faceup)	

3. Arrange the following body parts into a sequence for a massage of the front of the body. Begin with the face and finish the front of the body by massaging the torso. Successively number the body parts in the order in which they would be massaged.

_____ face	_____ right arm
_____ left arm	_____ right foot
_____ left foot	_____ right hand
_____ left hand	_____ right leg
_____ left leg	_____ torso
_____ neck	

4. Arrange the following body parts into a sequence for a massage of the front of the body. Begin with the right arm and finish the front of the body by massaging the left foot. Number the body parts in the order in which they would be massaged.

_____ face	_____ right arm
_____ left arm	_____ right foot
_____ left foot	_____ right hand
_____ left hand	_____ right leg
_____ left leg	_____ torso
_____ neck	

KEY CHOICES: Write the appropriate key word for each of the massage movements according to the correct sequence in the spaces provided.

effleurage	friction movements	petrissage
feather strokes	joint movements	

1. apply the oil
2. ______________________
3. ______________________
4. effleurage
5. ______________________
6. effleurage
7. ______________________
8. effleurage
9. ______________________
10. redrape

SHORT ANSWER: In the spaces provided, write short answers to the following questions.

1. In Swedish style massage, an oil or lubricant is used. Describe the three-step procedure for applying the lubricant from its container to the client's body.

   a. ______________________

   b. ______________________

   ____

   c. ______________________

   ____

2. How is contact with the client maintained when preparing to apply a lubricant?

   ____

   ____

3. Which massage strokes are directed toward the heart?

   ____

4. Which strokes can be directed away from the heart?

   ____

5. Why are strokes directed toward the heart?

   ____

6. Which part of the hand is used to apply gliding strokes to larger areas of the body?

7. Why follow deep friction movements with gliding strokes?

8. What is the first massage technique used after the oil is applied to a body part?

9. Which preliminary steps should be taken before a client arrives for a massage?

10. How should the client be greeted?

11. When should an information form be filled out?

SHORT ANSWER: In the spaces provided, write short answers to the following questions.

1. Name three areas of the body where lubricant is usually not needed.

2. Why are gliding strokes repeated between other massage strokes?

3. How many gliding strokes are usually applied between other strokes in a general massage?

4. When applying gliding strokes to the arm, in which direction is pressure applied?

5. When applying long gliding strokes to the leg with both hands, which hand leads?

6. What does the acronym ASIS stand for?

7. When extending the leg during joint movements, why is it important to keep one hand behind the knee?

____

8. What is the massage technique most likely to increase muscle length and increase range of motion?

____

9. Which special consideration must be given when massaging a woman's torso?

____

10. When working on the abdomen, what is the general direction of the massage movements?

____

11. What is the "caring stroke"?

____

12. What are the lightest gliding strokes using only the fingertips?

____

SHORT ANSWER: In the spaces provided, write short answers to the following questions.

1. Why is a client encouraged to drink plenty of water following massage?

____

2. How much water do experts suggest that people drink per day?

____

____

3. Clients sometimes experience adverse effects following massage. What are four possible adverse effects?

a. _______________

b. _______________

c. _______________

d. _______________

4. What is thought to be the cause of these adverse effects?

____

MULTIPLE CHOICE: Carefully read each statement. Choose the word or phrase that correctly completes the meaning and write the corresponding letter in the blank provided.

1. The most effective way to receive a relaxing Swedish massage is ______
   a) fully clothed
   b) partially clothed
   c) with all clothing removed
   d) wearing loose-fitting clothing

2. A client's modesty is protected with proper ______
   a) draping
   b) communication
   c) grooming
   d) clothing

3. The draping method that covers the table and wraps the client with a single linen is called ______ draping ______
   a) top cover
   b) full sheet
   c) diaper
   d) wrapping

4. Oil is applied with this stroke: ______
   a) petrissage
   b) tapotement
   c) effleurage
   d) friction

5. The first procedure when massaging a part of the body is ______
   a) effleurage
   b) getting informed consent
   c) applying oil
   d) undraping

6. The pattern or design of the massage that provides for a smooth progression from one stroke to the next is the ______
   a) treatment plan
   b) procedure
   c) sequence
   d) massage order

7. When developing a massage sequence, which of the following is important to keep in mind? ______
   a) superficial to deep and back to superficial
   b) adjacent body parts
   c) general to specific and back to general
   d) all of the above

8. A client with osteoporosis should not have a neck massage that includes ______
   a) petrissage
   b) friction
   c) joint movements
   d) effleurage

9. Percussion should not be applied to the back area over the ______
   a) spine
   b) kidneys
   c) lungs
   d) heart

10. When the massage is finished and it is time for the client to get up and off the table, the practitioner should ________
    a) leave the room and give the client privacy
    b) turn his back to prevent the client's embarrassment
    c) instruct the client to be careful when getting up
    d) assist the client into a sitting position and support the table, maintaining contact as the client stands up

11. If a client does not feel comfortable taking off all of his clothes to receive a massage, what should the therapist tell him? ________
    a) It would be best for the client to remove his clothes.
    b) Draping will be used to keep him modestly covered at all times.
    c) He should wear whatever he feels comfortable with.
    d) All of the above

12. If a client is unable to lie on her back with her legs straight out or head flat on the table, the therapist should ________. ________
    a) only massage them in the sitting position
    b) refer them to a doctor
    c) support the client's head and knees with bolsters and pillows
    d) give the massage with the client in a side-lying position

13. A reason for placing a support under the chest would be to ________. ________
    a) take the strain off of the cervical spine
    b) make breathing easier
    c) take the pressure off of the lower back
    d) all of the above

14. The reason for using draping when giving a massage is ________. ________
    a) to provide warmth for the client
    b) to keep the client modestly covered when giving a massage
    c) to allow the practitioner easy access to all areas of the client's body
    d) all of the above

15. To ensure that the client assumes the correct position when he gets on the table, the practitioner should ________. ________
    a) guide the client as he lies down
    b) maintain contact with the client as he sits on the table
    c) give the client clear instructions before he gets on table
    d) all of the above

16. Low back discomfort when a client is lying on her stomach can often be relieved by ________. ________
    a) elevating the head
    b) elevating the chest
    c) elevating the abdomen and pelvis
    d) elevating the knees

WORD REVIEW: The student is encouraged to write down the meaning of each of the following words. The list can be used as a study guide for this unit.

bolsters

____

____

draping

____

____

massage routine

____

____

prone position

____

____

sequence

____

____

shingles

____

____

side-lying position

____

____

supine position

____

____

CHAPTER 13

Hydrotherapy

COMPLETION: In the space(s) provided, write the word(s) that correctly complete(s) each statement.

1. The use of heat and cold is a powerful therapeutic agent because the physiologic effects are ____________.
2. The short application of cold is ____________, whereas prolonged application of cold ____________ metabolic activity.
3. The local application of heat causes the blood vessels to ____________ and circulation to ____________.
4. The application of heat causes the pulse rate to ____________ and the white blood cell count to ____________.
5. A generalized lowering of the body temperature is termed ____________.
6. The external application of heat to the body is called ____________.

KEY CHOICES: The following is a list of reactions to hydrotherapy. Write the appropriate key letter for each of the following conditions in the spaces provided.

C = Cold application
H = Heat application

_____ 1. hypothermia

_____ 2. vasodilation

_____ 3. reduced circulation

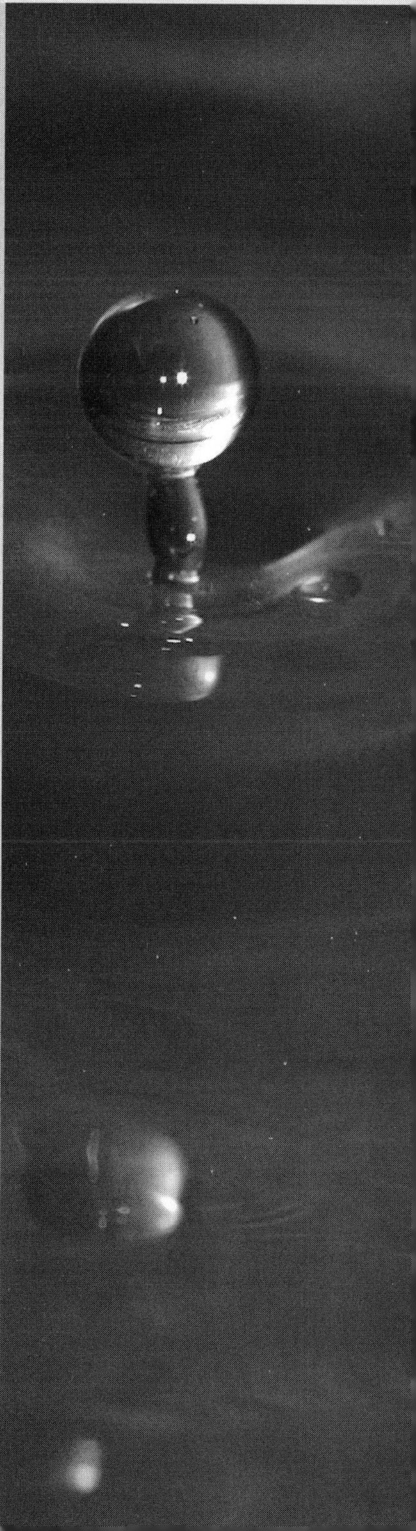

_____ 4. anesthetic effect

_____ 5. increased circulation

_____ 6. increased perspiration

_____ 7. numbness

_____ 8. increased white cell count

_____ 9. local muscle relaxation

_____ 10. analgesia

_____ 11. depressed metabolic activity

_____ 12. reduced nerve sensitivity

_____ 13. hyperthermia

_____ 14. decreased muscle spasticity

_____ 15. leukocyte migration into the area

TRUE OR FALSE: If the following statements are true, write *true* in the space provided. If they are false, replace the italicized word with one that makes the statement true.

__________ 1. When heat or cold is applied to the body, certain *physiologic* changes occur.

__________ 2. A *short* application of cold sedates metabolic activity.

__________ 3. The warming effect of the sun is due to *ultraviolet* rays.

__________ 4. The application of *cold* to a fresh soft-tissue injury reduces pain and swelling.

COMPLETION: In the space(s) provided, write the word(s) that correctly complete(s) each statement.

1. When a body part is submerged in water, it is called a(n) ______________.

2. The application of cold agents for therapeutic purposes is termed ______________.

3. The application of water to the body for therapeutic purposes is known as ______________.

4. The changes produced by water that is above or below body temperature are considered to be ____________ effects.

5. The upper temperature limit for water that is considered safe for an immersion bath is ____________.

6. The normal temperature of the body is ____________ or ____________.

7. The body's normal skin surface temperature is approximately ____________.

8. A bath in which only the hips and pelvis are submerged is called a ____________.

9. The acronym for a series of sensations resulting from the therapeutic application of ice is ____________.

10. The alternating application of heat and cold for therapeutic purposes is called ____________.

11. When the surface of the body is in direct contact with water, heat is exchanged by the process of ____________.

SHORT ANSWER: In the spaces provided, write short answers to the following questions.

1. List four variables that determine the nature and extent of the effects of heat or cold on the body.

   a. ____________________

   b. ____________________

   c. ____________________

   d. ____________________

2. What are the three forms in which water is used for therapeutic purposes?

   a. ____________________

   b. ____________________

   c. ____________________

3. Which properties of water make it a valuable therapeutic agent?

   a. ______

   b. ______

   c. ______

   d. ______

   e. ______

4. The three classifications of therapeutic effects of water on the body are

   a. ______

   b. ______

   c. ______

5. List five ways of applying moist heat.

   a. ______

   b. ______

   c. ______

   d. ______

   e. ______

6. The acronym PRICE stands for

   a. ______

   b. ______

   c. ______

   d. ______

   e. ______

7. List four economical methods of applying local cold therapy.

a. ______________________________

b. ______________________________

c. ______________________________

d. ______________________________

8. List the four normal reactions to ice therapy in the order in which they occur.

a. ______________________________

b. ______________________________

c. ______________________________

d. ______________________________

9. Baths can be classified according to the temperature of the water. What is the temperature range for the following baths?

a. cool bath—______ to ______ °F

b. tepid bath—______ to ______ °F

c. warm bath—______ to ______ °F

d. hot bath—______ to ______ °F

e. steam bath—______ to ______ °F

10. List the four ways that heat is transferred to the body.

a. ______________________________

b. ______________________________

c. ______________________________

d. ______________________________

MULTIPLE CHOICE: Carefully read each statement. Choose the word or phrase that correctly completes the meaning and write the corresponding letter in the blank provided.

1. A popular electrical apparatus used in massage is the ______
   a) heating pad
   b) vibrator
   c) adjustable table
   d) heat lamp

2. A short application of cold is ______
   a) anesthetizing
   b) chilling
   c) contraindicated
   d) stimulating

3. Thermal treatments below 32° F or above 115° F can cause ______
   a) tissue damage
   b) overstimulation
   c) reduced lymph flow
   d) burns

4. Prolonged application of cold leads to a physical condition called ______
   a) freezing
   b) hyperthermia
   c) hypothermia
   d) freezer burn

5. Heating pads and infrared radiation are types of ______
   a) moist heat
   b) dry heat
   c) diathermy
   d) solar gain

6. Hydrotherapy is the therapeutic use of ______
   a) heat
   b) water
   c) cold
   d) massage

7. Saunas and steam baths should be avoided by people with heart conditions or ______
   a) diabetes
   b) swollen glands
   c) arthritis
   d) muscle spasms

8. A local application of cold will ______
   a) cause reddening due to vasoconstriction
   b) increase leukocyte migration to the area
   c) increase the pulse rate
   d) have an analgesic effect

9. Cold applied for therapeutic purposes is called ______
   a) cryptology
   b) cryotherapy
   c) PRICE
   d) hypotherapy

10. Ice is used on some injuries to prevent ______
    a) swelling
    b) bruising
    c) pain
    d) all of the above

11. To increase circulation to an injured area and promote healing, alternate applications of ________ ________
 a) vibration and friction
 b) feathering and kneading
 c) heat and cold
 d) percussion and gliding

12. An economical alternative to commercial ice packs is a plastic bag containing a 2:1 mixture of crushed ice and ________
 a) vinegar
 b) isopropyl alcohol
 c) bleach
 d) antifreeze

13. Water is a valuable therapeutic agent for all of the following reasons EXCEPT ________
 a) it is inexpensive to use
 b) it is readily available
 c) it requires special equipment
 d) it absorbs and conducts heat

14. Water temperatures that are above or below body temperature have this effect: ________
 a) mechanical
 b) thermal
 c) chemical
 d) psychological

15. Sprays, whirlpools, and friction are examples of this effect: ________
 a) mechanical
 b) thermal
 c) chemical
 d) psychosomatic

16. Drinking water is an example of this effect: ________
 a) mechanical
 b) thermal
 c) chemical
 d) dietary

17. Cardiac conditions, diabetes, lung disease, and high or low blood pressure are examples of hydrotherapy ________
 a) contraindications
 b) complications
 c) indications
 d) benefits

18. The average temperature of the skin's surface is ________
 a) 96° F
 b) 92° F
 c) 86° F
 d) 94° F

19. Prolonged use of cold applications has this effect ________
 a) stimulating
 b) energizing
 c) depressing
 d) dizzying

20. Expansion of blood vessels following cold application is called a(n) ______
    a) primary effect
    b) secondary effect
    c) afterthought
    d) contraindication

21. A bath with a water temperature of 75° F to 85° F is considered ______
    a) cool
    b) cold
    c) tepid
    d) warm

22. A bath with a water temperature of 85° F to 95° F is considered ______
    a) cool
    b) cold
    c) tepid
    d) hot

23. A cold bath shocks the body's ______
    a) heart
    b) nervous system
    c) thyroid
    d) kidneys

WORD REVIEW: The student is encouraged to write down the meaning of each of the following words. The list can be used as a study guide for this unit.

Body wrap

____

____

conduction

____

____

contrast baths

____

____

contrast therapy

____

____

convection

convection

conversion

cryotherapy

hydrocollator

hydrotherapy

hyperthermia

hypothermia

ice massage

ice packs

____

____

immersion baths

____

____

moist heat packs

____

____

Radiation

____

____

sitz bath

____

____

vasocoolant spray

____

____

Massage in the Spa Setting

CHAPTER 14

SHORT ANSWER: In the spaces provided, write short answers to the following questions.

1. What is the Latin phrase from which the acronym *spa* was derived?

____

2. What does the phrase in the previous question translate to mean?

____

3. What is the Arabic meaning of *hammam*?

____

4. List the six major types of spas.

   a. ____

   b. ____

   c. ____

   d. ____

   e. ____

   f. ____

5. Which elements were included in the *kur* developed by Sebastian Kneipp in the 1800s?

____

6. What do Bath in England, Baden Baden in Germany, Montecatini in Italy, and Spa in Belgium have in Common?

____

COMPLETION: In the space(s) provided, write the word(s) that correctly complete(s) each question.

1. In Japan, springs used for communal bathing and personal renewal, including hydrotherapy, massage, and meditation are called ____________.
2. The most popular offering in spas in the United States today is ____________.
3. The average age of a spa client is ____________ with an average income of over ____________.
4. The number one reason that people list for making a spa visit is to ____________________.
5. The optimal number of massages that a practitioner performs a day in the spa setting is ____________.
6. When performing back-to-back massages, the practitioner or spa management should try to schedule a ____________ -minute break between massages.
7. An ancient Indian system of medicine that uses the application of herbs, oils, creams, massage, and exfoliation to rebalance the body's skin and internal organs is ____________.
8. A gentle massage technique that uses light, rhythmic, spiral-like movements to accelerate the movement of lymphatic fluids in the body is ____________________.
9. A treatment that is given with both guest and therapist submerged in warm (90°–98° F) chest-deep water where the therapist floats, stretches, and massages the guest is ____________.
10. The use of essential oils in massage oils, as inhalants, or with other modalities with the goal of affecting mood or improving health and well-being is ____________.

SHORT ANSWER: In the spaces provided, write short answers to the following questions.

1. Three reasons that it is difficult for massage practitioners to give high-quality therapeutic massages in a spa setting are

   a. ______________________________

   b. ______________________________

   c. ______________________________

2. What are three things that a practitioner can do to create a sense of timelessness within the very strict time structure imposed in the spa setting?

   a. ______________________________

   b. ______________________________

   c. ______________________________

3. What are three safety considerations when practicing hot stone massage?

   a. ______________________________

   b. ______________________________

   c. ______________________________

   ____

4. List the main contraindications for heated body wraps.

   ____

5. What are three characteristics that body wraps have in common?

   a. ______________________________

   b. ______________________________

   c. ______________________________

6. What are the main benefits of exfoliation?

   a. ______________________________

   b. ______________________________

   c. ______________________________

   d. ______________________________

7. Two main customer service skills therapists need in the spa setting are

   a. ______________________________

   b. ______________________________

8. What are four main teamwork skills required to work successfully in a spa?

   a. ______________________________

   b. ______________________________

   c. ______________________________

   d. ______________________________

COMPLETION: In the space(s) provided, write the word(s) that correctly complete(s) each question.

1. The term "*spa massage*" usually refers to a ____________________ or a ____________________.

2. Mary Nelson of Tucson, AZ, developed a method of using hot and cold stones as a part of the massage session called ____________________.

3. A spa treatment that combines paraffin and volcanic mud is ______________.

4. It is generally recommended not to use aromatherapy oils full strength or ______________, but rather in combination with a ______________ such as almond, sesame, grapeseed, or apricot oil.

5. Aromatherapy oils can be dispersed into the air of a room with a ______________.

6. When preparing for an aromatherapy massage, add approximately ______________ drops of essential oil to an ounce of massage lubricant.

7. Any spa treatment given with the intention of removing old skin cells is called ______________.

8. The upper part of a woman's chest, below the neck is the ______________.

9. Most body wraps are left in place for ______________ minutes.

10. The principle maneuver for all exfoliation techniques is a ____________________.

11. A waterproof treatment table with built-in drainage is called a ______________.

12. A shower stall with multiple shower heads aimed at the client from all sides and above is a ______________.

13. A long, horizontally aligned pipe with multiple heads aimed down to spray a client's body while she reclines on a wet table is a ______________.

MULTIPLE CHOICE: Carefully read each statement. Choose the word or phrase that correctly completes the meaning and write the corresponding letter in the blank provided.

1. The spa tradition is thought to have originated with the ________. ________
   a) Chinese
   b) Japanese
   c) Greeks and Romans
   d) Persians

2. The first modern spa that opened in the United States in the 1950s and focused on holistic health, fitness, diet, and overall well-being was ________. ________
   a) the Golden Door
   b) Saratoga Springs
   c) White Sulphur Springs
   d) Hot Springs, Arkansas

3. According to the International Spa Association's 2007 Spa Industry Profile, there were ________ spas in the United States in 2006 ________
   a) 2674
   b) 1964
   c) 16,280
   d) 14,600

4. The most popular service offered in spas is ________. ________
   a) body wraps
   b) massage
   c) hair care
   d) esthetics and skin care

5. A spa massage ________. ________
   a) is any body treatment given in a spa facility
   b) is a relaxing, Swedish style massage
   c) includes a body wrap or exfoliation
   d) may include any number of bodywork techniques

6. The challenge for many therapists working in spas to give high-quality therapeutic massage sessions consistently is ________. ________
   a) time constraints
   b) low expectations from clients
   c) inexperienced clients
   d) all of the above

7. Heated stones for stone massage are usually made of ________. ________
   a) granite
   b) marble
   c) basalt
   d) lava rock

8. The highest temperature for heating stones for stone massage is ________. ________
   a) 110° F
   b) 120° F
   c) 140° F
   d) 150° F

9. A spa treatment that applies a product to the skin with the intention of removing old skin cells is termed ________. ________
   a) exfoliation
   b) a skin wrap
   c) a salt glow
   d) a Swedish shampoo

10. Aromatherapy uses essential oils ________
    a) applied to the skin
    b) diffused into the air
    c) added to products
    d) all of the above

11. When mixing an essential oil with a carrier oil, add approximately ________ drops of the essential oil to the carrier oil. ________
    a) 1 to 2
    b) 5 to 7
    c) 12 to 15
    d) 20 to 30

12. The primary purpose of an aromatherapy wrap is to ________. ________
    a) nourish and cleanse
    b) heat and detoxify
    c) relax and improve mood
    d) purge and draw out impurities

13. The primary purpose of a seaweed wrap is to ________. ________
    a) nourish and remineralize
    b) heat and detoxify
    c) relax and improve mood
    d) purge and draw out impurities

14. The primary manipulation used when performing an exfoliation treatment is ________. ________
    a) long, light strokes toward the heart
    b) small circular movements
    c) vigorous back-and-forth scrubbing movements
    d) short strokes in the direction of blood and lymph flow

WORD REVIEW: The student is encouraged to write down the meaning of each of the following words. The list can be used as a study guide for this unit.

aromatherapy

____

____

Ayurveda

body wrap

décolletage

emulsion

Esalen massage

exfoliant

exfoliation

hammam

herbal wrap

hospitality industry

ISPA

LaStone therapy

Onsen

parafango

salt glow

sanitas per aqua

seaweed wrap

spa

spa massage

stone massage

Swiss shower

Vichy shower

Watsu

wet room

wet table

CHAPTER 15 Clinical Massage Techniques

COMPLETION: In the space(s) provided, write the word(s) that correctly complete(s) each statement.

1. Craniosacral therapy has been developed largely by ____________________.

2. The layer of the meninges that surrounds the central nervous system and contains the cerebrospinal fluid is the ____________.

3. Craniosacral motion is transmitted throughout the fascia of the body with flexion noted as a gentle ___________ rotation and ___________ of the body, and extension palpated as an ___________ rotation and a very slight ___________ of the body.

4. Massage styles that are directed toward the deeper tissue structures of the muscle and fascia are commonly called ___________ massage.

5. Rolfing was developed by ______________.

6. Neurophysiologic therapies recognize the link between the ________________ system and the ________________ system.

7. Alterations or disturbances in the neuromuscular relationship often result in _____________ and ___________.

8. A hyperirritable spot that is painful when compressed is called a ____________.

9. When a point is compressed and it refers pain to another area of the body, that point is considered a(n) ____________________.

10. If a point is hypersensitive when compressed but does not refer pain, it is considered a ____________________.

11. The technique used by massage therapists in which direct pressure is applied to the trigger point is known as ____________________.

SHORT ANSWER: In the spaces provided, write short answers to the following questions.

1. What are three types of neurophysiologic therapies?

   a. ____

   b. ____

   c. ____

2. Where are myofascial trigger points found?

   ____

3. What is the neurologic phenomenon that links a trigger point to its associated dysfunctional tissue?

   ____

4. How are taut bands of muscle located?

   ____

5. What are three common areas associated with the muscle where trigger points are found?

   a. ____

   b. ____

   c. ____

6. List four common procedures for deactivating trigger points.

 a. ______

 b. ______

 c. ______

 d. ______

 ______

7. What are three therapeutic modalities available to the massage therapist to reduce trigger-point activity and restore fascia and muscle to normal functional activity?

 a. ______

 b. ______

 c. ______

8. When pressure point release or ischemic compression are used to release trigger points, what determines how much pressure to apply?

 ______

9. Which method moves the body so that the attachments of the muscle housing and the trigger point are closer together?

 ______

10. How long is a position release position held?

 ______

11. When a trigger point has been released, which action should be taken on the muscle where it was located?

 ______

12. What is the preferred method of accomplishing the function mentioned in the previous question's answer?

 ______

SHORT ANSWER: In the spaces provided, write short answers to the following questions.

1. Who originally developed neuromuscular therapy (NMT) in the 1930s?

____

2. What are common abnormal signs associated with neuromuscular lesions?

   a. _______________

   b. _______________

   c. _______________

   d. _______________

   e. _______________

   f. _______________

   g. _______________

   h. _______________

   i. _______________

3. Besides trigger points, which other areas does NMT recognize that might be tender when palpated?

____

4. The main massage manipulations used in NMT are

   a. _______________

   b. _______________

   c. _______________

   d. _______________

COMPLETION: In the space(s) provided, write the word(s) that correctly complete(s) each statement.

1. A therapeutic procedure that is used to improve the functional mobility of the joints and goes by the acronym MET is ______________________.

2. The two basic inhibitory reflexes produced during MET manipulations are ______________________ and ______________________.

3. ______________________, is given credit for the modern development of MET.

4. All MET practices involve the ______________________ of the client.

SHORT ANSWER: In the spaces provided, write short answers to the following questions.

1. The three main variations of MET are

   a. ____

   b. ____

   c. ____

2. Which of the two variations of MET use postisometric relaxation?

   ____

3. Which of the two variations of MET use reciprocal inhibition?

   ____

4. Which condition responds best to MET?

   ____

5. What are the various outcomes from the different applications of MET?

   a. ____

   b. ____

   c. ____

6. MET has many variations in its application, depending on the condition of the target tissue, the condition of the client, and the intended outcome of the treatment. List those variations.

   a. ______________________________

   b. ______________________________

   c. ______________________________

   d. ______________________________

   e. ______________________________

   f. ______________________________

   g. ______________________________

   h. ______________________________

   i. ______________________________

   j. ______________________________

SHORT ANSWER: In the spaces provided, write short answers to the following questions.

1. The gentlest of soft tissue manipulations when addressing mobility restrictions from pain and soft tissue dysfunction are ______________________.

2. Three bodywork systems that incorporate this technique are

   a. ______________________________

   b. ______________________________

   c. ______________________________

3. How do these three techniques differ?

   ____

4. Strain-counterstrain (tender point) technique was developed by ______________________.

5. Describe the main treatment in strain-counterstrain technique.

   ____

   ____

   ____

6. Ortho-Bionomy was developed by an English osteopath named ______________________.

7. The hands-on manipulations used in Ortho-Bionomy are ______________________________

   and ________________________.

8. When practicing position release, which considerations are made while positioning the targeted body part?

   ____

   ____

   ____

   ____

9. After the correct position for release is achieved and held for an appropriate time, what is the appropriate way to release the move?

   ____

   ____

MULTIPLE CHOICE: Carefully read each statement. Choose the word or phrase that correctly completes the meaning and write the corresponding letter in the blank provided.

1. A bodywork technique that attempts to bring the structure of the body into alignment around a central axis is called ________. ________
   a) structural integration
   b) Trager
   c) MET
   d) NMT

2. Realignment of muscular and connective tissue and reshaping the body's physical posture is called ________. ________
   a) chiropractic
   b) centering
   c) Rolfing
   d) Trager

3. Craniosacral therapy was developed by ________
   a) Dr. William Sutherland
   b) Dr. Bruno Chikly
   c) Dr. John Upledger
   d) Dr. Arthur Pauls

4. A hypersensitive nodule located in a taut band of muscle that radiates pain when compressed is ________. ________
   a) a latent trigger point
   b) contraindicated for massage
   c) a satellite trigger point
   d) an active trigger point

5. Massage therapists can treat trigger points ________
   a) by injecting them with procaine or a saline solution
   b) by dry needling with acupuncture needles
   c) with ischemic compression, position release, and MET
   d) all of the above

6. Digital pressure applied directly into the trigger point is called ________. ________
   a) ischemic compression
   b) probing
   c) stretch and spray
   d) palpating

7. Using neurophysical muscle reflexes to improve the functional mobility of the joints is called ________. ________
   a) kneading
   b) NMT
   c) MET
   d) stretching

8. The technique based on the theory that as soon as a strong muscle contraction releases, the muscle relaxes is called ________. ________
   a) contract-relax
   b) antagonist contraction
   c) contract the opposite
   d) fibrosis reduction

9. Positioning and supporting patients in pain-free, comfortable positions is called ________. ________
   a) transition
   b) MET
   c) strain-counterstrain
   d) massaging

10. Position release techniques ________. ________
    a) bring the attachments of the affected tissue closer
    b) move away from pain into the body's preferred position
    c) are passive joint movements
    d) all of the above

11. The correct application of the natural laws of life is called ________. ________
    a) Swedish massage
    b) legality
    c) medicine
    d) Ortho-Bionomy

12. The procedure that gently moves contracted tissues into the direction of contraction while bringing the ends of the hypercontracted muscle tissue closer together is called ________. ________
    a) neuromuscular therapy
    b) tender point
    c) positional release
    d) reflex

WORD REVIEW: The student is encouraged to write down the meaning of each of the following words. The list can be used as a study guide for this unit.

active trigger point

____

____

____

antagonist

____

____

attachment trigger point

____

____

____

central trigger point

craniosacral therapy

deep-tissue massage

flat palpation

hypertonic muscle

hypotonic muscle

ischemic compression

latent trigger point

muscle energy technique (MET)

musculotendinous junction

myofascial trigger point

Ortho-Bionomy

pain scale

physiopathologic reflex arc

pincer palpation

position release

postisometric relaxation

preferred position

prenatal massage

PRICE

reciprocal inhibition

resistive soft tissue barrier

Rolfing

satellite trigger point

splinting

strain-counterstrain

still point

tendinoperiosteal junction

trigger point

Lymph Massage

COMPLETION: In the space(s) provided, write the word(s) that correctly complete(s) each statement.

1. The Danish practitioner credited with developing manual lymph drainage massage was __________________.
2. Thin-walled tubes that collect lymph from interstitial fluid in the tissues are called __________________.
3. White blood cells produced in the lymph system are known as __________________.
4. Small bean-shaped masses of lymphatic tissue located along the course of lymph vessels are termed ______________.
5. The principal massage manipulations used in lymph are ______________________________________.
6. Specialized lymph vessels in the walls of the small intestine called ______________ carry away a milky fluid called ______________.
7. The French doctor who developed methods to recognize the rhythm and flow of superficial and deep lymph is __________________.
8. Lymphocytes produced in the bone marrow that migrate to and mature in the thymus are called ________________.

SHORT ANSWER: In the spaces provided, write short answers to the following questions.

1. Where does lymph reenter the bloodstream?

____

2. What is the percentage of the interstitial fluid that is reabsorbed into the circulatory system becomes lymph?

____

3. What causes lymph to move through the system?

____

____

____

4. The main functions of the lymph nodes are

   a. _______________

   b. _______________

   ____

   c. _______________

   d. _______________

5. Most of the lymph nodes that drain the flow of superficial lymph are located in which areas of the body?

   a. _______________

   b. _______________

   c. _______________

6. What are the primary lymphoid organs where lymphocytes are produced?

____

7. What are the secondary lymphoid organs where lymphocytes reside in high concentrations?

____

8. How are lymph massage manipulations applied in terms of pressure, rhythm, and frequency?

____

____

9. In which direction is lymph massage given?

____

10. When lymph massage is done on the leg, where should the manipulations begin?

____

MULTIPLE CHOICE: Carefully read each statement. Choose the word or phrase that correctly completes the meaning and write the corresponding letter in the blank provided.

1. The ________ is considered to be a primary lymphoid organ. ______
   a) spleen
   b) lymph node
   c) bone marrow
   d) all of the above

2. Lymph massage movements ______
   a) begin and end at the site of local lymph nodes
   b) are circular or slightly elliptical
   c) use a light pressure and slow rhythm
   d) all of the above

3. There are approximately ________ lymph nodes in the human body. ______
   a) 40 to 100
   b) 200 to 400
   c) 400 to 1000
   d) 2,500 to 5,000

4. Small, thin-walled tubes that collect lymph from interstitial fluid are called ______
   a) lymph capillaries
   b) lymph nodes
   c) Peyer's patches
   d) lacteals

5. Lymph vessels in the walls of the small intestine that carry away fat are called ______
   a) fat blockers
   b) lacteals
   c) adipose ducts
   d) lymph capillaries

6. Submaxillary lymph nodes are located under the ______
   a) cranium
   b) tongue
   c) armpit
   d) stomach

WORD REVIEW: The student is encouraged to write down the meaning of each of the following words. The list can be used as a study guide for this unit.

angulus venosus

chyle

cisterna chyli

lacteals

lymph

lymph nodes

lymphatic capillaries

pre-collectors

watershed

CHAPTER 17 Therapeutic Procedure

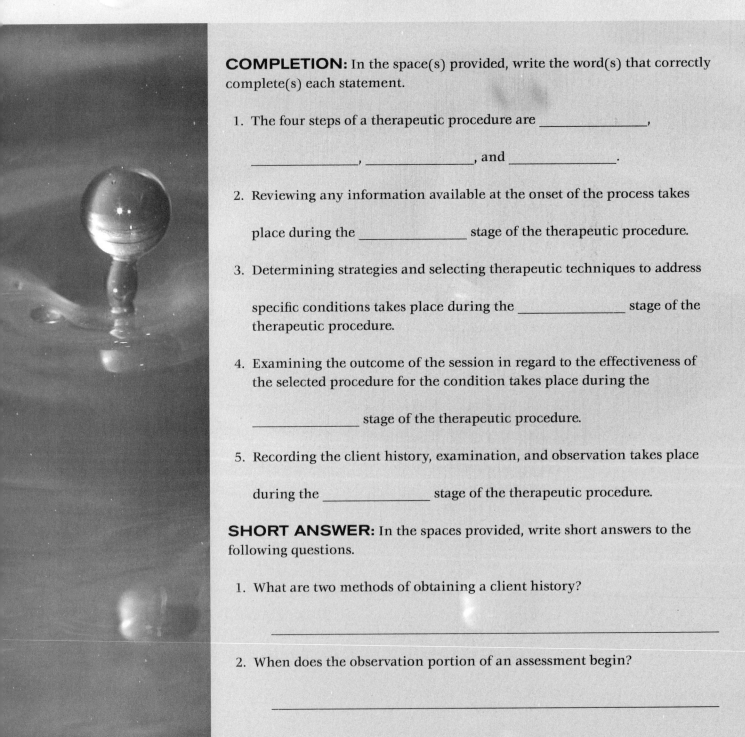

COMPLETION: In the space(s) provided, write the word(s) that correctly complete(s) each statement.

1. The four steps of a therapeutic procedure are ______________,

   ______________, ______________, and ______________.

2. Reviewing any information available at the onset of the process takes

   place during the ______________ stage of the therapeutic procedure.

3. Determining strategies and selecting therapeutic techniques to address

   specific conditions takes place during the ______________ stage of the therapeutic procedure.

4. Examining the outcome of the session in regard to the effectiveness of the selected procedure for the condition takes place during the

   ______________ stage of the therapeutic procedure.

5. Recording the client history, examination, and observation takes place

   during the ______________ stage of the therapeutic procedure.

SHORT ANSWER: In the spaces provided, write short answers to the following questions.

1. What are two methods of obtaining a client history?

   ____

2. When does the observation portion of an assessment begin?

   ____

3. What are three things that a therapist can observe while observing a client?

a. ______________________________

b. ______________________________

c. ______________________________

4. During the observation phase of an assessment, what does bilateral symmetry refer to?

____

5. When does the intake process begin?

____

6. What is included in the client intake process?

a. ______________________________

b. ______________________________

c. ______________________________

d. ______________________________

e. ______________________________

7. What are four portions of a common assessment protocol used for therapeutic massage?

a. ______________________________

b. ______________________________

c. ______________________________

d. ______________________________

8. What is the main difference between postural assessment and gait assessment?

____

____

COMPLETION: In the space(s) provided, write the word(s) that correctly complete(s) each statement.

1. Structural deviations, such as a tilted head, rotated hips, or a raised shoulder, are often the result of ______________________.

2. Posture is best observed when a person is standing and is best done from ______________ sides.

3. The action of a joint through the entire extent of its movement is called ____________________.

4. Three modes used in assessing the quality of this movement are ______________, ______________, and ______________ movement.

5. The English osteopath who developed a system of testing joints and soft tissue lesions was ____________________.

6. According to his definition, fibrous tissues that have tension placed on them during muscular contractions are called ____________________.

7. Tissues that are not contractile, such as bone, ligament, bursa, blood vessels, nerves, nerve coverings, and cartilage, are ____________________.

8. The quality of the sensation that the therapist feels as she passively moves a joint to the full extent of its possible range is termed ______________.

9. The results of testing that the therapist is able to see or feel are called ____________________.

10. The results of tests that the client feels, such as pain or discomfort, and the way in which the client reacts to the discomfort are considered to be ______________ findings.

11. When assessing ______________ movement, the client moves through a particular range of motion totally unassisted.

12. It is termed ____________________ when the practitioner moves the client's joint through full range of motion while the client remains relaxed.

SHORT ANSWER: In the spaces provided, write short answers to the following questions.

1. When range of motion is tested, which side should be tested first?

____

2. In which order should the three modes of testing range of motion be performed?

   a. ______________________________

   b. ______________________________

   c. ______________________________

3. Which tissues are involved during active movement?

   ____

4. If there is pain during active movement, what are four things that the therapist should note?

   a. ______________________________

   b. ______________________________

   c. ______________________________

   d. ______________________________

5. If there is a limitation to the movement during active movement, what are two things that the therapist should note?

   a. ______________________________

   b. ______________________________

COMPLETION: In the space(s) provided, write the word(s) that correctly complete(s) each statement.

1. There are three types of end feel that are considered normal. An abrupt, painless limitation to further movement that happens at the normal end of the range of motion, such as knee or elbow extension, is called ______________ end feel.

2. A cushioned limitation in which soft tissue prevents further movement, such as knee or elbow flexion, is called ______________ end feel.

3. It is called ______________ end feel, when the limitation is caused by the stretch of fibrous tissue as the joint reaches the extent of its range of motion.

4. Normal end feel happens at the ______________ of a normal range of motion and is ______________.

5. Sudden pain during passive movement before the end of normal range of motion was termed ______________ by Cyriax.

6. Abnormal end feel is indicated during passive movement when there is ______________ or ______________ in the movement.

7. Passive movement assessment indicates the condition of the ______________ tissues.

8. Full, painless passive range of motion indicates that the joint and associated structures are ______________.

9. Two indicators of dysfunction are ______________ and ______________.

10. Resisted or isometric movement is used to assess the condition of the ______________ tissues.

11. Indicators of lesions or dysfunction in the contractile tissue are ______________ and ______________.

12. Another name for resisted or isometric movement assessment is ______________.

13. Sensing the difference in tissue quality and integrity through touch is termed ______________.

14. A common palpable condition found in muscle that is usually associated with a lesion is a fibrous or ______________ band.

15. Examining the outcome of the process in relation to the expected objectives is called ______________.

16. The first sense of bind when manipulating healthy soft tissue is represented as the ______________ or ______________ barrier.

17. The end of comfortable soft tissue movement within the range of motion is represented by the ______________ barrier.

18. Movement beyond the ______________ barrier would cause tissue disruption or injury.

19. The acronym TART stands for ______________, ______________, ______________, and ______________.

20. A condition or illness that has a sudden onset and relatively short duration is considered to be ______________.

TRUE OR FALSE: If the following statements are true, write *true* in the space provided. If they are false, replace the italicized word with one that makes the statement true.

_______________ 1. Palpation is most effective when used in conjunction with and *before* assessing range of motion.

_______________ 2. When *passive* movement and resisted movement both give positive results, contractile tissues are involved.

_______________ 3. A *strong* and painful muscle test indicates a lesion in the inert tissue, possibly a torn ligament or fracture.

_______________ 4. The more severe the condition, the more severe the *pain*.

_______________ 5. *Taut bands* usually contain trigger points.

_______________ 6. In the acute phase of soft tissue injury, histamines are released, causing *vasoconstriction* of the capillaries.

_______________ 7. In the *acute* stage of soft tissue injury, gentle lengthening and cross-fiber techniques may be used.

SHORT ANSWER: In the spaces provided, write short answers to the following questions.

1. Which information is used in developing session strategies?

____

____

2. What takes place during the performance phase of the therapeutic procedure?

____

____

3. List the rehabilitative steps for restoring traumatized, injured, or dysfunctional soft tissue to ensure a long-lasting recovery.

a. ____

____

b. ____

c. ____

____

d. ____

e. ____

4. Which type of muscle tends to shorten, tighten, or develop trigger points and adhesions when under stress?

____

5. During the performance portion of a therapeutic massage, which techniques are effective to identify abnormal tissues?

____

6. During the performance portion of a therapeutic massage, which techniques are effective to reduce fascial constrictions?

____

7. When deep techniques are used, how much pressure is used?

____

____

8. List four common myofascial techniques

a. _______________

b. _______________

c. _______________

d. _______________

9. When does evaluation take place during a massage session?

____

____

____

____

____

MULTIPLE CHOICE: Carefully read each statement. Choose the word or phrase that correctly completes the meaning and write the corresponding letter in the blank provided.

1. The therapeutic procedure involves all of the following EXCEPT _______
   a) assessment
   b) planning
   c) performance
   d) psychological evaluation

2. The purpose of performing a client assessment is ______
   a) to diagnose the cause of the client's problem
   b) to reduce the chance of being sued for improper practice
   c) to establish a baseline of the client's functional ability to track improvement
   d) all of the above

3. Muscle tissues, tendons, and muscle attachments are called ______
   a) contractile tissues
   b) inert tissues
   c) fascia
   d) capsular patterns

4. Bones and ligaments are examples of ______
   a) contractile tissues
   b) inert tissues
   c) end feel
   d) capsular patterns

5. When assessing range of motion, first test the client's ______
   a) painful joints
   b) pain tolerance
   c) strength
   d) good side

6. Pain and how the client reacts to it is called a/an ______
   a) subjective finding
   b) objective finding
   c) active movement
   d) contraindication

7. Limitation of a joint movement because of the stretching of fibrous tissues is called ______
   a) hard end feel
   b) springy end feel
   c) soft end feel
   d) acute inflammation

8. The source of pain can be pinpointed through ______
   a) palpation
   b) hard end feel
   c) inert tissues
   d) range of motion

9. Determining if goals have been met is called ______
   a) goal tending
   b) processing
   c) evaluation
   d) assessment

10. When performing ROM assessment, the order of the tests that provide the most accurate information is ______
   a) palpation, passive movement, active movement, resisted movement
   b) palpation, active movement, resisted movement, passive movement
   c) active movement, passive movement, resisted movement, palpation
   d) passive movement, active movement, resisted movement, palpation

11. Which of the following takes place during the assessment? ________
    a) informed consent
    b) client and medical history
    c) deciding which techniques to use
    d) all of the above

12. Explaining policies and procedures, medical history, palpation examination, and informed consent are all part of the ________
    a) assessment
    b) treatment plan
    c) evaluation
    d) client intake

13. Observing a client's ability and willingness to move a body part through a range of motion is ________. ________
    a) assessing active movement
    b) assessing passive movement
    c) collecting subjective information
    d) collecting objective information

14. When soft tissue is manipulated, the first sense of bind represents the ________. ________
    a) anatomic barrier
    b) normal range of motion
    c) physiologic barrier
    d) restrictive barrier

15. Using the hands and sense of touch to assess the qualities of the tissues is ________. ________
    a) of little use
    b) termed palpation
    c) represented by the acronym TART
    d) done only with informed consent

16. An injury that begins with an event, causes some tissue disruption, and is fairly recent is considered ________. ________
    a) a chronic injury
    b) an acute injury
    c) a contraindication for therapeutic massage
    d) a biomechanical deviation

17. When a client is asked to actively flex the shoulder, he cautiously lifts his arm approximately 30 degrees, then stops quickly, winces, and grabs his shoulder. The practitioner should ________. ________
    a) perform techniques to relieve a spasm in the shoulder
    b) refer the client to a doctor for further evaluation
    c) note the reaction and perform further tests
    d) apologize and continue with a relaxing massage

18. When a client and practitioner have formulated a plan for six sessions, _______
   a) the plan should be strictly followed for the six sessions and then the results evaluated
   b) client priorities should determine what is done at every session
   c) slight modifications to the plan should be made according to session evaluations and individual pre-session interviews
   d) if there are no improvements after two sessions, the strategy should be abandoned

19. Evaluation is the part of therapeutic procedure that is done _______
   a) after every session
   b) after several sessions
   c) during the massage
   d) all of the above

20. The four parts of therapeutic procedure include ________. _______
   a) subjective, objective, assessment, planning
   b) planning, assessment, evaluation, performance
   c) history, assessment, planning, treatment
   d) subjective, objective, history, interview

21. The first part of the assessment involves ________. _______
   a) performing an interview with the client.
   b) palpation
   c) range of motion tests
   d) all of the above

22. A muscle injury in which there is intense pain at the time of injury, a palpable defect, a severe impairment of function, and little strength in resisted movement is a ________. _______
   a) first degree sprain
   b) second degree strain
   c) grade three strain
   d) third degree sprain

23. Which of the following should be done during the preliminary interview with the client? _______
   a) the client fills out intake and medical history forms.
   b) the practitioner asks questions to clarify information on the intake and medical history forms.
   c) the practitioner performs special orthopedic tests on the client.
   d) all of the above.

24. A muscle will stop contracting when ________. _______
   a) the nerve impulse to the muscle stops
   b) there is a nerve impulse to stop the contraction
   c) the opposing muscle contracts
   d) the muscle spindle signals too much tension

25. A muscle that is holding a body part so that other muscles that attach to that body part can contract and initiate movements is called a/an ________. ________
    - a) antagonist
    - b) stabilizer
    - c) neutralizer
    - d) prime mover

26. Bilateral symmetry and posture are assessed by ________. ________
    - a) orthopedic tests
    - b) palpation
    - c) observation
    - c) body diagrams

27. Manual resistive tests are performed by ________. ________
    - a) the client's attempting to move a body part in specific direction while the practitioner holds it in a neutral position, allowing no joint movement.
    - b) having the client move through a range of motion while the practitioner provides resistance
    - c) having the client lift a weight
    - d) the practitioner's moving the client through a range of motion while the client resists

28. When planning session strategies, which of the following should be considered? ________
    - a) the client's request for a relaxing massage
    - b) intake and medical forms that indicate back and neck pain
    - c) a doctor's report that indicates osteoporosis
    - d) all of the above

WORD REVIEW: The student is encouraged to write down the meaning of each of the following words. The list can be used as a study guide for this unit.

active movements

____

____

acute

____

____

anatomic barrier

____

____

assessment

asymmetry

bilateral symmetry

capsular pattern

chronic

client intake

contractile tissues

cross-fiber friction

deep gliding

directional massage

empty end feel

end feel

evaluation

fibrosis

functional assessment

gait assessment

hard end feel

hypertonic muscle

inert tissues

inflammatory response

ischemic compression

J-stroke

layer palpation

medical history

muscle energy technique

objective findings

observation

pain scale

palpation

passive movements

performance

physiologic barrier

planning

position release

postural assessment

postural distortion

PRICE

range of motion

resisted or isometric movement

resistive barrier

soft end feel

soft tissue barriers

soft tissue intervention

springy end feel

structural deviation

subjective findings

superficial gliding

TART

taut band

therapeutic procedure

trigger point

trigger-point massage

CHAPTER **18**

Athletic/Sports Massage

COMPLETION: In the space(s) provided, write the word(s) that correctly complete(s) each statement.

1. The 1972 Olympic gold medalist who was known as "the flying Finn" and who credited daily massage with his success was ______________.

2. The application of massage techniques that combine sound anatomic and physiologic knowledge, an understanding of strength training and conditioning, and specific massage skills to enhance athletic performance is termed ________________ or __________________.

3. The study of body movement is termed ______________.

4. In sports physiology, the ______________ principle states that to improve either strength or endurance, appropriate stresses must be applied to the system.

5. If the intensity of the athletic training exceeds the body's ability to recuperate, the result probably will be ____________________.

6. The rhythmic pumping massage manipulation that is applied to the belly of the muscle is called ______________.

7. Increasing the amount of blood available in a body area is called ______________.

8. If pressure on a tender point causes pain to radiate or refer to another area of the body, that point is considered a ______________.

9. The massage technique most often used on trigger points is _____________.

10. The amount of pressure that a therapist uses on a trigger point is determined by the

_____________________________.

11. ______________________________ is applied by rubbing across the fibers of the tendon, muscle, or ligament at a 90-degree angle to the fibers.

12. The British osteopath who popularized cross-fiber friction is _________________.

SHORT ANSWER: In the spaces provided, write short answers to the following questions.

1. Why does athletic massage enable athletes to participate more often in rigorous physical training and conditioning?

____

2. How does athletic massage reduce the chance of injury?

____

3. List four negative effects of exercise.

a. ____

b. ____

c. ____

d. ____

4. How long does it normally take for a muscle that has been stressed to the point of fatigue to recuperate?

____

5. What are two important effects of compression strokes?

a. ____

b. ____

6. In what direction is cross-fiber friction given?

____

7. How long is a cross-fiber stroke?

____

____

8. What does the acronym PNF stand for?

____

KEY CHOICES: Choose the massage technique that best fits the description or is most likely to produce the following effects. Write the appropriate key letter for each of the following massage techniques in the space provided.

A. compression
B. deep pressure
C. cross-fiber friction
D. active joint movement

_____ 1. softens adhesions in fibrous tissue

_____ 2. causes increased amounts of blood to remain in the muscle over an extended time

_____ 3. reduces fibrosis

_____ 4. adopted from proprioceptive neuromuscular facilitation

_____ 5. rubbing across the fibers of the tendon, muscle, or ligament

_____ 6. used effectively to treat tender points

_____ 7. a rhythmic pumping action to the belly of the muscle

_____ 8. therapist supports the body part in position while the client contracts his muscles

_____ 9. promotes increased circulation deep in the muscle

_____ 10. reduces the crystalline roughness that forms between tendons and their sheaths

_____ 11. helps to counteract muscle spasm, improve flexibility, and restore muscle strength

_____ 12. creates hyperemia in the muscle tissue

_____ 13. deactivates trigger points and increases function to the referred area

_____ 14. based on Sherrington's physiologic principles

_____ 15. stretches, broadens, and separates muscle fibers

_____ 16. encourages the formation of strong, pliable scar tissue at the site of healing injuries

_____ 17. based on reciprocal inhibition and postisometric relaxation

KEY CHOICES: Choose the athletic massage application that best fits the description. Write the key letter of the application next to the description in the space provided.

A = Post-event massage

B = Pre-event massage

C = Rehabilitation massage

D = Restorative training massage

_____ 1. focuses on the restoration of tissue function following injury

_____ 2. given within the first hour or two after participating in an event

_____ 3. breaks down transverse adhesions that might have resulted from previous injuries

_____ 4. warms and loosens the muscles, causing hyperemia in specific muscle areas

_____ 5. can locate and relieve areas of stress that carry a high risk of injury

_____ 6. stimulates circulation and at the same time calms the nervous system

_____ 7. reduces fibrosis caused by muscle injury

_____ 8. given 15 to 45 minutes before an event

_____ 9. is considered a regular and valuable part of the athlete's training schedule

_____ 10. enables the athlete to reach his peak performance earlier in the event and maintain that performance longer

_____ 11. allows the athlete to train at a higher level of intensity, more consistently, with less chance of injury

_____ 12. three to four times as effective as rest in recovery from muscle fatigue

_____ 13. shortens the time that it takes for an injury to heal

_____ 14. makes more intense and frequent workouts possible, thereby improving overall performance

_____ 15. prevents delayed onset of muscle soreness and reduces the time it takes for the body to recover from exertion

_____ 16. is fast paced and invigorating

_____ 17. accelerates healing so that the athlete's "down time" is cut to a minimum

_____ 18. helps to form strong, pliable scar tissue

_____ 19. given after the athlete has had a chance to cool down from the exertion of the competition or exercise

TRUE OR FALSE: If the following statements are true, write *true* in the space provided. If they are false, replace the italicized word with one that makes the statement true.

_______________ 1. Pre-event massage increases flexibility and circulation and *replaces* the warm-up before an event.

_______________ 2. During *pre-event massage*, adhesions can be eliminated to reduce the chance of injury.

_______________ 3. Post-event massage is given after competition and helps an athlete *to cool down*.

_______________ 4. *Post-event massage* is three to four times as effective as rest in recovery from muscle fatigue.

_______________ 5. *Restorative massage* can resemble pre-event or post-event massage.

_______________ 6. A *strain* involves the stretching or tearing of a ligament.

_______________ 7. A *grade I* strain is the most severe.

_______________ 8. As a muscle fiber contracts, the sarcolemma and the *endomysium* move as a unit.

SHORT ANSWER: In the spaces provided, write short answers to the following questions.

1. What is the first step when giving a post-event massage?

____

2. After a long race, what are some conditions that the therapist should watch for?

____

3. Which action should the therapist take if strains, sprains, abrasions, or contusions are apparent?

____

4. When interviewing an athlete for determining a training massage program, what are five important questions to ask?

   a. ____

   b. ____

   c. ____

   d. ____

   e. ____

COMPLETION: In the space(s) provided, write the word(s) that correctly complete(s) each statement.

1. Athletic injuries that have a sudden and definite onset and are usually of relatively short duration are considered to be ____________ injuries.
2. A muscle strain in which there is severe tearing and complete loss of function is called a grade ____________ strain.
3. The therapist's indicator of how intensely to work on an injury site is ____________.
4. Athletic injuries that have a gradual onset, tend to last for a long time, or recur often are considered ____________ injuries.

SHORT ANSWER: In the spaces provided, write short answers to the following questions.

1. Give six examples of acute athletic injuries.

   a. ____________________ b. ____________________

   c. ____________________ d. ____________________

   e. ____________________ f. ____________________

2. What effect does PRICE have on soft tissue injuries?

   ____

3. When can massage be started on injured tissue?

   ____

4. What are two goals that the therapist strives to achieve when working on chronic conditions?

   a. ____

   b. ____

5. List two positive effects of the swelling that results from tissue damage.

   a. ______________________________

   b. ______________________________

6. List six therapeutic modalities used in rehabilitation sport massage.

   a. ______________________________

   b. ______________________________

   c. ______________________________

   d. ______________________________

   e. ______________________________

7. List three negative effects of the swelling that results from tissue damage.

   a. ______________________________

   b. ______________________________

   c. ______________________________

KEY CHOICES: Identify the following conditions as either chronic or acute. Write the appropriate key letter in the space provided.

C = Chronic

A = Acute

_____ 1. dislocated shoulder

_____ 2. iliotibial band syndrome

_____ 3. shin splints

_____ 4. broken wrist

_____ 5. overuse syndrome

_____ 6. torn ligament

_____ 7. sprained ankle

_____ 8. tennis elbow

_____ 9. bruised hip

_____ 10. tendonitis

COMPLETION: In the space(s) provided, write the word(s) that correctly complete(s) each statement.

1. The tensile strength of connective tissue is provided by _______________.
2. The layer of connective tissue that closely covers an individual muscle is the _______________.
3. Connective tissue extends beyond the end of the muscle to become _______________.
4. The perimysium extends inward from the epimysium and separates the muscle into bundles of muscle fibers or _______________.
5. Each muscle fiber is covered by a delicate connective tissue covering called the _______________.
6. Soft tissue injuries result in the tearing of _______________ in the connective tissue.
7. Collagen fibers are produced by _______________
8. Collagen formation that reconnects the injured tissue forms _______________.
9. Collagen fibers that connect to structures other than the injured tissue form _______________ that restrict mobility.
10. Proper _______________ reduces the degree of secondary trauma following soft tissue injury.

MULTIPLE CHOICE: Carefully read each statement. Choose the word or phrase that correctly completes the meaning and write the corresponding letter in the blank provided.

1. Kinesiology is the study of
   a) muscles　　c) body movement　　_____
   b) cells　　d) muscle strength

2. Blood remaining in muscle for an extended period is called
   a) hyperemia　　c) hyperthermia　　_____
   b) hypertension　　d) ischemia

3. Compression strokes in athletic massage use the ________
   a) knuckles
   b) forearm
   c) fingertips
   d) palm

4. An active trigger point causes pain to ________ when palpated. ________
   a) radiate
   b) evaporate
   c) dissipate
   d) increase

5. Shaking and jostling are performed on muscles that are ________ . ________
   a) large
   b) small
   c) injured
   d) relaxed

6. The therapist-assisted active and resistive patterned movements used in the rehabilitation of disabilities are commonly known as ________ . ________
   a) MET
   b) PNF
   c) ROM
   d) PHD

7. MET helps to counteract ________. ________
   a) soft tissue injury
   b) headache
   c) sprains
   d) muscle spasm

8. Pre-event massage should be given this far in advance of an event: ________
   a) 30 minutes
   b) 2 days
   c) 2 hours
   d) 6 hours

9. The most beneficial form of massage for athletes is ________ massage. ________
   a) pre-event
   b) post-event
   c) restorative
   d) rehabilitative

10. A sprain with mild pain and minimal loss of function is classified as ________. ________
    a) Grade I
    b) Grade II
    c) Grade III
    d) Grade IV

11. A sprain with some tearing of fibrous tissue is classified as ________. ________
    a) Grade I
    b) Grade II
    c) Grade III
    d) Grade IV

12. Injuries that have a gradual onset or recur often are called ________. ________
    a) sprains
    b) occupational
    c) acute
    d) chronic

13. An injury in or between muscle fibers is called ________. ________
    a) macrotrauma
    b) microtrauma
    c) chronic
    d) acute

WORD REVIEW: The student is encouraged to write down the meaning of each of the following words. The list can be used as a study guide for this unit.

acute soft tissue injuries

____

athletic massage

____

____

____

chronic soft tissue injuries

____

____

compression strokes

____

____

____

cross-fiber massage

____

____

hyperemia

____

____

inflammatory response

____

____

intra-event massage

PRICE

postedemic fibrosis

postisometric relaxation

pre-event massage

proprioceptive neuromuscular facilitation

reciprocal inhibition

rehabilitative massage

restorative massage

sports massage

tender points

transverse friction massage

CHAPTER 19

Massage for Special Populations

COMPLETION: In the space(s) provided, write the word(s) that correctly complete(s) each statement.

1. The massage practitioner can sharpen his skills and stay current with new developments in the massage field through ____________________.

2. Massage given to a pregnant woman is commonly called ________________.

3. The main goal of prenatal massage is ____________.

4. During pregnancy, a woman's body experiences both ____________ and ____________ changes.

5. Massage directly on the abdomen during pregnancy is ______________.

6. During pregnancy, emotional mood swings and softening of connective tissues are caused by ____________.

7. Excessive weight gain; high blood pressure; swelling in the hands, legs, and face; and protein in the urine during pregnancy are signs of ____________________.

SHORT ANSWER: In the spaces provided, write short answers to the following questions.

1. What are two considerations when positioning a pregnant woman for massage?

   a. ____

   b. ____

2. Why is the supine position not recommended during the later stages of pregnancy?

   ____

3. List the major contraindications for prenatal massage.

   a. ____

   b. ____

   c. ____

   d. ____

   e. ____

   f. ____

   g. ____

4. List eight risk factors that increase the possibility of miscarriage during the first trimester of pregnancy.

   a. ____

   b. ____

   c. ____

   d. ____

   e. ____

   f. ____

   g. ____

   h. ____

MATCHING: Match the term with the best description. Write the letter or letters of the best description in the space provided.

A. first trimester

B. second trimester

C. third trimester

D. fourth trimester

_____ 1. Bonding is encouraged with infant massage.

_____ 2. Avoid all abdominal massage.

_____ 3. The baby doubles in length to about 20 inches.

_____ 4. The abdomen begins to protrude.

_____ 5. Massage helps to firm slack muscles and regain normal weight.

_____ 6. Weeks 14 to 26 of the pregnancy

_____ 7. Supine and prone positions are suitable as long as the client is comfortable.

_____ 8. The baby's head drops into the pelvis.

_____ 9. Use the semi-reclining or side-lying position for comfort and safety.

_____ 10. Provide massage only after the mother-to-be has received permission from her midwife or physician.

_____ 11. The mother will begin to feel the baby move.

_____ 12. Supine and prone positions are suitable as long as the client is comfortable.

_____ 13. The mother's body starts to produce the hormone relaxin.

_____ 14. Apply only light abdominal massage.

COMPLETION: In the space(s) provided, write the word(s) that correctly complete(s) each statement.

1. An early proponent of infant massage in the United States and the author of Infant Massage: A Handbook for Loving Parents is ____________________.

2. ____________ was the first official director of the International Infant Massage Instructors Association and helped incorporate the International Loving Touch Foundation.

3. The person best suited to administer infant massage is the ____________________.

4. Three benefits of infant massage for the infant are ____________, ____________, and ______________________________.

5. A full-body well baby infant massage usually lasts about ________ minutes or ________________.

6. The length of a massage for a young child depends on ________________.

7. A spinal cord injury in the cervical spine usually results in a condition called ________.

8. A spinal cord injury to the thoracic or lumbar spine usually results in a condition called ________.

SHORT ANSWER: In the spaces provided, write short answers to the following questions.

1. What are three strokes that can be used on a gassy or colicky baby?

   a. ________________

   b. ________________

   c. ________________

2. When massage for children under the age of eighteen is to be done, name two things that the parent or guardian should do.

   a. ________________

   b. ________________

3. List three benefits for massaging elderly clients.

   a. ________________

   b. ________________

   c. ________________

4. What are four considerations for providing massage for someone with auditory impairment?

   a. ________________

   b. ________________

   c. ________________

   d. ________________

   Alternate ________________

5. When providing massage to someone with paralysis, which considerations are made when massaging the paralyzed areas?

   a. ______________________________

   ____

   b. ______________________________

   c. ______________________________

6. When is an HIV infected person considered to have AIDS?

   ____

   ____

7. How is HIV transmitted from one person to another?

   ____

COMPLETION: In the space(s) provided, write the word(s) that correctly complete(s) each statement.

1. ______________, or proliferation of cancer cells, is the manner in which cancer spreads.

2. Cancers that are most lethal are those that ______________________________.

3. The four ways that cancer spreads are ______________________________, ______________________, ______________________, and ______________________.

4. The kind of tissue that cancer originally develops in determines the ____________ of cancer.

5. Cancer that has spread into regional lymph nodes and/or other tissues in the local area of the primary tumor is classified as stage ______________ cancer.

6. Three common medical treatments for cancer are ______________, ______________, and ______________.

7. Leg massage on a postsurgical patient is a contraindication because of an increased chance of ______________.

8. Surgical removal of regional lymph nodes can result in swelling, a condition called ______________.

9. The use of orally or intravenously administered drugs or chemicals to treat cancer is termed ______________.

10. For a person receiving the previously named treatment, the best time to receive massage is either ______________ the treatment or after the adverse side effects have subsided.

MULTIPLE CHOICE: Carefully read each statement. Choose the word or phrase that correctly completes the meaning and write the corresponding letter in the blank provided.

1. When a woman is pregnant, ligaments and other connective tissue tend to soften because of ________. ________
   a) estrogen
   b) relaxin
   c) progesterone
   d) stress

2. During the second and third trimester, the preferred position for a pregnant woman to receive a massage is the ________ position. ________
   a) prone
   b) supine
   c) seated
   d) side-lying

3. If an expectant mother is experiencing headaches, edema, and high blood pressure, she should ________. ________
   a) see her doctor without delay
   c) get a massage
   c) go to bed and rest
   d) drink more water and exercise

4. Signs of a DVT are ________. ________
   a) pain around the area
   b) redness and tenderness
   c) swelling distal to the area
   d) all of the above

5. During which portion of a pregnancy is the expectant mother more likely to experience nausea and sensitivity to some smells and tastes? ________
   a) the first trimester
   b) the second trimester
   c) the third trimester
   d) the entire pregnancy

6. What is the main focus of prenatal massage in the third trimester? ________
   a) pain relief
   b) relaxation
   c) preparation for delivery
   d) stimulate uterine activity

7. The first official director of the International Infant Massage Instructor Association was ________. ________
   a) Vimila Schneider McClure
   b) Fredrick Leboyer
   c) Diana Moore
   d) Tiffany Fields

8. The person best suited to perform infant massage on a baby is ________. ________
   a) the primary care giver
   b) a licensed massage therapist
   c) the infant massage instructor
   d) the baby's physician

9. What is the preferable location to perform infant massage? ________
   a) In a warm bathtub
   b) At the doctor's office
   c) On a massage table
   d) On a blanket on the floor

10. The length of a typical infant massage is about ________ minutes. ________
    a) 5
    b) 20
    c) 30
    d) 60

11. An important consideration when providing massage to children or adolescents is ________. ________
    a) their attention span
    b) having an adult in the massage room
    c) their body image
    d) all the above

12. When a client has a disability, how can the therapist determine which special needs the client has? ________
    a) Ask the client
    b) Ask the client's caregiver
    c) Ask the client's physician
    d) Consult the Internet

13. A complete spinal cord injury to the upper thoracic spine results in ________. ________
    a) paraplegia
    b) quadriplegia
    c) tetraplegia
    d) hemiplegia

14. Which of the following techniques is not appropriate when providing massage for someone who is critically ill? ________
    a) superficial effleurage
    b) MET
    c) Reiki
    d) light touch

15. The purpose of massage for the critically ill client is to bring ________. ________
    a) pleasure
    b) relaxation
    c) comfort
    d) all of the above

16. Massage for the critically ill client is a specialty massage ________. ________
    a) in which contraindications do not exist
    b) in which, depending on conditions, special precautions are taken
    c) done only in hospitals and nursing homes
    d) designed to enable a person to regain his health

17. The causative factor for the acquired immune deficiency syndrome is ________. ________
    a) an unhealthy lifestyle
    b) unprotected sex
    c) insufficient immunizations
    d) the human immunodeficiency virus

18. Which of the following is not a route of transmission the AIDS causing virus? ________
    a) transfusion of tainted blood
    b) unprotected intercourse
    c) airborne particles from a sneeze or cough
    d) transmission across the placenta to a fetus

19. The manner in which cancer spreads is ________. ________
    a) through airborne particles
    b) metastasis
    c) by human contact
    d) all the above

20. Cancer that is well developed and has spread to several organs in the body is termed ________. ________
    a) recurrent
    b) stage I cancer
    c) stage III cancer
    d) stage IV cancer

21. Cancer can spread within a person's body ________. ________
    a) through the bloodstream
    b) by directly invading neighboring tissues
    c) through the lymph system
    d) all of the above

22. Cancer is a disease that is often spread through the ________. ________
    a) genes
    b) lymphatic system
    c) air
    d) digestive system

WORD REVIEW: The student is encouraged to write down the meaning of each of the following words. The list can be used as a study guide for this unit.

AIDS

____

____

bonding

____

____

carcinoma

____

____

coagulability

____

____

contralateral

____

____

HIV

____

____

hemiplegia

____

____

leukemia

____

____

lymphoma

____

____

metastasis

____

____

myeloma

opportunistic infection

preeclampsia

prenatal massage

primary caregiver

quadriplegia

sarcoma

toxemia

CHAPTER 20

Massage in Medicine

COMPLETION: In the space(s) provided, write the word(s) that correctly complete(s) each question.

1. The early physicians, Avicenna and Rhazes, lived in ____________.

2. Medical gymnastics were created in Sweden in the early 1800s by ________________.

3. The Swedish Movement Cure was introduced to New York in the 1880s by the brothers ____________________ and ____________________.

4. Manual Therapies: A Treatise on Massage by ________________ was published in Boston in 1902.

5. While serving as the Director of Physiotherapy at the Harvard Medical School from 1921 to 1925, ________________ wrote the definitive text *Massage and Therapeutic Exercise.*

6. The use of massage in the medical field in the United States became nearly nonexistent after ____________.

7. In the 1960s and 1970s, massage began to reemerge as a part of the __________________________.

8. Health-enhancing practices that were outside of conventional allopathic medical practices became known as ____________ medicine.

9. ____________ is an acronym that stands for ______________________________ and encompasses many healing practices, philosophies, and therapies that conventional Western medicine does not include.

10. Therapies are termed as ______________ when used in addition to conventional treatments and as ____________ when used instead of conventional treatment.

11. __________________ combines CAM with allopathic medicine.

12. The most popular and requested CAM modality at most integrative medicine clinics is ____________.

13. Medically prescribed massage performed with the intention of improving pathologies diagnosed by a physician is termed ______________.

14. A document that is signed by the client and that is required to share confidential information with insurance companies, physicians, or attorneys is a ____________________.

15. A standard form recognized by most insurance companies used to submit claims is the ____________________ form.

16. ____________________ or ____________ were developed by the American Medical Association to categorize and quantify medical services accurately.

SHORT ANSWER: In the spaces provided, write short answers to the following questions

1. Between 1950 and 1970, where were most Swedish massage therapists employed?

____

2. When did the term *massage* first appear in medical literature?

____

3. What is contained in massage documentation in an integrative setting?

a. ____

b. ____

c. ____

d. ____

e. ____

4. What are some benefits of providing massage services to hospital staff?

a. ______

b. ______

c. ______

d. ______

e. ______

f. ______

5. What are some benefits of providing massage to hospital patients?

a. ______

b. ______

c. ______

d. ______

e. ______

6. What are the warning signs associated with cancer?

a. ______

b. ______

c. ______

d. ______

e. ______

f. ______

g. ______

7. Who can determine medical necessity?

______

8. Which elements should be contained in a prescription for massage?

a. ______________________________

b. ______________________________

c. ______________________________

d. ______________________________

9. Which types of insurance coverage are more likely to pay for massage?

____

10. Which information is needed from the client to contact the insurance company for verification?

a. ______________________________

____

b. ______________________________

c. ______________________________

d. ______________________________

e. ______________________________

f. ______________________________

g. ______________________________

h. ______________________________

MULTIPLE CHOICE: Carefully read each statement. Choose the word or phrase that correctly completes the meaning and write the corresponding letter in the blank provided.

1. The term *massage* first appeared in medical writings ________. ________
   a) during the times of the ancient Greeks
   b) during the Roman empire
   c) in the 1700s
   d) near the end of the 19th century

2. *Manual Therapies: A Treatise on Massage* was published in 1902 by ________. ________
   a) Per Henrik Ling
   b) Charles Taylor
   c) Douglas Graham
   d) James Mennell

3. Massage and physiotherapy were used for treating orthopedic conditions in the United States until about ________. ________
   a) 1900
   b) 1925
   c) 1945
   d) 1955

4. Massage and other healing practices that developed outside the Western medical model during the 1960s through the 1980s were considered ________. ________
   a) quackery
   b) alternative practices
   c) complementary medicine
   d) holistic medicine

5. Healing approaches that regard the entire person, including the spiritual, physical, mental, emotional, social, and environmental rather than just the symptoms, are considered ________. ________
   a) alternative
   b) integrative
   c) complementary
   d) holistic

6. Combining conventional Western medical practices with alternative and complementary therapies to best benefit a patient's health is ________. ________
   a) integrative medicine
   b) holistic medicine
   c) mind-body medicine
   d) all of the above

7. Providing massage services to a patient in a hospital requires ________. ________
   a) special training
   b) a medical license
   c) a physician's referral or prescription
   d) all of the above

8. The massage movements most frequently used by nurses are ________. ________
   a) Chinese
   b) Greek
   c) German
   d) Swedish

9. Massage is not performed on an area that is ________. ________
   a) bleeding
   b) swollen
   c) burned
   d) all of the above

10. A sore that has not healed normally, lumps underneath the arms or in the breasts, and a persistent hoarseness, coughing, or sore throat are ________. ________
    a) reasons to refer to a doctor
    b) warning signs of cancer
    c) contraindications for massage
    d) all of the above

11. A massage prescribed by a physician to address a diagnosed condition can be considered a ________. ________
    a) therapeutic massage
    b) medical massage
    c) wellness massage
    d) all of the above

12. A prescription for massage should contain ________. ____
   a) diagnosis of the condition
   b) an order for massage therapy services to be performed
   c) the frequency of treatments
   d) all the above

13. Which type of insurance is more likely to pay for medical massage services? ____
   a) major medical policies
   b) health maintenance organizations
   c) personal injury claims
   d) Medicare and Medicaid

14. What should a therapist do before providing services to a client with an insurance claim? ____
   a) perform a thorough assessment
   b) obtain verification from her insurance carrier
   c) contact her doctor for a prescription
   d) refer her to a doctor for a diagnosis

15. Which form must be signed by the client before a therapist can discuss her case with an insurance agent or other medical personnel? ____
   a) informed consent
   b) medical history form
   c) medical information release form
   d) assignment of benefits form

16. Why is the 1500 Health Insurance Claim form printed in red ink? ____
   a) to make it easy to read
   b) so it can be read by an optical scanner
   c) to make it easy to find
   d) all of the above

17. What are CPT codes? ____
   a) a system to categorize medical services
   b) current procedural terminology
   c) a list of allowable fees for medical procedures
   d) all of the above

WORD REVIEW: The student is encouraged to write down the meaning of each of the following words. The list can be used as a study guide for this unit.

agreement for payment form

____

____

____

alternative medicine

assignment of benefits form

CAM

complementary medicine

CPT codes

1500 Health Insurance Claim form

hospital-based massage

ICD-9 codes

integrative medicine

medical information release form

medical massage

mind-body medicine

NCCAM

NIH

verification for services

CHAPTER 21

Other Somatic Therapies

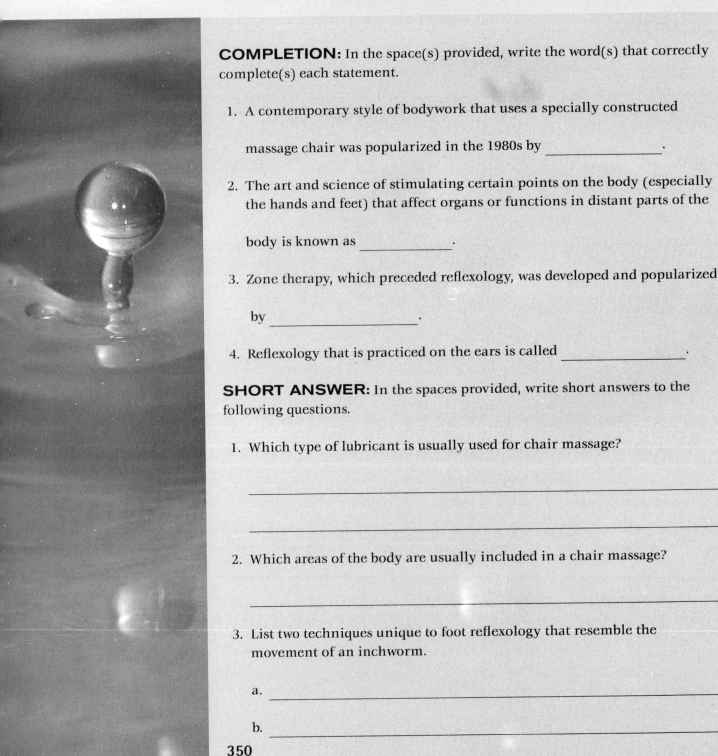

COMPLETION: In the space(s) provided, write the word(s) that correctly complete(s) each statement.

1. A contemporary style of bodywork that uses a specially constructed massage chair was popularized in the 1980s by _______________.

2. The art and science of stimulating certain points on the body (especially the hands and feet) that affect organs or functions in distant parts of the body is known as ____________.

3. Zone therapy, which preceded reflexology, was developed and popularized by ____________________.

4. Reflexology that is practiced on the ears is called ________________.

SHORT ANSWER: In the spaces provided, write short answers to the following questions.

1. Which type of lubricant is usually used for chair massage?

   ____

   ____

2. Which areas of the body are usually included in a chair massage?

   ____

3. List two techniques unique to foot reflexology that resemble the movement of an inchworm.

   a. ____

   b. ____

4. What alerts a reflexologist to places to work on the foot?

a. ______________________________

b. ______________________________

COMPLETION: In the space(s) provided, write the word(s) that correctly complete(s) each statement.

1. A traditional Chinese medical practice whereby the skin is punctured with needles at specific points for therapeutic purposes is known as ______________.

2. Religious philosophies of the Far East speak of ______________ or "the way" or "that which is all there is."

3. In Eastern philosophies, the opposing yet complementary aspects of existence are represented by ______________ and ______________.

4. In Eastern Asia, the vast web of invisible energy that intertwines all creation is known as ______________.

5. In the following exercise, list the names of the twelve organ meridians, whether each organ is yin or yang, and the element related to it.

	Organ/meridian	yin/yang	Element
a.			
b.			
c.			
d.			
e.			
f.			
g.			
h.			
i			
j			
k.			
l.			

MATCHING: Arrange the following words in two columns. In the first column, list words that correspond to *yin*. In the second column, write the words that correspond to *yang* adjacent to the contrasting word in the *yin* column.

active	back of the body	cold	contracting
dark	day	deficient	excessive
expanding	forceful	front of the body	high
hot	inner body	inside	light
low	lower body	night	outer body
outside	overactive	passive	underactive
upper body	weak		

YIN	YANG
______________	______________
______________	______________
______________	______________
______________	______________
______________	______________
______________	______________
______________	______________
______________	______________
______________	______________
______________	______________
______________	______________
______________	______________
______________	______________

COMPLETION: In the space(s) provided, write the word(s) that correctly complete(s) each statement.

1. The interaction of yin and yang creates a vibratory force or energy called ______________.

2. In traditional Chinese medicine (TCM), two common methods of assessment are

   a. ______________________

   b. ______________________

3. According to ancient philosophy, this vital force manifests itself as five interrelated elements. They are

a. ______________________ d. ______________________

b. ______________________ e. ______________________

c. ______________________

4. Qi moves through the body in specific channels called ______________.

5. There are ____________ bilateral channels that relate to the organs.

6. Along these channels are small areas of high conductivity called

______________________.

7. Several treatment systems that incorporate various manipulations (not needles) on acupoints are collectively called ______________.

8. The Japanese system of finger pressure massage is called ____________.

9. A technique in TCM of burning an herb, such as mugwort, over an acupoint or on an acupuncture needle is called ______________.

10. A form of Chinese bodywork that is based in TCM and incorporates methods to move energy along the meridians is ____________.

11. In the practice of Zen shiatsu, the primary assessment technique is ______________.

12. A traditional medicine system that originated in India and that uses herbs, massage, and diet as treatment forms is called ________________________.

13. A form of energetic bodywork that originated in Japan, in which the practitioner uses mantras and intention to channel energy rather than actual touch is called ____________.

14. Polarity therapy was created by ________________.

15. A form of energetic bodywork that is popular among nurses and is practiced in hospitals that seeks to balance the human energy field by the practitioner moving their hands near but not on the client's body is called ______________.

MULTIPLE CHOICE: Carefully read each statement. Choose the word or phrase that correctly completes the meaning and write the corresponding letter in the blank provided.

1. David Palmer developed the first specially designed massage chair in ________. ________
   a) 1885 c) 1986
   b) 1969 d) 1994

2. Which of the following strokes are not appropriate for chair massage? ________
   a) effleurage c) compression
   b) deep pressure d) percussion

3. The bodywork practice in which points in the hands or feet are massaged to affect organs or other parts of the body is ________. ________
   a) acupuncture c) reflexology
   b) shiatsu d) Reiki

4. Acupuncture and TCM originated ________ years ago. ________
   a) 2500 c) 1000
   b) 5000 d) 500

5. Traditional Chinese medicine was originally conceived by ________. ________
   a) Taoist monks c) the Yellow Emperor
   b) the king's physicians d) tribal shamans

6. According to Eastern philosophy, the fundamental substance of which everything is composed is ________. ________
   a) atoms c) the five elements
   b) yin and yang d) qi

7. Which of the following is yin? ________
   a) extrovert c) contracting
   b) masculine d) active

8. Which of the following is an example of the interaction of yin and yang? ________
   a) metabolism c) breathing
   b) digestion d) all of the above

9. Which of the following is not one of the five elements of traditional Chinese medicine? ________
   a) earth c.) fire
   b) water d) air

10. Which element do the spleen, stomach, yellow, and worry correspond to? ________
    a) fire
    b) earth
    c) water
    d) metal

11. The ________ meridian starts on the face and ends on the little toe. ________
    a) bladder
    c) gallbladder
    c) stomach
    d) kidney

12. In TCM, there are ________ bilateral organ-related meridians. ________
    a) six
    b) eight
    c) twelve
    d) twenty-four

13. A primary form of assessment in Chinese medicine is ________. ________
    a) blood pressure
    b) pulse
    c) posture
    d) temperature

14. A form of Chinese bodywork that is grounded in traditional Chinese medicine is ________. ________
    a) tuina
    b) shaitsu
    c) anma
    d) ayurveda

15. A Japanese form of bodywork that uses finger pressure to stimulate or balance qi flow is ________. ________
    a) tuina
    b) anma
    c) shiatsu
    d) Reiki

16. Energy vortexes aligned along front of the spine are called ________. ________
    a) acupoints
    b) chakras
    c) marma points
    d) all of the above

WORD REVIEW: The student is encouraged to write down the meaning of each of the following words and phrases. The list can be used as a study guide for this unit.

acupoint

____

____

acupressure

____

____

____

Ayurveda

chair massage

chakra

ki

moxibustion

organ meridian

pulse diagnosis

reflexology

Reiki

____

____

shiatsu

____

____

therapeutic touch

____

____

traditional Chinese medicine (TCM)

____

____

tuina

____

____

yang

____

____

yin

____

____

Part 4

Massage Business Administration

CHAPTER 22

Business Practices

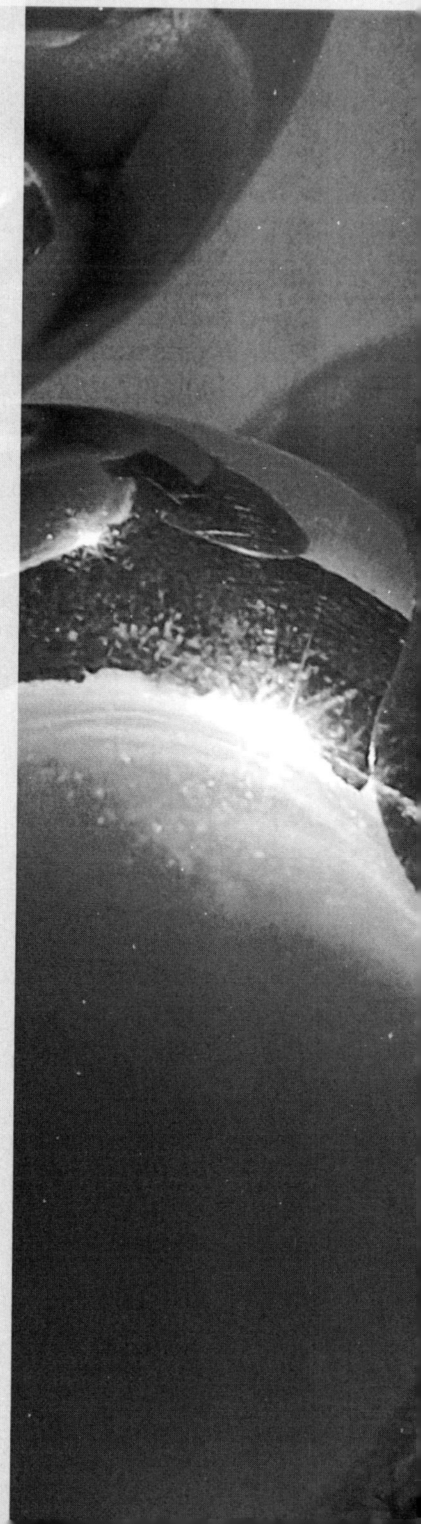

SHORT ANSWER: In the spaces provided, write short answers to the following questions.

1. When does business planning begin?

____

2. When does business planning end?

____

3. Name four important parts of business planning.

   a. _______________

   b. _______________

   c. _______________

   d. _______________

4. What are four common types of business operations?

   a. _______________

   b. _______________

   c. _______________

   d. _______________

COMPLETION: In the space(s) provided, write the word(s) that correctly complete(s) each statement.

1. A short general statement of the main focus of the business is called the

   ____________________.

2. Specific, attainable, measurable things or accomplishments that you set and make a commitment to achieve are termed ________________.

3. If you are an individual owner of a business and carry all expenses, obligations, liabilities, and assets, you are considered a ________________.

4. To establish a ________________, a charter must be obtained from the state in which the business operates.

5. Management of a corporation is carried on by a ____________________.

6. When a business is beginning, the expenses incurred before any revenues are collected are considered ________________.

7. Two primary reasons for the failure of small businesses are ____________________ and

   ____________________.

SHORT ANSWER: In the spaces provided, write short answers to the following questions.

1. If your business is a sole proprietorship, who is responsible for any losses or debts?

   ____

2. Which zoning requirements must be considered when choosing a massage business location?

   ____

3. List at least three important considerations when buying an established business.

   a. ____

   b. ____

   c. ____

COMPLETION: In the space(s) provided, write the word(s) that correctly complete(s) each statement.

1. If a business is operating under a name other than the owner's, a ________________ ________________ is required.

2. If the business sells products or if services are taxed, a ________________ must be obtained from ________________.

3. To ensure that the business meets zoning requirements, the ________________ ________________ should be contacted.

4. An employer identification number must be obtained from the ________________ if the business hires employees.

5. The identification number issued to licensed health care providers and used when submitting claims to medical insurance companies is called a ________________.

6. As a massage business owner, one should have adequate insurance against ________________, ________________, and ________________.

KEY CHOICES: Choose the types of insurance that best fit the description. Write the appropriate key letter next to the stated description in the space provided.

A. automobile insurance
B. disability insurance
C. fire and theft insurance
D. health insurance
E. liability insurance
F. professional liability insurance
G. workers' compensation insurance

_____ 1. protects the person from loss of income because they are unable to work because of long-term illness or injury

_____ 2. helps to cover the cost of medical bills, especially hospitalization, serious injury, or illness

_____ 3. provides medical and liability insurance to the driver and any passengers

_____ 4. is required if you have employees

_____ 5. covers the cost of fixtures, furniture, equipment, products, and supplies

_____ 6. covers costs of injuries and litigation resulting from injuries sustained on the owner's property

_____ 7. covers the medical costs for the employee if they are injured on the job

_____ 8. covers the vehicle and its contents, regardless of who is at fault

_____ 9. protects the therapist from lawsuits filed by a client because of injury or loss that results from negligence or substandard performance

COMPLETION: In the space(s) provided, write the word(s) that correctly complete(s) each statement.

1. The standards of acceptable and professional behavior by which a person or business conducts business are called _____________.

2. When setting fees for massage, consider the _____________ and the _______________.

3. A summary of all sales and cash receipts is called an _______________.

4. A ledger that records, separates, and classifies business expenditures is called a ____________________.

SHORT ANSWER: In the spaces provided, write short answers to the following questions.

1. If a massage business is operated out of a home, are all telephone expenses tax deductible?

____

2. For a self-employed massage practitioner, which three major records should be maintained?

   a. ____

   b. ____

   c. ____

3. Two important reasons for keeping accurate financial records are

   a. ____

   b. ____

4. Why is it advisable to consult an accountant when preparing taxes?

____

____

5. Which name is on the business checking account?

____

6. Which moneys are deposited in the business account?

____

7. For which purposes are checks written from the business account?

____

8. What is the purpose of a petty cash fund?

____

9. Where does petty cash fund money come from?

____

10. How long should canceled checks and bank statements be kept for tax purposes?

____

11. What is included in the income records?

____

12. Name ten things that should be included on an income receipt or invoice.

a. ____________________ f. ____________________

b. ____________________ g. ____________________

c. ____________________ h. ____________________

d. ____________________ i. ____________________

e. ____________________ j. ____________________

13. How many copies of the invoice should there be, and where do they go?

____

14. Information that is included in each entry of the disbursement ledger includes

a. ____

b. ____

c. ____

d. ____

e. ____

15. Which receipts should be kept and filed?

____

16. How long should receipts be kept?

____

17. When is it necessary to keep an accounts receivable file?

____

18. A record of money owed to other persons or businesses is kept in an ______________ file.

19. Items and equipment that are purchased to be used in the business for an extended time (more than a year) are called ______________.

20. Are the products that are for sale in the business considered business assets?

____

21. Which information should be kept in a record of business assets?

____

____

22. What are two methods of determining business-related automobile expenses?

____

23. What is usually kept in a client record?

a. ____

b. ____

c. ____

24. What is the importance of an appointment book?

____

____

COMPLETION: In the space(s) provided, write the word(s) that correctly complete(s) each statement.

1. The business activity done to promote and increase business is called ____________.

2. A segment of the population with similar characteristics that the practitioner might prefer to attract is her ____________.

3. Most promotional activities are ____________ in nature.

4. Any marketing activity that the practitioner must pay for directly is considered ____________

5. The practice of encouraging clients to come back for services repeatedly is known as ____________.

SHORT ANSWER: In the spaces provided, write short answers to the following questions.

1. List five marketing activities.

   a. ____________________

   b. ____________________

   c. ____________________

   d. ____________________

   e. ____________________

2. What is the advantage of selecting a target market?

   ____

   ____

3. What are two ways of determining a target market?

   a. ____________________

   b. ____________________

   ____

4. What are two objectives of promotional activities?

   a. ____________________

   b. ____________________

5. Give three examples of promotional activities.

   a. ______________________________

   b. ______________________________

   c. ______________________________

6. Give four examples of promotional materials.

   a. ______________________________

   b. ______________________________

   c. ______________________________

   d. ______________________________

7. What should be included on every piece of promotional material?

   ____

8. List four ways to promote business through public relations.

   a. ______________________________

   b. ______________________________

   c. ______________________________

   d. ______________________________

9. What are two main sources for obtaining referrals?

   a. ______________________________

   b. ______________________________

10. When a satisfied client refers a new person, what should be done?

    ____

11. When a health care professional refers a client, what should be done?

    a. ______________________________

    b. ______________________________

    c. ______________________________

12. What are the three Rs of referrals?

a. ____________________

b. ____________________

c. ____________________

SHORT ANSWER: In the spaces provided, write short answers to the following questions.

1. Which federal regulations must be observed when operating a massage business with employees?

a. ____________________

b. ____________________

c. ____________________

2. Which state regulations must be observed when operating a massage business?

a. ____________________

b. ____________________

c. ____________________

d. ____________________

e. ____________________

MULTIPLE CHOICE: Carefully read each statement. Choose the word or phrase that correctly completes the meaning and write the corresponding letter in the blank provided.

1. A positive self-image means that you ________. ________
   a) like yourself and what you do
   b) look beautiful
   c) wear expensive clothes
   d) are vain

2. Your public image includes all of the following EXCEPT ________. ________
   a) appearance
   b) business conduct
   c) expense reports
   d) customer relations

3. Clarifying your business's purpose, stating a mission, setting goals, and determining priorities is called ________. ________
   a) accounting
   b) business planning
   c) tax preparation
   d) job training

4. A short, general statement of the business's main focus is called a/an ________. ________
   a) goal
   b) business plan
   c) advertisement
   d) mission statement

5. A business that has one owner is called a ________. ________
   a) sole proprietorship
   b) partnership
   c) corporation
   d) limited liability company

6. A business that has stockholders is called a ________
   a) sole proprietorship
   b) partnership
   c) corporation
   d) subsidiary

7. Undercapitalization and poor management are the two main reasons for small business ________. ________
   a) expansion
   b) insurance
   c) failure
   d) advertising

8. When buying an existing business, make sure it is ________. ________
   a) well established
   b) reputable
   c) in a good location
   d) all of the above

9. The insurance that covers costs of injuries occurring on your property and any resulting litigation is called ________ insurance. ________
   a) disability
   b) liability
   c) homeowners'
   d) workers' compensation

10. Insurance that protects the therapist from lawsuits filed by a client because of injury or loss from negligence or poor execution of a professional skill is called ________. ________
    a) liability
    b) disability
    c) compensation
    d) malpractice

11. Insurance that covers the medical costs for employees injured on the job is called ________ insurance. ________
    a) workers' compensation
    b) malpractice
    c) liability
    d) disability

12. A ledger that separates and classifies every business expenditure is called a/an ________. ________
    a) inventory
    b) disbursement record
    c) profit/loss statement
    d) balance sheet

13. All of the following are business expenses EXCEPT ________. ________
    a) rent
    b) supplies
    c) advertising
    d) owner's salary

14. The marketing activity done in return for direct payment is called ________. ________
    a) publicity
    b) advertising
    c) bartering
    d) referral

15. Developing personal and professional contacts for the purpose of giving and receiving support and sharing information is called ________. ________
    a) hobnobbing
    b) networking
    c) advertising
    d) promotions

16. The best and least expensive way to create new business is through ________. ________
    a) referrals
    b) advertising
    c) public speaking
    d) client retention

17. Social Security and unemployment compensation are two regulations of the ________. ________
    a) state government
    b) federal government
    c) county government
    d) city government

18. Sales taxes, licenses, and workers' compensation are required by ________. ________
    a) state government
    b) federal government
    c) county government
    d) city government

19. A person hired on as her own boss is called a/an ________. ________
    a) employee
    b) bookkeeper
    c) independent contractor
    d) receptionist

WORD REVIEW: The student is encouraged to write down the meaning of each of the following words. The list can be used as a study guide for this unit.

accounts payable

____

____

accounts receivable

____

____

advertising

bank account reconciliation

bank statement

bookkeeping

business assets

business checking account

business expenditures

business goals

business license

client file

client retention

corporation

cost-of-goods

DBA

direct mail

disbursement ledger

EIN

entrepreneur

fictitious name statement

income ledger

independent contractor

inventory

invoice

LLC

limited liability company

marketing

massage license

mileage log

mission statement

outcalls

partnership

personal draw

petty cash fund

professional liability insurance

provider's number

record keeping

referral

Schedule C

Schedule SE